# Rescue Me

# Rescue Me

## My Life with the Battersea Dogs

## Melissa Wareham

W F HOWES LTD

This large print edition published in 2009 by
W F Howes Ltd
Unit 4, Rearsby Business Park, Gaddesby Lane,
Rearsby, Leicester LE7 4YH

1  3  5  7  9  10  8  6  4  2

First published in the United Kingdom in 2009
by Ebury Press

A CIP catalogue record for this book is available
from the British Library

ISBN 978 1 40744 944 9

Typeset by Palimpsest Book Production Limited,
Grangemouth, Stirlingshire
Printed and bound in Great Britain
by MPG Books Ltd, Bodmin, Cornwall

FSC
Mixed Sources
Product group from well-managed
forests, controlled sources and
recycled wood or fiber
SA-COC-1565
www.fsc.org
© 1996 Forest Stewardship Council

*This book is dedicated to my parents,
to Alison and to Marilyn.*

*And to an establishment that has
indelibly touched my soul.*

There is a scene in *Little Britain* where Marjorie Dawes, the pudgy Fat Fighters representative says,

'Ooh, I love a bit of cake, I do. I love cake. I just love a bit of cake.'

That's how I feel about dogs.

# CONTENTS

# AUTHOR'S NOTE

This book is a memoir of my time at Battersea Dogs Home, where I worked from February 1988 to September 2004. Any views expressed in this book are mine alone, based on my own experiences and recollections of that period and do not necessarily represent the views of the organisation. The experiences and characters are true to my memory and are written with love and affection. No one asks to be immortalised in print and I hope I have done them justice but if I have fallen short, I ask for their forbearance.

I have fond memories and great admiration for the work Battersea does. I understand that since I have left, the organisation continues to evolve – transforming itself into the modern, professional organisation it is today.

# PREFACE

# EVERY DOG HAS ITS DAY

Where else in the world would you go to work and find your first customer to be a singer who has performed to millions? He is looking for a mongrel to complement his existing female Border terriers. It has to be a boy as his two can be rather 'bitchy' around other girls.

Your next customer is Bill Turner, a pensioner from the local council estate. He has no family and is desperately lonely after his ageing Staffordshire bull terrier recently died. He is a big bloke, a real Londoner and is embarrassed to find himself sobbing.

Your third customer has big brown eyes, beautiful honey-coloured fur and 40 per cent burns to her body. Her previous owner doused her in boiling water because she urinated in the house after being locked up all day. You take her to meet her new owner. She gives her very best sit. Today is the first day of the rest of her life.

Your fourth customer is the Canadian ambassador. He and his wife had to leave their beloved Labrador behind when they moved to London. The void she leaves is enormous and desperately needs to be filled. They are potty about dogs and will take anything, but ask for one that won't bite visiting dignitaries.

You grab a quick bite to eat for lunch.

You return to find socialite Jemima Khan waiting patiently to see you. She has been brought up with dogs and wants her two young sons to inherit her passion. The youngest, however, seems more interested in eating the dog treats.

Your next customer is 12 weeks old, loves squeaky toys and is petrified of men. You introduce him to his new owner and hope she will help him forget the cruelty bestowed upon him by his previous master.

Next in line is a fellow down on his luck and with no fixed abode. He looks around at the dogs and vows to come back when he has found somewhere to call home. He says he cannot live without a dog in his life; they are the only real friends he has ever had.

Your eighth customer of the day is a feisty little chihuahua who was given up for being overly amorous towards the cat. He is meeting his new owners and their Irish wolfhound today. This embarrassing little problem is not expected to reoccur.

You end your day in a rather surreal fashion, sitting opposite Hollywood actor Kevin Spacey, who explains that he just adores dogs. He has relocated to the UK and would like to fill his home with at least four or five.

So where is this unique place? Exactly what kind of establishment sees such a broad spectrum of the human race, all in a day's work?

It is Battersea Dogs Home, the oldest and most famous dogs' home in the world.

I was lucky enough to work at Battersea for 15 years and it was there I learned that possessing a passion for dogs can break down barriers and unite people from all social backgrounds, races, religions and income brackets like nothing else.

Every day Battersea received an assortment of four-leggeds through its door. They included pedigrees and non pedigrees, all different colours, shapes, sizes and temperaments, much like the myriad of two-leggeds who kindly came to open their hearts and homes to one lucky hound.

A nation of animal lovers we may be but in juxtaposition to the compassion and generosity that surrounded me on a daily basis were 500 dogs, abandoned and bewildered.

This book celebrates the dogs – sometimes damaged beyond belief – that came through Battersea's door, the staff that mended them and the customers whose lives they enhanced and, in some cases, even saved.

It is an account of some extraordinary circumstances I found myself in – often completely unconnected to my everyday world of dogs – circumstances brought about simply as a result of my passion for dogs equalling someone else's.

This is a tribute to all the good that came out of one unique, genuine, caring, determined, proud establishment; a place as deeply ingrained in British heritage as the monarchy, fish and chips and cups of tea.

A place known simply as Battersea Dogs Home.

# CHAPTER 1

# LIKE A DOG WITH A BONE

Mr Wadman Taylor, head vet and manager of the world-famous Battersca Dogs Home, showed me up to his office and asked me to take a seat. The room was quite dark, with green leather chairs, wall-to-wall bookshelves and dog beds everywhere. The desk was piled high with paperwork. There were photographs on the walls of handsome hounds, proudly posing with large silver trophies. I couldn't decide if the room smelled more of dog or pipe tobacco but something about it made me feel strangely at home.

Two cairn terriers stood guarding their bed, which was between me and the seat I'd been asked to take. Was this my first test? Were the dogs part of the interview panel? Mr W.T. assured me they were harmless (with him maybe) but every step I took prompted their deep growls to become more frenzied, lip-curling, teeth-gnashing barks. A young 18-year-old, having had no previous exposure to this kind of dog behaviour, I wasn't exactly sure what to do. Somewhere in the darkest recesses of my mind the words 'show no fear' played as if on a continuous loop in my head.

I decided that I'd be damned if these two teeth-baring, overstuffed cushions were going to scupper my chances of landing my dream job.

I have always had a passion for dogs. Where it came from, I honestly don't know. We'd never had dogs in the family, but whenever I was due a free wish – from eating strawberries for the first time every summer, to seeing a black cat or catching snowflakes, it was always the same one: 'I wish that I had a dog.' I never imagined there might come a day when I'd have 700.

I have a running joke with my mother. If she had only bought me a dog when I was a kid, this strange obsession would be out of my system and I'd have a successful career in rocket science by now.

When I was six, in an attempt to placate me, my parents bought me a tortoise. A bloody tortoise! They named him Spiro. I did my best to love him, I really did. It's probably just as well I didn't form a strong bond with him. He was a demon vegetable muncher and escaped from his hutch on a regular basis in order to decimate my father's vegetable patch. One day poor Spiro ate one too many lettuces so my parents liberated him into next door's garden. With role models like those two, it's no wonder I ended up wanting a career in animal welfare.

Spiro tried his best, but dogs were my one true love – I just adored them. My earliest encounter with one was as a three-year-old, out shopping with my mother. She thought I was by her side but watched in horror as I strolled right up to an enormous German shepherd, tied up outside a shop.

Apparently we were nose to nose when, showing no sign of fear, I looked him squarely in the eye and gave him a resounding, 'Woof!' My mother stood frozen to the spot, praying that at best he wouldn't maim me and at worst, wouldn't swallow me whole. Thankfully he just yawned, displaying impressive fangs and turned away, bored.

Neither one of my parents has any kind of affinity with Man's Best Friend. If pushed (usually by me), my mother will pat a dog, but then asks, 'Where do I wash my hands now?' It's so embarrassing, especially when the dog in question is someone's pride and joy.

Unlike me, she lists culture and the arts amongst her interests. When I was a teenager, she would drag me off to museums, the opera, the theatre and galleries galore. The amount of hours I've spent agonising that I must be adopted. If I didn't look so much like her, I'd be sure my real mother is out there somewhere; a large woman living in the countryside, wearing wellies and a body warmer, cooking up tripe for her 15 hounds.

My father is just as bad. One summer in a Devon pub garden, a beagle decided to do number twos a little too close to our table. My dad immediately swore at the dog and then threw his pint of beer over the poor animal. The shame. I didn't know where to look.

It was painfully obvious I had no parental footsteps in which to follow but that didn't deter me from following my dream. I had never committed to anything before, in fact quite the opposite. I'd begin things and never finish them, get bored and go on to the next. But I was singularly and unequivocally devoted to a life with dogs.

My parents had worked hard to get where they were and having ploughed their hard-earned cash into a private education for me, some eyebrows, not to mention voices, were raised at my choice of career.

Don't get me wrong; their money wasn't by any means wasted. I loved my schooldays and believe they gave me a good grounding for life. However, at the time, I viewed the establishment as more of a social club than a place of learning.

My private school was as competitive as it was academic; always boasting top exam results. All I can imagine is they must have had a poor intake in 1981, the year they took me.

I was top of the class in two subjects: games and acting the fool. It's true that most people are either academic or sporty: not many are both. I loved zipping around the court, fleet of foot, whilst my academic peers stumbled around as if glued to the spot. I'd spend the other 90 per cent of my school life sitting at the back of the classroom struggling to keep up with simultaneous equations, Chaucer and the Periodic Table of Elements.

For six and a half years I hadn't given my career a second thought, but as my schooldays drew to a close, Mrs Hooper, my careers teacher threw herself into action. She'd ask me what I was interested in, what I was good at and what I liked to do but each of her questions was greeted with a screwed-up face and a shrug of the shoulders. We'd end every session without an inkling of success, absolutely none the wiser as to what was to become of me. When I left school, Mrs Hooper gave me a card. It read: 'We'll never forget you, although with time and therapy we might.'

The sad thing was I knew what I wanted to be. I wanted to be a vet but as year after year of failed exams rolled by, it was clear this was not going to be the case. I wasn't clever enough to be a Border collie, let alone a Border collie's doctor.

So whilst my peers were travelling the length and breadth of the country, attending interviews at universities of their first and second choice, I was boarding the number 36 bus and travelling over Vauxhall Bridge to attend an interview at Battersea Dogs Home; the workplace of my first choice.

I'd written to Battersea a week earlier to see if there were any jobs going. I didn't specify any particular area; I just wanted to work with dogs.

The minimal wage I was expecting to be paid

working for an animal charity would never put me on the world's Top 100 Rich List, but I was still living with my parents in Victoria so could probably survive.

I received a reply almost immediately. I'd landed my first job interview.

It was a bitterly cold February morning and it felt comforting to walk into the warmth of the reception of Battersea Dogs Home, the instant smell of dogs bringing a smile to my face. I gave my name and said I was there to see Mr Wadman Taylor. Coming out to greet me, he cut a distinguished figure in his tweed three-piece suit. He had a full head of white hair and a beard to match, from which he puffed away on his pipe. I felt like I'd wandered onto the set of *All Creatures Great and Small*

We made our way up to his office where I now stood, trying desperately hard to 'show no fear', never taking my eyes off the two snarling terriers in front of me. The bravado of my toddler days had clearly abandoned me. I took a step towards what felt like an impending and rather untimely death, or at the very least the loss of my toes. The snarling reached a crescendo. Suddenly the door was flung open and in strode Mr W.T.'s wife.

Mrs W.T., a little Scottish woman, stood all of five feet in her white coat and Hush Puppies. She was also a vet and although this husband and wife team ran the Home together, it soon became clear who was the boss. Both Mr W.T. and the dogs became deferential in her presence. One click of her fingers at the dogs and a smile and a wink at me and my first interview hurdles had been removed.

Keen to make up for my previous hesitance, I strode confidently to my chair and unwittingly sat on the oldest of the Wadman Taylor terriers. Blind and deaf, he produced a sound similar to that of a bagpipe, mid deflation. At this point I wondered if I should just get up and go home.

But it seemed no harm was done to my prospective career or the dog and we got on with the interview. Mr W.T. read my CV or rather my 'extended best bits school report' and asked if I'd thought of becoming a veterinary nurse. To be honest I had, but it required O level biology which I failed along with maths, history and home economics.

The thought of taking biology O level again or even having to go back to the world of education and academia was abhorrent enough to make me rule out veterinary nursing as a career. Actually, when explaining to my parents my chosen career path, my mother had suggested, 'If you have to work with animals, at least learn a profession that you can always fall back on. Why don't you become a veterinary nurse?' But there is something innate in all teenagers that when given parental advice, we either do completely the opposite or just ignore it altogether.

Rather than admit to Mr W.T. that I was too lazy to retake an exam and all the studying that would entail, I simply said, 'I faint at the sight of blood.'

He seemed convinced and we moved on.

Mr W.T. explained the workings of the Home to me. I had come to the interview with very little knowledge of Battersea so I was shocked to learn that during the previous year the organisation had taken in 23,000 stray and unwanted dogs.

I sat there open mouthed. Whatever happened to the British being a nation of animal lovers? Whatever happened to Man's Best Friend? This startling statistic made me even more certain I was doing the right thing. Someone had to look out for life's canine cast-offs.

That same year only 13 per cent of strays were claimed by their owners. Mr W.T. went on to explain that although Battersea endeavours to rehome as many dogs as possible, sadly some had to be put down. This was an area I hadn't even thought about and it shocked me to the core.

I asked a little haughtily what the reasons were that might warrant a dog being put to sleep. I imagined myself as their new champion, saving every dog that didn't make the grade.

Relighting his pipe, Mr W.T. said matter of factly, 'We put dogs down for two reasons. Firstly, if a dog's temperament was so unpredictable and dangerous that it would be irresponsible for Battersea to rehome it. Secondly, if it is deemed

8

kinder to put an animal to sleep, rather than let it suffer due to a medical condition that cannot be cured.'

That shut me up.

The spotlight turned on me again, as Mr W.T. asked what previous experience I'd had with dogs. Perhaps I'd had one as a child?

I had the feeling that my chosen career was about to grind to a halt before it had even begun as I tried to explain to him that what I lacked in experience, I made up for in hard work and enthusiasm.

How could my parents have done this to me? It was one thing that they didn't get animals but depriving me as a child was now sabotaging my future. Having to admit I had no dog experience whatsoever was embarrassing and left me feeling utterly deflated.

But Mr W.T. didn't seem too concerned and proceeded on to the subject of pay. He made it clear that although Battersea was a relatively wealthy charity, thanks to generous benefactors (which I took to mean dotty old ladies that left all their cash to the dogs rather than their despicable, money-grabbing relatives), the money was left for the care of the dogs. As such, if I were accepted as a kennel maid I would be paid £70 a week. It was more than I was expecting.

I'd be required to work from 8 a.m. till 5 p.m. and two out of three weekends. I would also be expected to work Christmas Day and other public

9

holidays. The dogs don't know or care that it might be a public holiday; they'd still need feeding and looking after. Perfectly reasonable, I thought.

Almost as an afterthought, Mr W.T. asked if I liked cats.

'Cats?' I replied.

'Yes. As well as 700 dogs, Battersea houses up to 100 cats at any one time.'

'I prefer dogs,' I said, immediately wishing I hadn't.

The interview came to an end and Mr W.T. asked if I'd like a tour of the Dogs Home. I could think of nothing I'd like more. After shaking my hand and telling me he would be in touch, I was handed over to a man called Fred.

At about 60 years old, Fred's looks were starting to fade but you could tell he had once been a handsome man. He walked with a pronounced limp and was accompanied by an ageing German shepherd called Tramp, who walked with exactly the same limp.

Fred asked me what I'd like to see.

'The dogs,' I replied.

He smiled and led me towards the stray kennels. Here the dogs waited patiently to be claimed by their owners but as I had just learned from Mr W.T., most would never come.

We walked down the Home's main thoroughfare towards the railway arches and I could hear muffled barking coming from some of the surrounding kennel blocks. The place was much larger than I had imagined but I still couldn't believe there were 700 dogs here, shoved between the gas works and the railway arches in central London.

As we approached the door of a building that resembled an aeroplane hangar with a rail track running over it, I had mixed feelings of anticipation and trepidation. Although I was about to see my favourite things in the whole world, I wasn't sure I was prepared to see them caged and abandoned in such large numbers. Fred pushed the big, heavy, metal door and we entered. The block was about three-quarters of the length of a football pitch with high, arched ceilings. A central aisle ran its length with approximately 50 kennels on either side.

The first thing that struck me as I entered the large, old-fashioned kennel block wasn't the smell or the noise, as most people might think it would be. Mid-morning, the smell was more of disinfectant than dog and the residents were mostly quiet. Instead, what struck me was how these beautiful, intelligent, faithful, once-loved companions could have ended up being discarded in such a cold and callous way.

There were some stunning dogs, all different shapes, colours, sizes, ages and breeds. Puppies all in kennels together wreaking havoc, oldies fast asleep and others just sitting on the concrete floor, shaking with fear and looking a little lost.

I didn't get the feeling most people get when

they walk into Battersea Dogs Home. I didn't want to take them all home or, for that matter, even just one. Apart from the fact my mother would have evicted me, I felt I had to do more, much more.

Back then in 1988, Battersea Dogs Home was as people imagined it: dark, dank and dungeon-esque. Although the dogs were always very well looked after and had heating and blankets, the kennels were extremely basic, unchanged from when they were built pre-World War II.

Fred informed me that there were 16 kennel blocks in total, all single-storey and each holding between 40 to 160 kennels, with a corridor running down the centre.

The partition between some kennels had been removed to create extra-large kennels that catered for the giant breeds, but the majority measured six feet by four. This was capacious for a chihuahua but a little cosy for larger guests or those sharing accommodation. The front of the kennel was made up of reinforced wire mesh, criss-crossed to form squares about two centimetres wide. The remaining three sides were lacquered wood panels from floor to waist-height with the same wire mesh running from waist-height to the ceiling. The kennel floor was concrete, cold and bare.

Each kennel was equipped with a heavy metal water bowl, a fibreglass bed at the back and an electric heat lamp that hung down from the ceiling, right above the bed. I noticed one particularly large German shepherd sitting tall and erect in his bed, head directly underneath the lamp, an ear either side. He reminded me of one of those ladies under the dryer at an old-fashioned hairdressing salon.

The acoustics in the kennel block were appalling and when one dog barked, the rest piped up, quickly reaching fever-pitch. I made a mental note that this was not the place to come with a hangover.

Some job seekers might have been put off by these conditions. Indeed many visitors were deterred from coming to Battersea Dogs Home for fear it would be too upsetting. During my time at Battersea, however, the kennels were transformed from these dungeon-like dwellings into multi-million-pound pooch palaces. But on this day with Fred I was far from deterred, and looking into the faces of all those dogs I saw exactly what I had to do. If I couldn't be a vet, I'd help dogs in another way.

I arrived back home to find a nail-biting mother hoping I'd come to my senses and that my career in rocket science could now commence in earnest. But my interview at Battersea Dogs Home had just confirmed for me what I already knew. I was single-minded. I was like a dog with a bone.

An anxious wait by the letterbox ensued. Two days later it came: the offer of a job as kennel maid. It was official; I'd gone to the dogs!

The next 15 years were to become a roller-coaster ride of unique experiences; a journey that would catapult me through the whole gamut of human emotions and deposit me in situations I could never in my wildest dreams have foreseen.

# CHAPTER 2

# GONE TO THE DOGS

I was told to arrive at 7.45 a.m., ready to begin work at 8 a.m. sharp. I rang the bell and tentatively pushed the staff gate open. I stepped over the threshold and entered my new world.

Everyone is nervous when they begin a new job and I was no exception, but when I walked through that gate, I felt an instant calm wash over me. Everything felt right as though this was where I was meant to be. I remember that feeling distinctly.

I closed the gate behind me and turned to see an Alsatian cross hurtling towards me, off lead, barking his head off. This was going to be interesting. There was no one around to rescue me so I tried reasoning with him. I found myself telling him to give me a break; this was my first day. He didn't understand English. We stood at stalemate for what seemed like ages.

Eventually, a tall woman with long hair came out and called the dog. I later discovered the dog had come into the Home emaciated a couple of years previously and was named Slim Jim. He was now verging a little on the podgy side and

15

was known simply as Jimmy. He lived at Battersea Dogs Home and was devoted to June, the tall woman who turned out to be one of my fellow kennel maids. June had nursed Jimmy back from the brink and he'd never forgotten her kindness. He followed her everywhere and wasn't afraid to put the staff in their place with a nip on the bum, should they misbehave.

I explained to June who I was and, without saying a word, she trundled off, Jimmy in tow, and returned two minutes later with the supervisor.

No nonsense and matter of fact, to me Dot was the stereotypical mad dog lady. She looked me up and down and when she heard my private school accent, probably wondered how long I'd last.

Sharing an office with the slightly more senior Fred, Dot was short and thin with a sallow complexion. She had a little black-and-tan mongrel, who, like Jimmy and Fred's dog Tramp, was a Battersea yard dog and lived at the Home. Tina was a pleasant-enough dog, but Dot kept her all to herself.

Dot introduced me to Jacky who was going to train me. I smiled nervously at Jacky who, in response, stubbed her fag out and looked me up and down in the same way Dot had. But unlike Dot, Jacky gave me a warm smile. There was something about Jacky I instantly liked; she was friendly, efficient, extremely practical and, according to Dot, very good at her job.

16

As Jacky and I approached the same kennel block I'd been through on my tour a week earlier, she said, 'Right, the dogs have been left to their own devices since 5 p.m. last night. They need cleaning out and feeding.'

I couldn't wait.

When she opened the kennel block door, I was almost floored by the aroma.

'Bit rich, isn't it?' Jacky said with a wink.

We entered the Unders kennel block, so named because it sat underneath the railway arches. It was dark (not helped by the early February hour), noisy and smelly. A hundred hungry, barking dogs sounded more like a thousand, compounded by rush-hour trains travelling directly above us every minute. (The rail network seemed so much more efficient from down here. There seemed to be a million trains going back and forth, yet the story is completely different when you're standing on the platform, waiting in the rain.)

When I saw my first dog, the noise of the barking and the smell of what dogs do immediately evaporated. He was a little black-and-white mongrel, about six months old.

I could barely contain myself. 'What's his name?' I shouted to Jacky.

'He doesn't have one,' she yelled back. 'He only came in yesterday and he's a stray. You can name him if you want.'

I knelt down to his level and he pushed himself against the bars. His ears and paws were way too big for him. He had soft, fuzzy puppy fur and big brown eyes that implored me to touch him. But something in those eyes was also holding him back and I wondered if he had been bit before. I raised my hand through the bars to pet him but he flinched. Jacky explained that I should always start by stroking a dog on its chest rather than its head as this is less threatening for them.

I gently stroked his chest, working my way up to a scratch behind one of those outsized ears. He loved it.

'I'm going to call you Sunny,' I said and he wagged his bum at me.

Jacky yanked me from my Disney moment by shoving a broom, a bucket and a kennel key into my hands.

'Looks like Sunny's got an upset stomach,' she said. 'Make sure you get it all up.'

This was it. I held my breath and thought of England.

As I cleaned out Sunny's kennel, I was aware that a yellow head with a grey face had popped up from the kennel next door and was looking at me through seal-cub eyes.

'Hello. Who are you?' I heard myself say as though expecting a reply. She gave me a concerned squeak. 'Hang on; I'll be with you in a minute,' I reassured her.

I left Sunny's kennel (in a much better state than I had found it, I might add) and went next door to clean out his neighbour. Before I entered her kennel, I had a quick scan of her card which was clipped to the outside. As well as the usual necessary information it read 'loves a cuddle'. That made two of us.

The old girl was sitting down, wagging her tail at me and as I bent down to give her a pat, she leaned back and balanced on her haunches as if begging. She then burrowed her soft snout under my chin, put a paw either side of my neck and gave me a big hug! That was it: I'd fallen hook, line and sinker.

She must have been housetrained as her kennel was spotless and required more of a dusting than a full spring clean. Only a few were like this and most, especially the ones with two or three dogs in them, looked like they'd played host to an all-night party. It was everywhere; all over the floor and the walls and when I entered the kennel, the dogs were so pleased that they jumped up and it was all over me! Three crazy youngsters were jumping all over me with the filthiest paws in the world. But how could I mind when they greeted me with such unbridled love and enthusiasm.

Jacky had warned me not to go in with certain dogs. She pointed out the less trustworthy individuals and said she'd clean them out. One was a Rottweiler that looked like a big, sad bear.

I felt so sorry for this majestic-looking beast, caged and unhappy. I approached his kennel to offer a few kind words. He lowered his head and his lips began to twitch. He let out a deep growl warning me off, yet when Jacky approached him, he gently came towards the bars, ears back, tail wagging.

She explained that with time and patience the dogs get to know and trust you. They'd been badly let down by someone and, understandably, it took a while for them to trust again.

An hour and a half of hard scrubbing later, all the kennels were clean and I was filthy. Next it was feeding time. At school, I'd done a bit of work experience at a kiddies' playgroup, handing out orange juice and biscuits to 40 three-year-olds. I thought that experience wouldn't be dissimilar to this. I was wrong. This was far worse.

Jacky told me that when there was more than one dog in a kennel, I should stand in with them, placing the bowls at opposite ends of the kennel. This would stop them going for the same bowl, causing all-out war.

Easier said than done. I put the two bowls down at opposite ends but both dogs dived into the same one. They were eating as though they'd never seen food before, heads deep down in the bowl, but at the same time (and I'm not sure how this was possible) they were scrapping with each other. Food was flying everywhere. I didn't know what to do. I looked around for Jacky but she was at the other end of the block. I didn't want to seem incapable by calling her over and with the racket of barking dogs she probably wouldn't have heard me anyway. No, I would deal with this on my own.

I looked down at my charges.

'Sit! Down! Heel?' I uttered weakly. They took no notice of me. They had finished one bowl and were diving into the other, still fighting and eating at the same time. By the time both bowls were empty, they were covered in food and so was I. It all happened in the blink of an eye. But there were still another 98 hungry mouths to feed. How would I survive? Mostly, by throwing the bowls down, shutting my eyes and hoping for the best. I would like to report that by the time the last two canine bellies were filled, I had the hang of feeding time at Battersea Dogs Home but I hadn't, and my nerves were shot to pieces.

At 10 a.m. it was time for our break and, boy, had we earned it. The canteen was a humble affair but it did a mean fry-up. I'd always loved a full English breakfast and it seemed to taste even better after such hard physical work. It was also very cheap, subsidised to help with our modest wages.

As I was tucking in, Jacky told me I'd done well. This was a novelty; I'd never heard this kind of praise during my school-days. I was in my element and loving every minute. This wasn't the career my parents had envisaged, but it was going a long way to making up for my dogless childhood.

★   ★   ★

The Home opened to the public after breakfast and the majority of people headed straight for the rehoming kennels. Jacky and my section housed the strays so only people who'd lost their dog came into Unders.

I watched as a handful of people trudged through our kennel block. Some had expectant looks on their faces, some angry looks and others just looked desperately worried.

One such angst-ridden face turned a corner and found her dog. It was my friend, the hugging mongrel with the seal-cub eyes. There was instant recognition from both parties who wailed and wept with delight at the sight of each other.

I found out her name was Tulip and she was 12 years old. Tulip had been on the same walk without incident for the whole of her life, but yesterday had decided it was time for a little adventure. For reasons known only to her, Tulip had run out of the park and boarded the back of the 159 bus. A horrified Mrs Tulip witnessed the whole event but was too far away to catch the bus and her shrieks went unheard by the conductor, who was upstairs taking fares.

Tulip ended up in the West End and was brought into Battersea Dogs Home by a dog lover, who recognised a lost dog with early senility when he saw one.

I told Mrs Tulip that her dog had been a model guest. Not that I knew. I'd been at Battersea for less time than Tulip, but she looked like she needed to hear something good about her otherwise dotty dog.

I was thrilled that Tulip had been reunited with her owner and thought this meant one less kennel to attend to. I didn't bargain on this prime real estate vacancy being filled within minutes, this time by a grumpy-looking boxer. It seemed that as soon as one dog vacated a kennel, another moved in straight away.

The time between breakfast and lunch was spent washing up food bowls, filling up water bowls, cleaning out the kennels as required and just being with the dogs. And I couldn't get enough of them. Urgent noses, impatient paws, eager tails and earnest tongues greeted me at every turn.

As well as their indoor quarters, the dogs had large outdoor exercise yards in which to breathe some fresh air. We spent a large chunk of our time rotating them from inside to outside, playing with them and cleaning the outdoor kennels.

Many of the dogs were housetrained so would endearingly wait until it was their turn to go outside. If they were friendly, we'd mix five or six dogs together in the outside yards. This way they could tear around and tire each other out, making for happier and better-behaved inmates in the afternoon. We could also take dogs for a walk within the parameters of the Home, although time only permitted us to walk a few dogs as we couldn't leave the kennel block unattended for too long.

If I thought feeding time was tough, walkies was a whole new ball game. If you so much as dangled one lead in a kennel block, the whole place exploded into hysteria with hyperventilating hounds all trying to get noticed and yet there I was, a novice on my first day, standing outside a kennel, dangling three leads and feeling sick with nerves. I wasn't afraid of the dogs, it was just that they were literally hurling themselves at the door in an effort to be taken out for a walk.

I watched Jacky as she confidently walked into the next-door kennel, pushed the three large, leaping dogs down, commanded them in a loud voice to sit and expertly clipped three leads on with little fuss. She walked them down to the end of the kennel block and waited for me.

I swallowed hard, trying to steady my hand as I fed the key into the lock. The dogs were turning somersaults with excitement and a wrestling match ensued as I tried to clip three leads on to three collars, whilst in the middle of a tangle of twelve paws, six ears, three tails, three noses and three tongues. In amongst all of this, how was I supposed to find the three tiny metal rings on which to hook my trembling leads? As I found out for myself, taking more than one dog out at a time is something only the very experienced should attempt. Those who are not – me – invariably lose at least one of the dogs and spend the next ten minutes running around Battersea Dogs Home trying to catch it.

The first dog shot through my legs like a greyhound out of a trap with me in hot pursuit. I had, of course, forgotten to close the kennel door on the other two and as I sped down the kennel block intent on catching the first, the other two overtook me. Jacky was at the other end of the block holding her three dogs and watched in horror as three more (plus me) came hurtling towards her. She managed to catch two of them but the third evaded her and ran out the door.

Thankfully, he didn't get too far and I was relieved to see someone grab hold of him. My relief turned to shame as I realised who it was.

'Hello there!' Mr Wadman Taylor called to me, between puffs on his pipe as I sheepishly approached him. He patted the dog, which incidentally was under his control in less than a millisecond. Here was the man who had given me a job, taken a risk on me – foolishly, some might say – witnessing my howlers first-hand.

'How are you getting on?' he warmly enquired.

Wasn't it obvious? Without looking up, I mumbled something in the affirmative, leashed the hound and scuttled back to Jacky who, even with all her prowess, was struggling to control five dogs.

Seeing how flustered I was, Jacky took four and I walked the remaining pair of crazed hounds, tongues hanging out and eyeballs on stalks. Even with just these two, I was flung around the Home like a pinball. The flinging didn't cease until the end of the walk when I returned to the block with both arms considerably longer than before.

At Lunchtime, Battersea's little canteen was full of the public so the staff went down the road either to the kebab-cum-pizza shop, the sandwich café or the sweet shop, owned by an Indian couple with a young son. I bought a sandwich from the café then went into the sweet shop for a drink, some crisps and a chocolate bar. As soon as I walked into that shop I was in heaven, wrapped up in the smell of Indian cooking; my all-time favourite food.

My maternal grandfather was Indian, making me a quarter Indian, but my upbringing was traditionally British with one exception: I was fed curry from the moment I was weaned. Some might say that *was* a traditionally British upbringing. My grandmother cooked the most incredible curries but when I was little she'd water mine down, worried they were too powerful for a delicate young stomach. I knew instantly and would push the diluted variety away in favour of the full-strength curry on my mother's plate.

The first time I walked into that sweet shop, it was like going home. I took a deep breath and smiled in ecstasy. The lady shopkeeper looked delighted, if a little shocked. I told her it smelled delicious and asked what it was. She ran upstairs as fast as her legs would carry her and came down with the most amazing samosas I'd ever tasted.

From that time on we became firm friends and she always brought me a little something from her kitchen upstairs whenever I went into her shop. Her husband's face wasn't quite as sunny whenever he saw me. I guess he thought I was eating his hard-earned dinner; fair enough, too.

That first day, we took our lunch back to the Home and sat in the staff quarters, which left a lot to be desired. There was a TV, a cooker, some dilapidated furniture and not much else. The cooker was for cooking the dogs' lunch, and tripe, pasta and rice sat bubbling away on the stove top. Eating lunch to the smell of boiling tripe was going to take some getting used to.

The only good thing about this staff area was that dogs were permitted. There were about ten staff in the mess room, all of whom had their favourite dog with them. As I unwrapped my lunch, 20 ears pricked up. In a flash, ten bums had assembled themselves on the floor in front of me in a display of very best sits. Long stalactites of drool dribbled from hopeful mouths as 20 eyes bored into my sandwich. I discovered that eating quickly was a prudent strategy.

Amongst the ten dogs brought up to the staff canteen for a treat were a few that were terrified of their own shadow. Jacky explained that they were being socialised by their respective staff member. She said that it wasn't so much being around people that brought them out of their shell as being around other dogs that were not afraid of people and that, within a few days, these former nervous wrecks would be tearing around the room just like all the others and teaching a new set of neurotics that life wasn't so bad after all.

After spending an idyllic hour immersed in dogs, it was time to head back to work. I was looking forward to seeing my dogs again until Jacky informed me it was time for the midday feed. Being the new girl, I was made to carry the tripe down the stairs, gagging at every step.

In order to vary the dogs' diet, this meal was different from the breakfast slop and seemed far more palatable. The rice, pasta, biscuit and tripe were emptied into a large trolley and Jacky stood over it and told me to get stuck in. I asked what utensils I should use to mix it with.

'The things on the end of your arms,' she replied.

I held my breath, bent down and started to mix. If my home economics teacher could see me now.

The dogs had three meals a day due to most of them being underweight. Even the dogs that weren't underweight usually lost some condition due to the stress of being in such an unfamiliar kennel environment. Jacky explained that the particularly skinny dogs were fed again through the night by Charlie, the night security man.

The lunchtime feeding routine was much the same as breakfast – a deafening din of hungry, barking dogs. I soon learned which dogs and their kennel mates needed supervision during feeding time, in particular two Alsatian crosses named Joe and Jasper.

I fared a little better during this feeding time and only ended up in the middle of seven fights (Joe and Jasper being one), with just half the amount of lunch in my hair as breakfast.

After we had cleared the lunchtime bowls away, Jacky pointed out a bedraggled-looking mongrel called Harry, desperately overdue for a bath. As we walked him down the block towards the grooming room, Joe and Jasper started bickering again. A loud 'Oi' from Jacky distracted them enough to quell the quarrel. She told me she had been trying to separate them for the last week but there were no empty kennels and no other dogs suitable to switch them with. Lack of space was always a huge pressure on both staff and dogs alike.

We got Harry into the bath. Jacky asked me if I'd ever bathed a dog before. I was embarrassed to tell her I'd never even walked one before today, let alone bathed or fed one.

Harry was covered in fleas so we gave him a medicated bath. Most dogs I'm sure hate the bath, but Harry was only too pleased to be the centre of attention. He was a scrawny little fellow with big pointed ears, a long tail and a sable-coloured coat.

Harry stood still for me as I massaged the

shampoo into his coat. I could feel every single rib and now that his fur was wet, I could see them too. Silently, I thanked him for being so well behaved. If I couldn't control dogs on land, I was sure as hell that I wouldn't be able to in water, which would just add to the day's other mortifying moments. He responded by staring at me with devoted eyes that after a while began to shut. As I was massaging him, Harry was falling asleep.

We finished bathing him and I hoped to God I hadn't caught anything. I imagined going home on my first day and telling my mum we might have a small flea problem.

Harry had been in the *Daily Telegraph* the day before, in a story featuring the overcrowding problem at the world's most famous dogs' home. No publicity was bad publicity and Harry was expected to find a new home as a direct result of his newspaper appearance. Two days later he moved into the rehoming section and did just that.

Before I knew it, it was four o'clock and we were giving the dogs their last meal and settling them down for the night. Most had clean blankets and for those that liked to eat their blankets, we shredded newspaper to put in their beds.

The staff was responsible for cleaning their own quarters at the end of each day and as this was my first day, the mopping duty fell to me. I did what I thought was right, but was rumbled straight away by Dot who took one look and said, 'You've never mopped a floor before, have you?'

Granted, I hadn't but not wanting to admit we had a cleaning lady at home, I innocently asked, 'Why do you say that?'

'Because if the Home's cat comes in here, she'll drown!'

At that point the rest of the staff started coming into the locker room to change and go home.

'Blimey, those toilets flooded again?'

I hoped this over-zealous mopping wouldn't blot my copybook on my very first day.

I jumped on the train and as I walked back into our swanky Victoria apartment, I was struck by how my home life and my new world of work were the complete antithesis of each other. Perhaps my life mirrored that of some of the dogs I'd spent the day with. Had they also come from comfortable homes to a rougher, tougher existence? It was as though I was leading some kind of double life but I felt richer for having found the more modest part.

My mother didn't so much greet me at the door, as stand there telling me to strip. She had run a bath into which I was frog-marched. I didn't think it was the best time to mention Harry and his little social problem.

At dinner I waxed lyrical about my day. My mother was quiet and seemed a little tense. I suppose this was very different to the first day of

31

university she'd imagined me telling her about ever since I was little.

I was in the dog house – the Battersea dog house – and this was going to take time and patience, from both sides.

# CHAPTER 3

# HIS BITE WAS WORSE
# THAN HIS BARK

I made my way home from the hospital with my arm bandaged and in a sling and awaited my fate. My mother was going to kill me.

Three months into my Battersea life she was more uptight than ever and this little episode would do nothing to reassure her I'd chosen the right career path. It was bad enough that after my expensive education I was working at a dogs' home, but now I was maimed for life. In my book, one fang mark to the arm hardly constituted the need for reconstructive surgery but my family has always had a penchant for the dramatic.

When she walked through the front door and saw me her reaction resembled that of a roller-coaster ride. The upward climb was concern – this wasn't so bad. She levelled out with sympathy – the calm before the storm perhaps? And finally – realising I would live – the predictable hair-raising descent into how this would never have happened if I had taken a nice clean office job.

But when it became clear the next morning that the wound had not stopped bleeding, she did what mothers do best: she cared. When it mattered, she put her feelings aside and accompanied me back to the hospital.

The doctor was an elderly Indian man with extremely strong-looking bi-focals, who insisted on calling me Miss War-e-ham. He informed us that although his colleague, who treated me the day before, had followed the correct procedure and not stitched the dog bite for fear of infection, the wound had become infected nevertheless. He would have to cut some skin away and I would need to go on a drip to flush the anti-biotics straight into the infection.

All I heard was 'on a drip' and the room began to spin. I envisaged myself lying in a hospital bed with tubes coming out of me, as the Last Rites were administered.

The doctor wanted to keep me in for five days. I'd never stayed in hospital before. I didn't know whether to laugh or cry so I cried. My mum wiped away my tears. I felt seven years old.

Joe and Jasper were just about small enough to be kennelled together but they had a love-hate relationship. At night they'd curl up in the same bed, resembling a scene from the lid of a chocolate box but during the day they were like impossible siblings, constantly bickering.

The dogs at Battersea were usually kennelled with at least one or two others, not just to combat the overcrowding, but also because it was highly beneficial for them. Dogs are social creatures that flourish when in the company of people and other dogs. The shy ones were put in with friendly, confident dogs to help encourage them out of their shell, neutered males were doubled with females and vice versa, youngsters were mixed together and the geriatrics formed their own club.

Unless very young, bull terriers were given separate quarters as they didn't always like to share. Large dogs received the same treatment: two Great Danes to a kennel would simply be impractical.

I was in the kennel block kitchen preparing the dogs' lunchtime feed when I heard a blood-curdling scream. I dropped everything and ran down the block to find Joe and Jasper tearing chunks out of each other.

In the short time I'd been at Battersea, I had learned that dogfights usually consisted of a lot of noise, slobber and drama but were rarely serious. Every once in a while, however, things turned nasty. I couldn't understand it – there was nothing around that might have triggered the argument, no toys or food, blankets or people to fight over. To this day, I don't know what caused one of the worst dogfights I'd ever seen during my 15 years at Battersea.

On my first day, Jacky had taught me never to break up a dogfight with my bare hands, advice that turned out to be most valuable when I think back to that very first feeding session. Instead, she told me I should use distraction tactics: shout at the dogs, bang a metal food bowl on the door, put my foot in between them and if it came to it, throw a bucket of water over them.

At one time or another over the past 12 weeks I'd had to employ all of these methods, with perfect results every time. But this time was different.

Having attempted all of the above without success, I began to panic. They say once bitten, twice shy and until that point I hadn't been on the receiving end of any canine's canines so had nothing to be shy of. Jacky had taken a couple of dogs out for a walk and there was no one else around so without a thought for life or limb, I grabbed both dogs by the scruff of the neck. Joe (or it could have been Jasper in the melee) whipped his head around and, thinking I was the other dog grabbing hold again, sank his teeth deep into my arm.

Instantly, I knew this was bad. Realising I needed help, I let go of the dogs and ran out of the kennel without even shutting the door. I had blood cascading down my sleeve and a sick feeling rising in my stomach.

Halfway down the block I was aware, albeit in a dreamlike state, of Joe and Jasper running past me. It seemed that in the end, their freedom was more important than their fight.

June found me and took me to Dot.

Although I hadn't been at Battersea for long,

I'd heard the folklore. Whenever someone was bitten, Dot administered first aid in the form of sinew-stinging surgical spirit and then sent you straight back to work. Thankfully a tetanus jab was obligatory before starting work at Battersea Dogs Home.

Realising what had happened, Dot smiled a demonic smile and pulled out the biggest bottle of surgical spirit I'd ever seen. She rolled my sleeve back. Being the squeamish sort, I chose not to watch. She took one look, put the surgical spirit straight back in the cupboard and asked Gerry, the maintenance man, to drive me to St Thomas' hospital. I don't know if that made me feel better or worse.

I remember two things from that short car journey along the Embankment; the overwhelming pain in my arm and asking Gerry to pull over while I threw up. We arrived at Accident & Emergency; Gerry dropped me at the door and promptly buggered off.

I sat in the waiting room for five hours, watching the television that was clamped to the top corner of the wall between the window and the ceiling and realised I now had a pain in my neck that was almost as bad as the pain in my arm. I was not having a good day.

By then it was evening. Jacky had finished work and kindly came to check on me. She watched as the doctor had a three-minute poke around the wound, bandaged my arm, stuck it in a sling and sent me home with some antibiotics. He told me to come back in the morning if the wound hadn't stopped bleeding.

The next morning I stood in the hospital with my bloody arm while a nurse checked me in for what was to be a five-night stay in hospital.

I asked my mum to phone Battersea and let them know I wouldn't be in for a few days and to explain the reason why. She gave this responsibility to my brother, who only told half the story. He got through to Jacky and told her I was back in hospital, this time on a drip. The news spread like wildfire and by the time Chinese whispers had run their course, I was all but dead.

My mum left and I took in my new surroundings. It was all a bit surreal. My ward consisted of eight beds, all of which were taken. The only other person vaguely my age was a girl who I later found out was a bicycle courier. She'd had an argument with a lorry and come off second best. Her legs were in a bad way and she slept for most of the time.

Hospital was an experience of extremes for me. The food was extremely bad but the nurses extremely kind, the wake-up call was extremely early but the view extremely fabulous. My ward overlooked the Thames and stood directly opposite the Houses of Parliament.

At about 6 p.m., eight of my colleagues tiptoed, ashen faced, through the corridors of St Thomas' hospital, looking for their fallen comrade. From my bed I could see them asking the nurse for directions to me.

When they found me sitting up in bed watching TV and eating chocolates, their faces turned from worry to relief to scorn. I tried to explain it wasn't my fault that my brother had over-dramatised the details of my condition. In the end I won them over with chocolate. They produced a cuddly gorilla and another mountain of chocolate. I was deeply touched.

Two weeks later I was back at work with a new-found respect and a lovely three-inch scar. There was no psychological damage to speak of, but when I encountered my first dogfight since the Big One, I went to pieces. I put it down to post-traumatic stress but it's true what they say: the best cure is to get straight back on the horse, or in my case the hound.

During my time at Battersea there were only a handful of serious dog bites, largely due to the staff being expert dog handlers, their ability to read dogs and their speed at getting out of the way. Catherine was just that little bit too slow on one occasion and found herself on the receiving end of one rather nasty bite.

A little slip of a thing and as quiet as a mouse, Catherine was Battersea's dog groomer. Her job was to pick out the most bedraggled, dirty and matted creatures and restore them to their former glory. She had an inner calm that the nervous and aggressive dogs seemed to respond to, which was just as well as some of the candidates for a shampoo and set were not altogether friendly. Taking no notice of the size of their attitude or their teeth, Catherine would just plonk them straight in the bath. Most of them were too shocked to react. Most of them except for Dingo.

Catherine decided he needed a bath; Dingo had other ideas. He was massive, covered in filth and grease and when she picked him up to put him in the bath he lashed out, catching her in the face. Catherine was getting married in a week's time and walking down the aisle looking like she'd been in a bare-knuckle fight wasn't the bridal look she was going for.

In an automatic reaction, Catherine held her hands up to her face but blood poured from behind her hand, gushing down her arm and dripping from her elbow.

In the calm of Dot and Fred's office, Catherine slowly removed her hand to reveal the extent of her injuries. Thankfully, Dingo had missed her eye and bitten the fleshy part around the eyebrow.

Having survived my own dog-bite trauma, Dot picked me to accompany Catherine to St Thomas' hospital. It was 8.15 a.m., too early for the day's accidents to have taken their toll and thankfully the waiting room wasn't too full. There were about 15 people before us, so we took our seats and waited patiently. Catherine held bandages and swabs to her face and I found myself once again straining my neck to watch the TV.

Next to us was an elderly Irish fellow with his arm in a makeshift sling. He was a little the worse for drink and when he saw Catherine his eyes widened and he said, 'For the love of God, what happened to you?'

Catherine told the man she worked at Battersea Dogs Home and had just been attacked by a dog. She added that she hoped the wait wouldn't be long, as she had to get back to work.

'Jesus, Mary and Joseph,' he exclaimed, 'you're going back? If a fella had done that to ye, you wouldn't be going back to him, surely?'

Catherine thought about this for a moment and answered, 'You're right, but being a battered wife is slightly different from being a battered kennel maid.' She motioned to her injury and continued, 'This goes with the territory and even though we're not paid danger money, I'll be returning to my Battersea batterer with a handful of choc drops to see if we can't work it out.'

After an hour or two, the doctors put Catherine back together again and one week later (with the help of some strategically placed make-up) she walked down the aisle with only the merest hint of her disagreement with Dingo.

One of the things I like best about dogs is that when they love you, they really love you. I noticed that special quality on my very first day at

41

Battersea, especially at break time when the staff brought their favourites into the canteen. I'd watch with envy as the dog looked doe-eyed at its handler, its happy-o-meter swaying from side to side, and desperately wanted to be the recipient of that tail-thumping, unconditional love. I just wasn't sure how to find it.

Still not having much of a clue about dogs, I deferred to my more experienced colleagues. I chose June because judging by Jimmy's love for her, I knew she must be the expert. She explained what I needed to do.

I had to find myself a dog from the kennels, not just any old dog, she explained, but one that needed a little extra love. I must then gain its trust and take it out whenever I had any free time. June assured me a bond would soon build. I was extremely excited at the prospect of a single dog loving me as much as I loved its entire species.

The next opportunity I had, I took a walk through every kennel block at Battersea Dogs Home searching for 'the one'. I imagined it must be the same for new owners who come looking to adopt a dog.

Then all of a sudden there he was. Our eyes met; I was smitten.

He was a Border collie cross, smaller than a pedigree and about a year old. He was in the veterinary section with a bad case of kennel cough – a highly contagious form of dog flu, rarely serious but requiring antibiotics. Maybe it was because he was looking so sorry for himself or it could have been the fact that he was terrified, but this dog definitely seemed to need a little extra love.

I slowly opened the door. He backed away. Although I hadn't been at Battersea for long, one of the first things I'd learned was how to approach a nervous dog.

I knelt down, side on to him, avoiding eye contact. I threw him some treats, which he took. After ten minutes he had plucked up the courage to take a treat from my hand.

He was a bit whiffy but too nervous for anyone to have bathed yet. Because of his black and white colouring and his extremely rich aroma, I named him Pepe Le Pew after the cartoon skunk.

Over the next few days I spent all my free time with Pepe. It took a while for him to trust me but the day he turned the corner was worth waiting for. Until then it had always been the same. I'd go to the kennel, he'd back away, I'd throw the treats, he'd take them. By the end of each session I could give him a cuddle but at the start of every new session, we'd be back to square one.

But today was different. As I walked through the block of barking, coughing dogs, I could see he was at the front of the kennel, straining to see the kennel block door, as though he was waiting for me to come through it. When he saw me he let out a half howl, half squeal. He was up on his back legs, tail wagging, doing a two-legged dance from left of his kennel to right. Perhaps it was just because he was feeling better but I hoped it was because he was genuinely pleased to see me. Whatever it was I didn't care because for the first time, Pepe Le Pew was a happy dog and I felt my canine love reciprocated.

Our bond became stronger over the following weeks and we slipped into the routine of a walk at lunchtime and a long walk in the park every day after work. I even risked his displeasure by giving him a bath. He didn't appreciate it but he still loved me. I was the happiest person in the world.

Then the moment I'd been dreading finally came. Pepe was given a clean bill of health by the vets and he moved into the rehoming kennels. Of course I wanted him to go to a proper home and never have to go back into a kennel, but I couldn't bear the thought of not seeing him again.

I knew he would be chosen quickly; after all he was young and good-looking and had the softest eyes I'd ever seen. Just two days after arriving in the rehoming kennels, Pepe was chosen.

I had written on his card that he was my favourite and could the rehomer who rehomed him please come and find me so I could say goodbye. I was in awe of the rehomers; dealing with all those people, maybe having to say no and making huge decisions about a dog's future was more than I could imagine.

Scottish Mark, the rehomer, walked into my

block with an apologetic smile on his face. As soon as I saw him, I knew what he was going to say. I didn't even give him a chance to say it.

'Are they nice?' I asked.

'They're lovely,' he replied.

He told me Pepe's new owners were a retired couple that lived in Barnes with the husband's mother.

I went with Mark to the rehoming section. He opened Pepe's kennel and clipped the lead on him but as he began to lead Pepe towards the exit, Pepe looked at me, a little unsure. I gave him a reassuring stroke and we continued on.

I waited outside the meeting room whilst Mark introduced him to his new owners. Twenty minutes later he came out.

'Does he like them?' I asked.

'He was a little shy at first, but he's really taken to the ladies.'

'Can I come and meet them?

'Of course you can, lassie. In fact, they want to meet you,' Mark said, holding the meeting room door open for me to enter.

When Pepe saw me, he threw himself at me. I caught him mid-leap and he licked my face.

'I think he wants to go home with you!' said the husband.

I liked them straight away, especially Granny who was barking mad and kept asking to see my teeth. I really wanted them to take him but at the same time I didn't; I would miss him so much.

When they broke the news that they would like to take Pepe home, I was embarrassed to find myself crying. The wife put her arm around me and made me promise to come and visit them. This made me feel much better and we agreed I'd see them all again in three months, when Pepe had settled in.

They paid for Pepe and signed on the dotted line. They bought him a lovely new red collar and lead which I put on him, kissing the top of his head as I did.

As they walked away with Pepe, he kept turning around to look at me. He even put his brakes on a couple of times. I'll never forget the look on his face. It was as if he couldn't understand why I was letting these strangers take him away, as if I was just another human that was abandoning him. It was awful. I had to go back inside. I didn't realise this was just the first of many times my heart would be broken.

I counted the days until three months was up. True to their word, Mr and Mrs Hall phoned me and invited me over for lunch the following Saturday. I had visions of a tearful reunion between Pepe and me and felt quite nervous as I rang the doorbell. A loud bark came from upstairs, followed by deep growling. He never barked like that when he was at Battersea. I checked the address again. Had I got the wrong house? It sounded like a Rottweiler lived here.

Mrs Hall opened the door, gave me a hug and

46

invited me upstairs. Pepe was standing on the top step. He was barking his head off, pleased to see me – or so I thought.

When I reached the top he launched himself at me, though not in an 'I've really missed you' kind of way, more in a 'get out of my house, intruder, or I'll kill you' kind of way.

Then the little bugger jumped up and sank his teeth into me.

Mr Hall grabbed him and told him off, but this only made him worse. He launched another attack. If Mr Hall hadn't stopped him in time, he would have done some serious damage. He put Pepe in another room and slammed the door on him.

We all stood there in a state of shock until Granny broke the silence with, 'He's got lovely teeth.' I know; I'd just seen them at very close range.

Mrs Hall cleaned my wounded hand and dressed it. I'd only just recovered from the last dog bite. My mother was going to have a field day.

We went into the garden and sat down around the lunch table trying to make sense of what had just happened. We'd all lost our appetite, except Granny who was tucking into everything.

Mr and Mrs Hall couldn't understand it. They had given him everything, rarely told him off, spoilt him rotten and allowed him to do whatever he wanted. Right – now I understood. From the little I'd picked up in my short time at Battersea,

I realised that they felt sorry for Pepe and had overcompensated by never disciplining him, instead indulging his every whim. They'd even bought him his own sofa. His own sofa!

As a direct result of their overcompensation, Pepe Le Pew had become the alpha male and saw himself as top dog. As we talked, I discovered this wasn't the first time something like this had happened. One night, Pepe had been lying on the Halls' bed and when Mr Hall tried to get in, Pepe went for him.

I asked if he'd ever gone for anyone else.

'Only Tracey, our daughter. Actually, she should be joining us for lunch any minute.'

Poor Tracey, I hoped she was wearing her suit of armour.

I was desperately disappointed. I'd waited three long months to see my boy again and now he was locked away to stop him from savaging me. This was unacceptable. I was determined to see Pepe on my terms, not his, which involved too many teeth.

I suggested one of them put Pepe on a lead and bring him out. The plan was that we'd all ignore him and get on with lunch and after a while I'd try feeding him some ham from the table.

He came out as though nothing had happened. I asked Mr Hall to hand me Pepe's lead. I told Pepe to sit; he completely ignored me. I repeated myself in the sternest voice I could muster whilst at the same time hoping I wouldn't be torn to pieces.

He immediately sat so I gave him some ham and he gave me his paw. We were back to our old selves. He even gave me a sloppy wet kiss.

Our plan had worked a treat. He was relaxed and happy so we let him off the lead. Big mistake. At that moment Tracey arrived.

The garden was at the front of the house. Tracey pulled up, got out of her car and walked towards us. She was a big girl, with loud earrings and the highest heels I'd ever seen. She clomped towards us, earrings swinging, heels grinding into the pavement, shouting, 'Coo-ee!'

I must say, even I was a little spooked but not as much as Pepe who launched himself at Tracey.

She saw the oncoming black-and-white bullet, swore and turned tail, hotfooting it back to the car, trying not to break her ankles in those shoes. Pepe was hot on her stiletto heels. The rest of us just sat there open mouthed. It was like watching a car crash.

She only just made it and slammed the car door behind her as Pepe threw himself at the little Honda. She opened the window a crack and screamed a string of obscenities as she drove off.

I explained to the Halls that Pepe's behaviour was a serious concern. If he bit someone that wasn't one of the family (or me), he might have to be put down. I told them they must come to Battersea and see one of the behaviourists. They had to realise, though, that the change would have to come from them as well as Pepe. From now on,

Pepe was to be treated as a dog. Of course they should love him and look after him but no more spoiling, no more letting him get away with murder (literal or otherwise) and definitely no more sofas.

'But that seems so cruel; he's our baby,' said Mrs Hall. I wasn't getting through.

'It isn't cruel and he isn't your baby, he is your dog. If you carry on treating him as your baby he'll end up being put to sleep,' I said in desperation.

I felt terrible being so stern with these good people. All they had done was what any new dog owner would do: open up their home and spoil the cuddly new addition to their family. But I'd seen so many dogs brought into Battersea for this exact same reason and now I was witnessing it first-hand.

It took six months of hard work on everybody's part but thankfully, with help from Battersea, a major catastrophe was averted and Pepe returned to being the friendly, affectionate dog he once was. I received a photograph in the post. Tracey, her earrings and Pepe were all cuddled up together. What I was most delighted and relieved to see was that they were curled up on the floor, and Pepe's sofa was nowhere in sight.

# CHAPTER 4

# RESCUE ME

Kevin Spacey, a customer of Battersea Dogs Home, was once quoted as saying that his idea of heaven was to walk through his front door and be buried under a pile of dogs as they manically come to greet him. Mr Spacey is a man after my own heart.

The dogs and I shivered our way through my first few months at Battersea. It was a harsh winter and heat lamps, blankets and shredded newspaper did little to keep out the cold in those draughty old-fashioned kennel blocks. Even with my wellington-booted feet shoved into three pairs of socks and the dogs wearing their outsized knitted jumpers, it was teeth-chattering stuff.

Thankfully, I didn't have too long to wait before spring descended on Battersea, with summer hot on its heels. The Home's solitary tree, treated more as a natural place for leg-cocking than a thing of natural beauty, was abundant with pink blossom.

The mood across the United Kingdom brightens with the onset of spring and summer and my little corner of the British Isles was no exception as all of us, both two-legged and four, gambolled into the warmer weather. Having completely recovered from my dog bite, the feel-good factor was in full swing; however, the happy days were somewhat tempered by the sharp rise in unwanted dogs coming into the Home.

I had wrongly assumed that Battersea's busiest time would be Christmas and was finding out first-hand that it was in fact the summer months. I was intrigued, so canvassed opinion as to why this might be. Having clocked up decades of experience at the Home, I decided to ask Fred first. His answer made a cruel kind of sense.

He said that firstly, summer is when most people go away on holiday and, having usually left it far too late to organise boarding kennels (often booked up months in advance), people find they suddenly have a four-legged problem on their hands. They face a choice of cancelling their hugely expensive family holiday and losing their money or going on holiday and losing their dog. Sadly, as was evident to me, many chose the latter.

I was told about one bright spark that went away on a summer break, leaving his dog home alone for the week. He left seven bowls of food out – one for each day, thinking the dog would pace itself. Needless to say the dog ate all the food in the first five minutes and the RSPCA were called by a concerned neighbour five days later.

Secondly, Fred went on, by the summer that cute, fluffy little Christmas-present puppy is about eight months old. The once-tiny, vulnerable little ball of fur, with its greeting-card looks, is now gone and in its place is a much larger marauding beast, capable of wreaking a whole lot more havoc.

I was learning as much about humans as I was about dogs and didn't like what I saw.

At times during that busy summer, I could barely get through the kennel door for dogs. Four or five youngsters would be up on their hind legs, clamouring for attention. Sometimes they'd climb on each other's heads to gain that extra bit of height. Having battled my way into the kennel they'd be all over me, paws everywhere, licking tongues, sniffing noses and tails wagging so furiously they could have had someone's eye out.

I loved watching them bound around, fearlessly bumping into things and falling on their faces. They really are the dog equivalent of teenagers; gangly and awkward and just too big for themselves. They have wonderful saggy, baggy, wrinkled skin, almost as though they're wearing a romper suit that's five times too big. There's all that loose skin, those huge paws and eyes, all those differing car types and of course that wonderful smell of dog.

Sometimes, just because I could, I'd kneel down, cover my face from sharp claws and bury myself under those crazy kids as they climbed all over me.

It was during those times, when Battersea was at its busiest, that I'd think of Kevin Spacey.

53

Ironically, there he is with all the money in the world and there I was without two pennies to rub together, actually living his dream.

I'd been at Battersea for six months now but was still having trouble controlling most of the manic mutts under my care. Much of the time it felt like they were handling me instead of the other way around. I couldn't help feeling like the outsider – as though I was some kind of novelty, but I undertook all my responsibilities with gusto, which wasn't always easy, depending on the task. For this sheer bloody-minded persistence, and the fact that I'd been hospitalised during active service, I was beginning to earn myself brownie points and friends.

Ali Taylor was just one of Battersea's larger-than-life characters. She lived on a tough estate in north-west London, and often came into work with tales of gunshots ringing out, blue flashing lights, sirens screaming and police raids at all hours of the day and night. I'd sit listening, wide eyed and open mouthed; this didn't happen where I lived.

Ali wasn't like the friends I'd had at school and to begin with I was a little scared of her. She didn't suffer fools gladly and was a tough, straight-talking Londoner but had the kindest heart I think I'd ever come across.

Having always had dogs she had an innate understanding of Man's Best Friend and kindly –

and frequently – showed me where I was going wrong.

Whenever I bathed a dog, I'd come off second best and have to spend the rest of the day in damp clothes. Ali took pity on me and the first thing she taught me was how to avoid these soakings. I was all ears, concentrating hard, expecting there to be some science involved.

'When he starts to shake his coat out, just grab him by the scruff. It's not brain surgery,' she said, throwing her eyes heavenwards as though everyone knew this.

The next time I bathed a dog I tried the Ali Taylor method and it worked a treat. I grabbed the Airedale's scruff and his shake stopped in its tracks; just like putting your finger under someone's nose to stop them sneezing.

The second thing she taught me was how to tell a dog's age by looking at its teeth. Our guinea pig was a fat, elderly Labrador.

'Anything under five months will have needle-like puppy teeth. Watch your fingers on those!' she advised me. 'If the dog has its adult teeth but they are nice and white and its gums nice and pink, the dog is probably under 12–18 months old.'

OK, I think I can remember that.

'If the teeth are starting to discolour and have signs of wearing down, the dog is usually approaching middle age.' Ali then pulled the fat Labrador's chops right up and back so that I could see all his pearly whites – which were anything but.

'See how discoloured his gums are and how his back teeth have worn right down? Even his front teeth aren't too clever,' she said.

I peered into the Labrador's mouth which was a bit whiffy, to put it mildly. His teeth were shocking; all brown and cracked. Slobber began to drip from his jowls.

'This one's probably a stone chewer,' Ali pointed out. 'Going by his teeth, I'd say he's about ten years old,' she expertly predicted as the Labrador shook his head and covered us both in drool.

Once Ali felt that I'd grasped the finer points, she lined up a few friendly hounds to test me on. I passed with flying colours.

I may not have gone to university but my education was far from over.

At school, my teachers had taught me Reading, 'Riting and 'Rithmetic. Now I was discovering another set of 'R's as I learned that Battersea's main aims were to Rescue, Reunite, Rehabilitate and Rehome.

All four Rs were as vital as the other, although the ease with which they were undertaken varied enormously. For example, it was not difficult to reunite a lost one-year-old, female Nova Scotia Duck Tolling Retriever (probably the only one in the country) with someone who had been on the phone ten times that day, frantically looking for their lost one-year-old, female Nova Scotia Duck Tolling Retriever.

It was, however, somewhat more of a test to rehabilitate an antisocial ten-stone mastiff that had no interest in being social and would rather see to it that you never played the piano again.

In order to be able to reunite, rehabilitate and rehome, Battersea first had to rescue. This was the only one of the four Rs that required little effort. Sadly the dogs just fell into Battersea's lap. Most strays came in via members of the public, who found them and kindly took them to their local police station, from where Battersea's animal ambulances collected them.

Some strays, like the dotty bus-hopping Tulip, were brought directly into Battersea by the member of public that found them, which meant that the dog didn't have to spend any time in a police kennel. It's all very well for human felons to languish in a cell if they have committed a crime, but for an innocent hound to spend a night in the nick just doesn't seem right.

Copper, a little Jack Russell terrier, was a prime example. He spent four days in a police kennel and, forgotten, had had to lick condensation from the walls just to stop from dehydrating. Thankfully, better late than never, someone remembered Copper and called Battersea straight away to come and rescue him.

Not long after, a tiny poodle left me wondering how certain policemen ever managed to deal with big burly criminals.

I still hadn't quite got the hang of walking more

than one dog at a time and was being returned to my kennel block at breakneck speed by two long-legged hounds I had attempted to take for a civilised stroll. Just before I disappeared into my block, I saw three large policemen bringing in a small white poodle. The poodle stood shaking at the other end of a grasper (a long metal pole with a loop on the end used when dealing with particularly aggressive dogs; the pole keeps its user away from gnashing teeth at the other end. Graspers were only used at Battersea in extreme cases, because they can cause distress to some dogs).

That was all I managed to see before being bundled through the door and out of sight of the policemen. As I was putting hound-from-hell number two back into his kennel, he somehow managed to squirm his way out before I had a chance to close the door. Here we go again, I thought, I'm never going to get the hang of this, as he bolted out of the block like a bat out of hell. I had visions of running the length and breadth of the Home, past Dot – her eyebrows as usual raised to the heavens, trying to catch this canine Houdini. But just as he was halfway out of the kennel block door, Mickey, a senior member of staff who had been standing just outside my block, grabbed him. I'm not sure whether this was good or bad luck. On the upside Dot would never know I'd let my thousandth dog escape but on the downside I wasn't exactly showing signs of potential to the other senior staff.

'First one today?' Mickey asked, handing him back to me.

'First one all week,' I replied, clipping the lead back on to Houdini whilst trying to recover my ropey reputation. She couldn't help smiling as she reminded me it was only Tuesday morning. As she looked away I saw her smile fade, replaced by a concerned frown.

'What are those silly buggers doing with that poodle?' she asked rhetorically.

As Mickey marched over to the three policemen I thought, this should be good. After the largest of the officers gesticulated that the poodle had tried to attack them, there was a heated exchange of words. Mickey slowly knelt down to the same level as the cloud-like ball of fluff, gently stroked the poodle, picked it up, gave the police their grasper back as well as a filthy look for good measure, tutted, turned on her heel and stomped off. The three of them stood rooted to the spot, looking at their shoes like naughty schoolboys. If they were guilty of using unnecessary force, than so was Mickey.

Battersea Dogs Home's fleet of rescue vehicles consisted of five vans, also known as animal ambulances. Every day of the year, they collected anywhere between 10 and 30 stray dogs from police stations within the M25. That may sound like a lot but in my early years that figure could treble, with drivers having to make two police station runs a day. On one particularly dark day the intake exceeded 100.

Back in the very early days (even before my time), 1909 to be exact, two motorised vans and six horse-drawn vehicles were hired to collect the strays from London's streets. It wasn't until 1911 that they began collecting dogs directly from police stations.

At Battersea Dogs Home the canine is king and nowhere was this more evident than in the animal ambulances. The part of the ambulance where the dogs sat was air-conditioned; the driver's cab was not. That first summer I watched as the drivers returned from their rounds not only frazzled by London's traffic, but also from the extreme temperatures they had to endure in their cab. The dogs meanwhile stepped out of the back of the ambulance as fresh as daisies.

Part of my job as a kennel maid was to receive the dogs from the drivers, hold them whilst they were vaccinated and then take them to their kennel. With a hairstyle like Cousin It from the Addams Family and a penchant for large stroppy dogs, the diminutive Pauline headed the team of ambulance drivers. She still has the same hairstyle and fondness for moody mutts today. It was through working at Battersea that Pauline met, fell in love with and married Martin, her fellow ambulance driver. Pauline is a dog-handling expert and I do not use the word lightly. In all her years of service at Battersea she has never once been bitten which to me definitely constitutes expertise.

I was a little apprehensive the first time I was called upon to assist her unload her vehicle. I had visions of slathering Rottweilers, sabre-toothed German shepherds and snarling Dobermanns all waiting with 'I dare you' expressions on their faces. I needn't have worried, when Pauline flung open the back door of her ambulance, I was greeted by a sea of smiley hounds with wagging tails. Even more than that, I was struck by the amount of dogs she had managed to fit in. She had comfortably managed to squeeze 15 dogs of all shapes and sizes into an area roughly ten feet by six. The top half of the van was fitted with eight cages for small dogs and puppies, and below them, at ground level, were two cages where large, aggressive dogs could be securely stowed. Running around the inside of the van at hip height was a rail that more sociable dogs could be tied to.

Pauline was an old hand and, working so closely with dogs every day, had gained a sixth sense for who the potential troublemakers might be. She explained to me that a good rule of thumb when putting dogs in such close proximity together was to always put opposite sexes next to each other. Even when secured to a rail, having two males face to face can result in squabbling and driving around the M25 whilst a punch-up takes place in the back of the van should be avoided at all costs.

We were down to offloading the last two dogs

on Pauline's van. They were small terriers so she brought them off together and handed one to me. Not wanting to screw up in front of her, I held on to mine as tightly as I could. As the veterinary nurse vaccinated the other one, he screamed and turned to bite her. She let go of him and he charged at my dog. In a flash, there was a full-blown dogfight at my feet. I stood there paralysed, remembering back to my hospitalisation. All I could summon up was my most shocked expression and a muted squeak. Pauline dived in and within a couple of seconds had the pintsized pugilists under her expert control. Panic over. I longed for the day when I might emulate this fearless dog handler. There was no room for scaredy cats at Battersea Dogs Home.

The arrival of the animal ambulances became one of my favourite parts of the whole day because although it was sad to see so many new arrivals coming in, when those van doors were opened up it was always a surprise. I was often delighted with what I found, sometimes a little terrified but never disappointed.

I had seen dogs come in via members of the public, police officers and Battersea's very own animal ambulances but I had also seen men and women in green uniforms bringing dogs in. I asked my guru, Jacky, who they were.

I discovered that each local authority had a dog warden whose full-time job, amongst other things, was to round up strays, educate people about responsible dog ownership and enforce dog-related by-laws such as making sure people scoop their dogs' poop. Sometimes they collected dogs directly from owners who could no longer care for them, but mostly they brought in the dogs found straying on their patch.

Tony was by far the chattiest dog warden. During my first few months I discovered that new faces were generally ignored by those on Battersea's periphery, with very few exceptions. One of those exceptions was Tony, who talked to anyone and everyone. On approximately my third day at the Home, Tony had stopped me in my tracks (whilst carrying a heavy pot of tripe) and proceeded to tell me, in minute detail, all about a Border collie he'd been trying to catch for 'what seems like for ever!' Thinking it rude to just walk off, I put my pot down and offered him the attention my up-bringing had taught me was polite. I was quickly swept up in his tales of cat and mouse and hung on his every word until Dot walked by and asked me why I was depriving a hundred hungry hounds of their lunch?

Apologising to both Dot and Tony I picked up my cauldron and headed back to my block.

'What's the dog's name?' I shouted from the door.

'Dunno what 'is real name is but I've called 'im Quick and I don't 'ave to tell you why!' Tony yelled after me.

From then on, whenever I saw Tony I asked for a Quick update. Not really understanding the concept, Tony would launch into a lengthy discourse about his nemesis, whilst I kept a weather eye out for Dot.

No one really knew where Quick had come from. He had just appeared out of the blue one day, on a vast expanse of common ground in south London. Countless members of the public had tried to catch him and after failing miserably, they'd phoned Tony.

As soon as Tony saw Quick, he knew catching him was going to be difficult. The dog was lightning fast and spooked out of his wits. Usually dogs like this settle after a few days and either approach a human or at least allow one to catch them. Not Quick. Something bad had happened to him and he wasn't about to allow himself to be caught. Quick was in it for the long haul.

This poor beleaguered dog warden had been trying to catch Quick for so long that now, months down the track, it had become a running joke between us. Whenever Tony came in with a stray that wasn't a collie, I'd say, 'No luck then?' to which he would always reply, 'Nah, not yet but I'm getting closer.'

'Sure you are, Tony.'

Catching Quick became almost as much of an obsession with me as it was with Tony. I couldn't wait for the next instalment and sat transfixed as he regaled me with increasingly ingenious ways how he was going to do it. He started showing me complicated diagrams involving ropes, pulleys and boxes and had even devised a plan involving his wife's Sunday roast leg of lamb. It reminded me of Wile E. Coyote trying to catch Roadrunner.

'Don't worry, I'll 'ave Quick in the back of me van by close of business, Friday,' he'd say. But many, many Fridays came and went, Quick always coming out on top in this fascinating battle of wills.

Then one day, after three months of failed attempts, Battersea received a phone call from a hyperventilating Tony.

'I've got 'im, I've got 'im. 'E's in the back of me van. I'm coming in,' he wheezed down the phone.

When Tony arrived at Battersea I was waiting there to greet him and the infamous Quick.

'So how did you do it?' I asked him. 'Which one of your schemes got the better of him?'

'You won't believe it. I was 'avin' me lunch at the common, sitting on the ledge at the back of me van, when bugger me if Quick didn't appear from nowhere, jump up next to me and wolf down me sandwich. I didn't want to startle 'im so I offered 'im a bite of me KitKat which 'e nearly bit me 'and off for. I took it dead slow but held out me 'and to stroke 'im and 'e let me. I reckon old Quick 'ad 'ad enough of the open road.'

I peered into the back of the van and wasn't at all surprised that this was the case. Looking back at me was a thin, raggedy collie with matted fur and exhaustion written all over his face.

I took him straight to a warm kennel, gave him a blanket and some food and as he finished his last mouthful, Quick fell asleep.

In almost equal number to strays came 'Gifts to the Home'. Historically, strays had always out-numbered gifts by three to one, but towards the end of my time at Battersea strays and gifts made up roughly half and half of Battersea's canine intake. The term 'Gift' was a rather ludi-crous title I'd always thought. The theory behind the name was that people gave their dogs as 'gifts' for Battersea to sell and therefore make money from. Never mind the fact that by the time Battersea had vaccinated, neutered, micro-chipped, fed and housed the animal for however long, the cost of doing all that was about eight times more than Battersca would receive from the meagre £85 rehoming fee. Battersea's yearly bill for dog and cat food alone was over £120,000.

Never having owned a dog before, I was astounded at how many crimes they were capable of commit-ting. I knew a lack of housetraining might bring a dog to Battersca and perhaps chewing up expen-sive personal belongings could lead a hound into hot water but some misdemeanours were really quite surprising.

They ranged from fighting with other dogs and beating up the cat, to attacking the children and howling all day. Some poor dogs found themselves dumped through no fault of their own. Moving house and emigrating were particularly popular, as was my own personal favourite: allergies. Even though in some cases they had had the dog for many years, all of a sudden they seemed to be having an allergic reaction to it.

One quiet afternoon, after I had administered the lunchtime feed – this time with most of the food going down the dogs instead of all down me, and it was too wet to walk them, Jacky asked if I'd like to watch the intake process. This was a job shared between the rehomers and the more experienced kennel staff. That day, two of my colleagues were handling the intake but judging by the amount of dogs seeking sanctuary at the world's most famous dogs' home, this section was woefully undermanned.

As Jacky and I walked into the waiting room where people give up their pets, we were greeted with pandemonium. Two dogs were fighting, another was growling at everything that moved, three young kids were running wild and a cat was desperately trying to squirm out of its owner's arms. We'll take the dogs and the cat but they can keep the kids, I thought to myself. The cat was our priority; if it got loose there'd be big trouble. I ran to find a cat box whilst Jacky asked who was first.

By the time I'd returned and we had wrestled the cat into the box for its own safety, Jacky had handed each owner a form to fill out, giving as much information as possible about their dog or cat. I flicked through the comprehensive form and found that the questions ranged from the animal's medical history, to how it reacted towards children, other animals and even fireworks.

I found some of the people to be terribly shifty but couldn't put my finger on why. Jacky took me aside and explained that when bringing dogs into Battersea to be rehomed, owners often lied in an attempt to justify what they were doing either to themselves or to us. They might say that the dog had bitten someone when it hadn't. Conversely, the dog really might have bitten someone but the owner wouldn't mention it in case it hampered the dog's chances of finding a new home.

The first in line was a tattooed lady, bringing her dog in because it had bitten her child. This was not an unusual occurrence in itself and some of the friendliest dogs in my own kennel block had been brought in for snapping at kids, often as a result of being teased at the time. This case was different. The dog had put the seven-year-old child in hospital and left her requiring 28 stitches to the face, as well as plastic surgery.

As soon as I heard this, I took a step back from the dog. My comfort levels didn't improve when I heard the woman say she wanted Battersea to rehome her dog. Jacky told her that with this kind of history, it would be irresponsible for the Home to do so and that the only sensible option would be to put the dog down. With this, she started effing and blinding. She stormed off with the dog who incidentally tried to bite me as it went past, missing by an inch, shouting she'd 'effing well tell everyone that Battersea just wants to put dogs down' and that she'd 'effing well rehome the dog herself'. The mind boggled. How could she give that dog to someone knowing what it had done to her child and that it could do the same to someone else's?

Occasionally, Battersea was called upon to collect dogs from private addresses and on one such occasion Pauline asked if I would like to accompany her. I was already sitting in the van before she'd finished her sentence. I loved those vehicles because they were all about the dogs. The seats themselves resembled smooth-haired hounds from all the hair ingrained into them. A box filled with recycled collars sat in the foot-well, each waiting to adorn a new arrival. Half-empty packets of Schmackos were stuffed into every corner of the cab, ready to entice reluctant strays. But best of all was the overpowering smell of dog.

The fact that Pauline's delightful English bull terrier, Emmie, sat in the cab with us was a bonus. Emmie was the sweetest-natured bull terrier I'd ever met. She was rotund, had a smiley face and whenever I squeaked at her, her pointy ears shot skyward.

We pulled up outside a run-down house where the police were waiting to let us in. A neighbour had alerted them when she hadn't seen the occupant for days and unopened milk bottles were piling up outside the front door. The police had entered the house an hour before we arrived to find the occupant dead and his dog fiercely guarding the body. Remembering the poodle incident, I wasn't altogether surprised the police had called Battersea; it was going to be a hell of a job to coax the dog away without being bitten.

I'd never seen a dead body before and tried to focus on the dog to stop myself from fainting. He was a one-year-old, large black cross-breed Labrador called Roscoe. Because of the circumstances, Pauline was reluctant to use a grasper to move him. This poor creature's world had been turned upside down and without his beloved master things were only going to get harder for him.

It was going to take a long time to gain Roscoe's trust and the police, who kept trying to hurry Pauline up, were not helping matters. In their big black coats and helmets, and with booming voices and impatient gestures, they intimidated Roscoe. Pauline told them in no uncertain terms that they were hindering proceedings rather than helping, and to wait outside.

Roscoe was starving and greedily took the treats Pauline threw to him. He seemed soothed by her gentle voice telling him he was a good boy. She avoided any confrontational eye contact which also helped to put him at ease. Two hours later he was eating treats from her hand but Roscoe never once took his eyes off his lifeless master.

Pauline managed to slip a lead on Roscoe but when she tried to lead him out of the house, he dug his heels in and wouldn't be parted from his owner. He was incredibly strong and if she managed to coax him one step away, Roscoe would effortlessly drag her small frame back until he could plant himself firmly in the crook of the dead man's arm, with his head resting on his master's chest.

Pauline realised another tactic was needed. Out of the corner of her eye, she saw the man's hat hanging by the door. She dropped Roscoe's lead, walked over to the door and picked up the hat. She called Roscoe over. At the sight of his master's hat, he came bounding over and before he had time to think, Pauline grabbed his lead and took him and the hat outside. Once away from the body, Roscoe was the friendliest, most gentle animal you could possibly wish to meet, but he never let that hat out of his sight.

'How did you know that would work?' I asked.

'Emmie's the same,' she replied. 'Whenever I put my coat and hat on, she knows it's time for walkies and is out of the door before you can say Hong Kong Phooey. Don't know why I didn't think of that an hour and a half ago!'

We got Roscoe back to the Home and although he wasn't technically a stray, I took him to a kennel in my block. Battersea had an obligation to try and track down any relatives of the deceased that might want to keep Roscoe. I was pleased about this and hoped he would go off and live with someone he already knew; at least this would provide some form of normality and continuity in his life. I was also glad because whilst this search took place he couldn't go up for rehoming and would remain in my block where I could take care of him.

When I put Roscoe into his kennel he made a beeline for the bed at the back, not to get into it, rather to burrow behind it so he could hide between it and the wall. He stayed like that for days, only moving when I took him out for a walk.

My heart went out to him – his pain became my pain. Inevitably, I fell in love with Roscoe.

By now, I was beginning to feel as much a part of Battersea Dogs Home as the dogs it rescued. In many ways, when I thought about where I could have ended up, I felt that Battersea had rescued me too.

The dogs that Battersea received varied enormously, from Great Danes and Irish wolfhounds to chihuahuas and Yorkshire terriers, from geriatrics on their last legs to newborns and sometimes heavily pregnant bitches, thrown out by cold-hearted owners.

Whatever the dogs' vital statistics, if they were unwanted by their owners, they were wanted by Battersea. Its door was always open – 24 hours a day, 365 days of the year – which was just as well considering the thousands that came through it annually.

It took a long time for me to come to terms with the amount of dogs Battersea had to deal with and the heartless way in which their owners disposed of them. A six-week-old puppy found dodging traffic on the Great West Road, another poor unfortunate under the floorboards of a deserted flat and a pit bull terrier fished out of the Thames, to name but a few.

All of this was hard to swallow for someone whose lifelong dream was to have a dog. I vowed that when I left home I'd have my own dog, but I'd wait until I felt responsible enough to do it properly. To my dog, whoever he or she may be, wherever or whenever he or she may be, I would commit 100 per cent, totally and utterly.

# CHAPTER 5

# FRIENDS REUNITED

Boss the Border Collie had gone missing six long months ago, after his family's car was stolen with Boss in the back seat. A few days later the police found the car but there was no sign of Boss. Although his distraught owner knew she would never stop looking for him, she realised the chances of finding him were growing increasingly slim.

I was glad to be working in the stray section at Battersea Dogs Home. This was the dogs' very first taste of Battersea life and I wanted to do everything I could to make sure it was as palatable as possible. It was hard not to become attached to the strays in our care and Roscoe aside (who'd leapt into place as my top dog), we couldn't help but have favourites. Jacky liked a challenge and often befriended the troublemakers like Smithy, a white German shepherd who terrified me. I chose the altogether soppier individuals, but friend or foe, we were all too aware that after seven days they would move on; either claimed by their owners or sent on to the rehoming section.

Over the years, the number of dogs reunited with their owners improved dramatically and of the 10,000 dogs that annually passed through Battersea's doors towards the end of my service, 48 per cent were claimed. But back then I found it impossible to believe that only 13 per cent of the dogs were claimed by their owners each year, although with Unders bursting at the seams that figure certainly felt real enough. This 13 per cent were genuinely lucky in love. The remaining 87 per cent, some 20,000 dogs, were callously abandoned rather than genuinely lost.

Roscoe wasn't having much luck being claimed either and both Battersea's investigations and those carried out by the police failed to find any relatives with whom Roscoe could be reunited. In addition to this setback, he wasn't enjoying Battersea life. I was doing my best to keep him buoyant but it wasn't me he wanted, it was his owner. This was obviously never going to happen and he became more depressed by the day, eventually resorting to howling in an attempt to summon his late pack-leader. When Roscoe began to go off his food and lose weight, I realised he needed more help than I could give him.

On the whole, my own daily howlers were becoming fewer and further between and with a combination of Jacky's expert guidance and my unbridled enthusiasm, I had almost mastered feeding, walking and generally controlling the dogs in our block.

In recognition of this achievement (feeble by most standards), Mickey asked if I'd like to shadow her whilst she showed the people who had lost their dogs around the Home. I hadn't yet earned my stripes to go it alone but through shadowing my seniors I was steadily working my way around all aspects of the Home. I was having all of the fun without any of the responsibility and that suited me just fine.

As Mickey and I walked towards the waiting area I could see a crowd of people eagerly peering back at us. Two of them looked furious, one looked hysterical and a small group, a family of four, just looked rather sad. It transpired that this was the sixth and seventh time respectively that the angry people had collected their wandering hounds from Battersea, incurring claim fees for vaccinations and housing each time. The distraught person was looking after her friend's dog and had let it off the lead assuming it would come back. The spaniel had other ideas and was last seen running north.

First in line was the rather sad-looking family whom Mickey greeted warmly, as if she knew them. They had been coming to Battersea three times a week religiously for the past six months and phoning every day since their dog went missing. By now, they knew Battersea's routine intimately and waited until the animal ambulances had returned from collecting the day's strays before coming to see if one of them might be their beloved Boss. The rest of the family stayed in the waiting area whilst Mum came with us.

As we walked around the kennels, she explained to me that the kids desperately wanted Boss back and insisted upon coming to Battersea but seeing all those unwanted dogs every time, none of whom was Boss, was just too upsetting for them. This didn't worry her as much as not knowing what had happened to her dog. What if he was dead or, worse still, being abused by someone? We had gone around three-quarters of Unders when she stopped and lingered at one kennel. In the back was a pathetic-looking wretch, shaking like a leaf and terribly underweight. I held my breath. It was Quick.

Mickey asked her if she thought this was Boss. She looked at the dog's card.

'No, he's too thin,' she murmured, 'and this one's name is Quick.'

Mickey explained that Quick was just a name the dog warden had given him and also gently reminded her that her dog had been gone for six months and would probably look a little different to how he looked when she last saw him.

The lady knelt down, put her hand to the bars and ever so softly said, 'Boss?'

The dog stopped shaking for a few moments, lifted his unkempt head up from the concrete floor and tilted it to one side.

'Boss?' she said again, this time a little more audibly and with greater conviction.

The dog stood up, still hesitant, still unsure, but increasingly alert. My heart was racing.

It took a few moments to really register but once it did, the dog launched himself at the kennel door in an explosion of relief and recognition, tail wagging and squealing. His owner screamed; she was shaking and sobbing. I could feel the tears rising up in me and had to swallow hard. I had to hold myself together and stop my hand shaking long enough to unlock the kennel door so that neither had to spend another second apart.

She threw herself at him and he at her. Tears turned to joy and joy turned to laughter, which soon became cries of, 'Boss, where have you been?'

Still shaking, she just kept repeating over and over between sobs, 'I've found you. I've found you.' She and Boss were both euphoric and, in an instant, the agony of those lost six months was forgotten for ever.

I called Tony, the dog warden.

'Where are you?' I asked, breathless.

'As it 'appens, I'm pulling up to your front door.'

'Come to the stray block straight away.'

Tony pulled up just in time to see Boss and his owner exiting the kennel block.

'Quick!' he shouted.

'His name is Boss,' I explained to Tony.

'Much better name. Don't you look happy, boy?'

And he did. Boss couldn't take his eyes off his owner, nor she him. When we walked into reception, the rest of Boss's waiting family looked up.

For a moment nobody moved, too stunned to comprehend that after six months they had found their missing family member. And then they were all over him, screaming and crying too. I looked at Boss whose expression was as close to a grin as I'd ever seen on a dog's face.

Tony explained to his owner the fun and games he and Boss had had over the past three months.

'Only three months?' she asked, looking puzzled. 'He's been gone for six.'

We didn't know where Boss had been or what he went through in those first three months, nor will we ever know. The most important thing was that today he was going home.

It's not just ordinary people that mislay their mutts once in a while; it can happen to real live saints too.

We knew Bob Geldof lived in the area from having seen him countless times at the petrol station on the corner. He also walked his dog in Battersea Park and his daughters attended the school a stone's throw from the Home.

It was a fairly routine day at Battersea Dogs Home. About 30 strays had been picked up by Pauline and the other drivers that morning and I'd only managed to lose one whilst escorting them to their new temporary home. Jacky and I fed and watered them along with the other 70 dogs in our care. All of the new kids had then flopped straight into their beds, to rest their weary travellers' bones.

All of them except for one, a happy, chubby golden retriever that sat by his kennel door, holding a teddy bear in his mouth and wagging his tail at anyone who was interested.

You couldn't help but stop and commend these triers. Not only did they look particularly endearing but they worked so hard just for someone to notice them. I whispered to him that he didn't have to try so hard, not yet anyway, the rehoming kennels were a whole week away. He never made it that far.

I was sitting in the retriever's bed giving him a cuddle when Dot walked past.

'I know you haven't done this on your own yet, but it's time to put all that shadowing to good use. It's very busy in the Lost Dogs' area,' she said. 'Can you show some claimants around?'

Although I was a little nervous, I was happy to be growing into my Battersea shoes but as I left the retriever's kennel, he let out a pitiful howl.

'It's all right, boy,' I reassured him, 'I'll be back,' and threw him a couple of Schmackos.

First in line was a young lady who said she had lost the family's golden retriever. It couldn't be, I thought. Sure enough, she stopped right outside my friend's kennel. There was a slight problem, however. He hardly paid any attention to her and seemed more pleased to see me! This concerned me because when verifying a claimant really was the owner of a dog, our main indication was the animal's reaction towards them. Usually when a dog saw its owner, especially in such unfamiliar surroundings as Battersea Dogs Home, it would go completely mad, leaping around like a gazelle and howling like a lunatic. The same reaction applied whether the dog only saw its owner that morning or, like Boss, six months ago. Not so in this case.

I checked the lady's form and it became clear why the dog's reaction was not more intense. She had ticked the box stating that she was not the owner, but a representative of the owner. I asked what her relationship to the owner was, to which she replied she was nanny to his children. In these cases the representative had to return with a photograph of the dog and a letter from the owner, giving their permission for it to be released. We might have also phoned the owner for verbal confirmation.

I scrutinised the form only to read that the owner of the dog was none other than Bob Geldof. I had always liked the Boomtown Rats and thought it would be pretty cool to meet the orchestrator of Live Aid, so I mischievously told her the rules stated only the owner could claim their dog. She said he was out looking for the dog but she'd let him know and he'd probably be in before closing time. He had better hurry, I said, the doors shut in half an hour.

Within 20 minutes Bob was at Battersea and I made the most of my cheeky meeting with him. The topic of conversation could have been music, politics or Live Aid but instead we talked about our mutual love: dogs.

We chatted as we went up to the kennels to retrieve his retriever and Bob told me how one of his girls had left the back gate open and the dog had made a bid for freedom, well, the park anyway. He was clearly delighted and relieved that his dog was safe at Battersea. He asked me who had found him and I explained that a member of the public walking his own dog in Battersea Park had found him and brought him straight into the Home.

Bob was fascinated by how big Battersea was and likened it to Doctor Who's Tardis. He drove past the Home every day and commented on how no one would ever believe it was so huge inside.

With genuine interest, he asked many questions about the Home: how it ran, how it was funded, how many dogs came in every year.

We walked up to his dog's kennel. The dog had taken my advice and given up trying to impress people with the teddy-bear routine and was now fast asleep in his bed. Bob called him. No response. He called a little louder. No response. Then he said in his thick Irish brogue, 'Would you wake up, you lazy bugger, Daddy's come to get you.'

With that the dog's eyes popped open and he was on his feet in a second. Not forgetting to pick up his teddy bear, he threw himself at the kennel door, singing like a soprano. Now that's the reaction I was looking for.

A similar reaction came from Bob who immediately dropped down to the dog's level and threw his arms around his long-lost pal. The dog's tail wagged furiously in a circular motion; any more vigorously and he was in danger of shooting into orbit and taking Bob with him.

Even though his dog had only been lost for a few hours, Bob became a little emotional. He told me the dog was his mate, his sanity and the only other boy in a house full of girls.

Bob signed the paperwork, put a large donation in the box and the two boys happily trotted home together.

In time, Battersea's database became computerised, but back in 1988 when Bob Geldof was claiming his retriever, no one had heard of a hard drive and a mouse was something you might encounter in the storeroom. Back then there was just a huge old-fashioned, handwritten ledger to cope with 23,000 dogs arriving each year.

With the dawn of computer technology, the unenviable task of not only implementing the computerised database, but also getting the staff, many of whom were completely technophobic, to some level of computer literacy fell to Sue 'Oaky' Oak who went on to work at Battersea for 16 years as head of IT. The poor thing nearly had a nervous breakdown in the process, coming close on many occasions to pressing the 'escape' button:

The only thing that kept Oaky sane was her love

of Battersea's cats that she tirelessly socialised up in her office. In order to keep the cats from escaping, Oaky had to have a floor-to-ceiling cage door installed. To any non-Battersea person passing by, she must have looked like an exhibit in the zoo, either that or some kind of Hannibal Lecter-type psychopath, caged for the safety of the general public.

In the end, Oaky's many mini-meltdowns were worth it and the efficiency of this age-old institution improved dramatically. Every single dog and cat that arrived at Battersea was entered on to a growing database and it was possible to reunite lost dogs with their owners at the click of a mouse and, just for fun, find out how many German shepherds came in from Shepherd's Bush. The possibilities were endless. The powers that be realised reuniting lost dogs with their owners was now a full-time job and Battersea's Lost Dogs & Cats Department was born.

This department consisted of five humans, and a Rottweiler called Kane. They worked from 8 a.m. till 8 p.m. every day of the year, checking their enormous database of lost dogs against the flood of phone calls from frantic owners. The sophisticated state-of-the-art computer software matched in minute detail the dog's colour, sex, age, breed (or breed cross), size, distinguishing features, collar and the area it was lost or found, with desperate parents hanging on at the other end of the phone.

The Lost Dogs & Cats Department received about 18,000 calls a year, some from owners whose dog or cat had gone missing, others from people who had found a dog or cat. The team not only helped thousands of hounds at Battersea find their way home, they also managed to reunite approximately 1,000 dogs a year with their owners at police stations, thus never having to set foot inside the Home. This saved them and their owners time, heartache and expense, and eased the space problems of an often-overcrowded Battersea Dogs Home.

One of the busiest times for the Lost Dogs & Cats Department was Guy Fawkes Night, or should I say Guy Fawkes fort-night, which increasingly became the case. For the dogs at Battersea this was a horror fortnight. The staff did the best they could by blacking out windows at night and turning up radios to drown out the increasingly loud bangs but they often came into work the next morning to find dogs that had injured themselves in frantic efforts to escape the confines of their kennel.

For the capital's pet population, Guy Fawkes is terrible news, as are religious festivals like Diwali that occur throughout the year. Dogs and cats cannot understand the concept of fireworks but many of them somehow know that they have to do whatever it takes to get away from them.

Around these times Battersea's stray numbers doubled, with phone lines to the Lost Dogs &

Cats Department jammed by distraught owners. Thankfully most of them were reunited with their owners almost as quickly as they came into the Home.

I cherished the moments when old friends were reunited but in my early years at Battersea I also learned that sometimes new-found friends were brought back together too.

It was 1989. The Berlin Wall had fallen and so had I, for a dog called Marley.

Marley was a rough-coated lurcher languishing in my kennel block. She was only a pup and with her big 'who me?' eyes, her ears at half mast and her shaggy grey fur, she looked as though she had been pulled through a hedge backwards. She was bewildered by the whole Battersea experience and was terrified of all the other dogs, especially those that were bigger than her, which was practically all of them. I had kennelled her with another youngster which helped them both relax and it wasn't long before they had forgotten their worries and were jumping all over one another without a care in the world.

Marley had been brought into Battersea by Jade, a member of the public who had found her wandering down a busy London street.

Jade had just moved out of home and was living in rented accommodation with her boyfriend Mark. She was missing her family dog like mad and when she saw this seemingly abandoned puppy with the big brown eyes, Jade didn't think twice about scooping her up, taking her home and keeping her.

Mark had other ideas.

'What if her owner is looking for her? We have to take her to Battersea Dogs Home.'

'But if she isn't claimed we can keep her, right?' came Jade's reply, more a statement than a question.

Mark remained vague and the next day drove Jade and the newly named Marley to Battersea.

Providing they met the rehoming criteria, anyone that found a dog had first refusal to rehome it if it remained unclaimed. When Jade dropped Marley off with us, she made it very clear that she wanted to come back for Marley if her owners didn't come forward.

By law, all stray dogs had to remain at Battersea Dogs Home for seven days in order for their owners to find them, a law introduced by Queen Victoria, Battersea's very first patron.

During that week, Jade worked tirelessly on Mark until he succumbed. They phoned Battersea on Marley's seventh day. A tense wait ensued whilst the receptionist went to check if Marley had been claimed.

'Have you got a grey puppy in here called Marley?' Carol yelled from the door of Unders.

'What? I can't hear you,' I mouthed from the other end, pointing at my car.

Carol walked down to me and asked again.

'Yes, she's here,' I pointed. 'Has her owner come?' I asked.

'No, but the person that found her wants to keep her,' Carol shouted over the din of the dogs.

Happy days, I thought to myself as I looked at the innocent puppy chewing her kennel mate's ear.

Four chewed fingernails later, Jade heard Carol come back on the phone.

'She's still here. Come down tomorrow and fill out the rehoming forms.'

Jade and Mark were first in the queue the next morning. Their rehoming interview with Keith, one of the rehomers, went relatively smoothly and because they lived in a flat they were passed for a small- to medium-sized dog. Keith came to my block to collect Marley but when he saw her, his face dropped.

'Oh my God, she's a lurcher. They just said she was a small grey puppy.'

'What's the problem?' I asked.

Lurchers usually have greyhound or deerhound in their ancestry, which means it's a pretty safe bet they'll reach a fair size.

'I don't think their accommodation is big enough to cope with her when she's fully grown,' Keith said. Then he asked me how big I thought she would grow to be. This was novel; I was being asked my opinion about a dog. Trying to look serious and knowledgeable I put my hand to my chin, raised my eyebrows and answered, 'Lurcher size, I'd say.'

'Very helpful. Large lurcher or small lurcher?' Keith pressed.

'Oh, probably around medium-sized lurcher,' I replied, hoping it didn't show that I didn't have a clue.

Back in the interview room, Jade was breathless with excitement at the prospect of becoming Marley's proud owner. But when Keith returned without her, she was crestfallen.

He explained what the problem was, to which she informed Keith she had a large flat and asked if she could reserve Marley whilst Battersea carried out a home visit in order to see how spacious her flat was. He couldn't justify holding Marley back for up to a week whilst the home visit was carried out. Battersea was bursting at the seams with both dogs and customers and Keith knew that Marley could be rehomed that same day. He remained steadfast but so did Jade.

Keith realised he had a battle on his hands but he also recognised that these were caring, dog-savvy people that would give Marley a fantastic home. Reasoning to himself that Jade could have just kept Marley instead of doing the right thing and bringing her to Battersea, he did an about turn and reunited Jade with her beloved Marley. She burst into tears, thanking Keith profusely. He didn't want thanks; just for Marley not to grow too big.

A couple of years later Jade returned to Battersea, this time as an employee. She brought Marley into work with her one day. Marley had, indeed, grown up to be a Lurcher but to my shock and amazement she had the legs of a Jack Russell terrier! We still laugh about it to this day.

Imagine what would have happened, though, if after Jade and Mark had taken Marley home, Marley's true owner came forward demanding his dog be returned to him. I was learning that nothing at Battersea, except for perhaps the Dalmatians, was ever black and white.

Duke came into my block three weeks after Marley went home. He was a good boy but unremarkable in every way; just one of the thousands of black-and-tan mongrels Battersea received every year. He behaved impeccably during his week with me, always waiting to be let out for his morning ablutions, never snatching treats and always sitting when I offered him his food. This was much more than could be said for many of my other tenants.

Duke waited patiently to be claimed by his owner. He waited and waited; for seven days he waited but no one came. The obedient, middle-aged Duke sailed through his temperament assessment and was put up for rehoming. Within a week he was chosen by a kind couple with a 12-year-old son.

We loved them, they loved him, and he loved them. They skipped off into the sunset and everyone was happy. That was until his original owner turned up at Battersea brandishing a photo of Duke. I stared at the photo, knowing this dog had been in my kennel block and then rehomed to a new family.

Having had many days shadowing my senior colleagues without incident whilst they dealt with claimants, I had only recently been given the responsibility of going it alone. Bob Geldof was my first; why did my second have to be the most complicated scenario ever?

Duke had been in his new home for four weeks. His previous owner had had him for four years. When I quizzed the original owner as to why he hadn't come forward sooner, he explained that he and his wife were on holiday with their 12-year-old daughter and had literally just arrived home.

Their good-for-nothing adult son was supposed to be looking after the dog whose real name was Arthur. When asked why the good-for-nothing son hadn't come to Battersea to look for Arthur himself the man replied with words that cannot be put into print.

Just to be sure, I asked the man if he had any other photos of the dog. He produced a whole album containing pictures of their prized Arthur. I stared at dozens of photos of the exact same dog that had been in my block for a week. There were snaps of Arthur on the beach, Arthur at a birthday party, Arthur eating Christmas dinner, Arthur posing with Granny and many, many more. The 12-year-old daughter was hopping up and down on the spot desperately trying to hold back the tears. There was no doubt about it; they were the true owners.

I pulled the man aside and explained the position to him.

'There's no easy way to tell you this. Your dog was here but he was rehomed four weeks ago. When a stray comes into Battersea it stays here for seven days to give the owner a chance to claim it. Once those seven days are up, the dog becomes the property of Battersea Dogs Home who then passes ownership to the new owner when the dog is rehomed. The dog belongs to them now,' I grimaced. 'It's up to them whether they give Arthur back or not.'

'But we've had him since he was a pup. My daughter will be heartbroken if they don't; we all will.'

They've got a 12-year-old too, I thought to myself and whichever way this goes, one child is going to be inconsolable. I phoned the new owners.

I counted four rings before the phone was picked up. All I said was that I was calling from Battersea Dogs Home and before I could explain the situation the man launched into how wonderful Duke was. He waxed lyrical for ten minutes and when I finally managed to get a word in, not surprisingly, he was crushed by the news.

'But he's been marvellous and we're all in love with him. He's changed our lives. You see, my son struggles with emotional problems and Duke has turned him into a completely different person. His therapist put the remarkable change down to Duke.'

Great. Trust me to have to deal with the one where there's a therapist involved. It got worse. The man went on to tell me that his wife had been suffering from depression and had to take medication to help her cope with her son's problems but now that her son was happier, so was she. In fact, 'she was weaning herself off the medication but this news would definitely send her back on to the full dosage'. This unremarkable black-and-tan mongrel dog was turning out to be a saint. He should have been named Mother Teresa, not Arthur or Duke.

All I could do was explain the facts to the new owners; that the other family had had Duke/Arthur/Mother Teresa since he was a puppy, the 12-year-old daughter was beside herself and that it really wasn't the owner's fault that his dog found its way into Battersea in the first place. I told them the decision was theirs and let them sleep on it.

It must have been a terrible night for both parties and as I went to bed that night I wondered how this drama would play out. The new owners had given no clue as to which way their decision might go, stating only how much they loved 'their Dukey'.

The next morning I phoned the new owners. There was a long pause and a deep sigh.

'We've decided to give him back.'

I realised I'd been holding my breath and exhaled.

'It's not their fault,' the man sniffed. 'And if this had happened to us we hope that we would be given our dog back too. Besides, they've loved him for four years; we've only loved him for four weeks. We're on our way.'

Whilst I knew that no dog could replace Duke, I promised to find them a cracker of a dog to help ease their pain.

I called Arthur's original owners. They must have been sitting on the phone; it hardly rang before being snatched up.

Arthur was reunited with his family amid a flurry of tail-wagging, treats and tears. I introduced the other family to the new dog I'd found for them. Luckily they fell in love with their new charge, a female whom I named Teresa. As both parties left the Home, I poured myself a stiff drink.

# CHAPTER 6

# REHAB – NOT JUST
# FOR CELEBRITIES

I was getting to grips with all aspects of life at Britain's best-loved dogs' home and as the months and years rolled by, I was no longer the hapless kennel maid covered in dog food, whose charges were in charge of her. Gone was the tentative spring lamb that was herded into submission on a daily basis and in her place was a wily old sheepdog, growing in confidence, knowledge and expertise. I had gained a feeling of self-worth I'd never felt at school and without realising it I'd been rehabilitated from a girl who failed exams into a useful and productive member of society.

Fred and Dot must have thought so too because they rewarded me with my very own kennel block in the rehoming section. The thing I loved most about my relocation was being able to build relationships with the dogs. In the stray section they'd move on after seven days but here in sales, they might stay for weeks, months or even, God forbid, years.

In kennel number one was Benjamin, a beautiful

cream lurcher with big brown eyes and unruly fur. He welcomed me into my new block with the utmost tail-thumping vigour and as many kisses as I could handle. Although this kennel had been his home for a whole year, he wasn't bitter; he was hopeful. My heart would break watching him get up from his bed and trot towards the front of his kennel every single time someone walked past. He'd look up at them imploringly but they'd usually just walk on by. I didn't understand why. If I could, I would have taken him home in a heartbeat. I'd do the next best thing – I'd make Benjamin my project; I'd find him a home.

As happy as I was to have my own sales block, it wasn't long before I realised the move was bittersweet, and I shed many tears waving favourite after favourite off to begin their new lives.

I wouldn't say my mother was warming to my new life but she had at least given up on the prospect of further education and the mention of universities and polytechnics was becoming a thing of the past. Every now and then, however, she'd tell me about one friend or another that was looking for a 'bright young person to work in their office'.

I didn't know exactly what this office work entailed but I doubted it would include being surrounded by 700 dogs on a daily basis and as far as I was concerned, nothing on earth could beat that. Even though it was hard to regularly witness the way mankind abandoned its own best friend, I was glad just to be at Battersea to try and make life seem a little better for the dogs in any way I could.

By now, it was clearer to me than ever that I was leading a double life: one, the world of my family, in a central London apartment, enjoying Royal Ascot and membership of the Hurlingham Club, the other a life of clocking on and off, minimum wage and defeated, destitute dogs.

In a strange way, I felt lucky to be living two different lives all wrapped up into one and wondered how many other people experienced this same clash of completely opposing worlds within one existence. These collisions always seemed most stark during landmark moments in my life.

Three years after landing my dream job, Nelson Mandela was released from prison and I turned 21.

My birthday fell on one of my rare weekends off and all my best friends at Battersea including Jacky, Ali and Keith had managed to beg, borrow, steal or swap the day off. They had clubbed together to whisk me away on a magical mystery day trip; my only instruction was to be at Victoria station at 9 a.m. Easy, I lived five minutes' walk away.

Before I left for the station, my family wished

me happy birthday. The one stipulation my mother had was that I be back home by 6 p.m. for the family celebration.

As planned, I met my pals at the station. They'd already bought my train ticket and some iron rations for the journey. When we reached the platform they covered my eyes so I couldn't read the destinations board and whenever the announcer came on the tannoy during the train journey, they'd sing a rousing rendition of Happy Birthday to drown him out. Altogether this happened eight times – the other passengers looked on, unimpressed.

About two hours later, we stepped out of the train and into the brilliant sunshine of Southend-on-Sea. I'd seen so much of Europe and other parts of the world but I'd never been to Southend. I was ridiculously excited. The destination had been Keith's idea. He lived there and undertook the massive commute to Battersea on a daily basis. I guess when you had it that bad, you really had it bad. I knew how he felt and wouldn't have ruled out such a commute myself.

It was a beautiful June day and the sea was like a millpond. The sun shone high in the sky and a warm breeze gently caressed our lily-white London limbs. It was good to be away from the hustle and bustle and I really felt as though I was on holiday. If I closed my eyes, I could have been in St Tropez. We headed straight for the beach, rolled up our jeans and dipped our pale toes into the freezing cold water. Suddenly St Tropez seemed a little further away.

For lunch we had fish and chips followed by candyfloss and doughnuts. Appetites satisfied, we made for the amusements. The last time I'd spent a decadent afternoon throwing money away was when I was eight years old. It wasn't half as much fun back then; my dad gave me a strict budget of one pound, after which he ceased to fund my habit. On my own terms, however, I could foolishly fritter away as much as I wanted. I must have spent at least a fiver on the grabbing machine alone. For my efforts I won a small monkey wearing boxing gloves, which was probably worth a tenth of what I'd spent grabbing it.

When we decided we had wasted enough money at the amusements, we headed for the fair so we could waste some more. By the end of the afternoon we had whiplash from the waltzers, dislocations from the dodgems and sore stomachs from laughing like hyenas. We giggled our way around every ride without a care in the world. I hadn't felt this type of gay abandon since I was a child, devoid of responsibility and unaware of the stresses of the real world.

We checked our watches and decided we had just enough time for a quick game of bingo before heading home. My pals were experts, dabbing the numbers away on six cards at a time. I was a bingo virgin and it was all I could do to manage one card. Needless to say I didn't win anything.

I didn't care though; I had my 'Kiss Me Quick' hat, a boxing monkey and some wonderful memories to take home with me.

I made my 6 p.m. deadline – just. I jumped into the shower and changed from my jeans, T-shirt and trainers into my dress, jewellery and high heels.

My family and I piled into the Jaguar and it wasn't long before we pulled up outside the Savoy. I figured the other part of my double life was about to commence.

A maître d' showed us to our table and carefully placed starched napkins, of the finest quality, on our laps. As he handed us the menus, I looked at the prices and nearly fell off my chair. Thank God it was my birthday; if I had been paying, we wouldn't have progressed past the bread rolls.

We ordered our meals and cracked open a bottle of champagne. As usual, my grandmother was the life and soul of the party and as she flirted with the waiter and I sipped my champers I took in my opulent surrounds. We had one of the best tables in the restaurant which had stunning views of the Thames with London by night as its backdrop. I spotted a couple of celebrities and a prominent MP dining alongside us. It was a fabulous evening and a birthday to remember.

My truly unique twenty-first birthday was spent in two entirely different worlds, with two entirely different sets of people and I loved them both. I felt so lucky and proud to be part of such a wonderful family; both my own and Battersea's.

Some dogs came into Battersea so emotionally damaged and broken that it could take weeks for them to feel brave enough to hold eye contact with a human being, let alone stop shaking. This kind of abject terror came from being abused, extremely under-socialised or, in some cases, both, and needed careful, expert handling.

Enter the Rehab department. To the uninitiated, their title might have conjured images of weaning dogs off class A drugs and booze and, in truth, this might have been an easier task than that faced by the eight-strong Rehabilitation team.

Under extremely challenging environmental conditions (inside the kennel block trains rattled overhead every five minutes whilst, outside, jumbo jets roared along their flight path to Heathrow), the team set about the highly specialised job of reconstructing shattered canine psyches.

In these instances the team would take as long as necessary to regain the dog's trust and remind it that most humans really weren't that bad. However, the never-ending conveyor belt of distrusting dogs dumped on Battersea's doorstep would serve as a dismal reminder that some humans really *were* that bad.

As well as caring for the more sensitive canine souls, Rehab was also on hand to train the aggressive dogs. Dogs showing extreme aggression were put to sleep, as Battersea took its responsibility to the public very seriously. However, when assesors spotted aggressive tendencies that could be worked on, they would refer them to the Rehab team who'd use their knowledge and experience to identify the trigger behind the dog's aggression and ultimately retrain it out of its antisocial behaviour.

Sometimes simply setting paw inside Battersea Dogs Home could be tricky enough for a dog. Even to us humans, a kennel environment is a noisy one but imagine what it must be like for a dog, whose superior hearing and highly developed sense of smell magnifies everything. On top of this, it also has to deal with the sight of hundreds of other dogs of all shapes and sizes. Just how would the average canine brain process all this extraordinary information?

The only dogs that never seemed to have a problem adapting to kennel life were ex-racing greyhounds. Having been kennelled for their entire lives, they tended to settle down in their beds, delighted at the prospect of having a blanket, probably for the first time ever.

But many dogs, even usually happy and well-balanced hounds, could retreat into themselves in a kennel environment, becoming solitary and morose. These dogs needed a little extra time and socialisation from the Rehab team before they could go off to the rehoming section and offer up their very best side for potential new owners to see.

One such dog was Roscoe, the poor mutt that Pauline and I found clinging to his dead owner in my very early days at Battersea. Already confused by his owner's week-long lack of vital signs, Roscoe was led away from the old man, brought into the Battersea madhouse and put straight into a kennel.

I was still very new and inexperienced back then, which probably explains why, even after a week in my block, Roscoe still hadn't rallied. For the whole week he hid behind his bed and the bags under his eyes suggested he wasn't sleeping at night. He'd started to lose his appetite so I tried him on the tastiest food I could think of. I bought him sausages from the canteen and curry from home (some dogs are mad about it) but Roscoe wasn't impressed.

I had fallen for him in a big way and spoiled him at every opportunity, but in my amateurish approach, I was making no headway. What Roscoe needed was therapy from the experts. I hoped that the love I had given him when he was in my kennel block had helped in some small way but it was time to bring in the heavyweights. The next day, Roscoe was to move into the Rehabilitation department. It was the end of the day and as I said goodnight to all my dogs, I made a special fuss over him, probably more for my sake than his.

'I'll miss you, boy, but I'll come and visit you in Rehab every day,' I told him and was surprised to find my eyes filling up with tears. He looked up at me and heaved a heavy sigh. This dog was seriously depressed. I kissed him on the head, turned out Unders' lights and shut the door behind me.

The Rehab team soon discovered that Roscoe was not like many of the dogs brought to them. He didn't try to bite anyone, he didn't wreck his kennel and he didn't howl night and day. He wasn't aggressive, terrified or disobedient. He was simply grief-stricken and no amount of coaxing, food, toys, kind words or otherwise would bring him around.

I took Roscoe out every day in my lunch hour. I groomed him, walked him in the park and shared my lunch with him. Occasionally he would wag his tail when he saw me coming but these fleeting moments of happiness never lasted more than a few seconds.

Ann, the Irish Head of Rehabilitation, was in the staff canteen one day when Pauline walked in with a cup of tea.

'How's life in the naughty dog department?' Pauline asked.

'Fine, thanks. How's the open road?'

'Good, thanks, except that traffic gets worse by the day. Hey, how's that dog I brought in, Roscoe, the one whose owner died?'

'Not coping so well,' Ann replied.

'Oh, that's a shame. Hat not helping then?'

'Hat? What hat?'

'His dead owner's hat. It was the only thing he responded to when I was trying to get him out of that house so I brought it in with him.'

'I've never seen it,' Ann replied. 'Where could it be?'

A Battersea-wide search began involving Ann, Pauline, me and 20 other staff. Finally the hat was found in the veterinary department of all places.

We took it straight to Roscoe. As usual, he was holed up behind his bed. At the jangle of Ann's kennel key, his ears pricked up and two brown eyes appeared just above the top of the bed.

He must have smelled the hat before he saw it and for the first time, Roscoe's tail began thumping frantically against the wall. When the hat was placed on the floor in front of him, Roscoe became a different dog. Gone was the morose hound with the hound-dog eyes and in its place was an exuberant dog with a wagging, upright tail and bright, keen eyes. He leapt out from behind the bed, ferociously sniffing the hat and turning it over and over with wild-eyed enthusiasm, finally coming to rest with it in his mouth like a wide-brimmed security blanket.

This was Roscoe's motivation; his reason for getting out of (or from behind) bed. He stood at the front of his kennel, tall and handsome, proudly showing off his most prized possession. All Roscoe needed now was someone to fill that hat, so the very next day Ann updated his notes and packed

105

him off to the rehoming kennels to find that very person.

I visited Roscoe every lunchtime in the rehoming section and at midday every day he'd push himself up against the bars, in anticipation of my arrival. I couldn't help smiling as I was greeted by this huge dog with soppy eyes, holding a hat in his mouth and wagging his tail so hard I thought it might come off.

I looked at his sale card. It read:

'Roscoe: Friendly, obedient, well-socialised one-year-old Labrador cross. Not too keen on cats but loves people and other dogs. New owner must be energetic, have a garden and like Trilby hats.'

I remembered all my favourites with great affection. I was three years into my Battersea life and by now had some two-legged favourites as well, one of whom was the straight-talking Ali Taylor.

It was Ali's knowledge and experience that saw her scale the ranks to reach the position of Head Behaviourist at Battersea Dogs Home. This was dangerous territory and I made a mental note not to follow in her footsteps. Part of Ali's role was to undertake the daunting task of assessing large, antisocial dogs that had been referred to her by the assessors or the Rehab team, in order to determine whether they were safe to rehome.

Ali lived with her dad, a colourful and lovable, long-suffering fellow. I use the term long-suffering as Ali would quite literally bring her work home with her – a pastime she still indulges in today. She wouldn't think twice about bringing home a fiery Dobermann to see if there was any truth behind its display of aggression. Poor Mr Taylor would innocently saunter out of his bedroom only to be chomped on by a moody dog that believed Mr Taylor was invading *his* house.

One sunny afternoon at Battersea, I was going about my kennel business when Ali called out to me.

'Oi, whatcha doing?' she asked.

'Just going on my break.'

'Oh no you're not. You're coming with me.'

'Where are we going?' I asked, feeling a little anxious. I must have had a sixth sense for impending doom.

'To meet the devil.'

Satan, a large German shepherd displaying particularly aggressive tendencies, was referred to Ali as no one else felt confident enough to get him out of his kennel, a rare occurrence at Battersea.

When dealing with potentially dangerous dogs, staff were trained to always take someone else along. Quite understandable but why did that someone have to be me? I had never really been wary of dogs until I began life at Battersea Dogs Home. It was here that I learned to have a healthy respect for them because – as my stint at St Thomas' hospital confirmed, I saw first-hand exactly what some of them were capable of.

I'd like to think it was this healthy respect that had kept me from being bitten ever since. In reality all my wariness did was earn me the reputation of being a complete coward.

After shooting down every possible excuse I could muster as to why I was too busy to come and meet the devil, Ali dragged me over to the section of kennels that housed the dangerous dogs. She gave me Satan's card to read on the way. His owner had brought him in as she was emigrating – a likely story.

I heard Satan before I saw him. He sounded like a cross between a lion, a Tasmanian devil and a grizzly bear. We walked into the block and approached his kennel. He was as large as he was black, sitting at the back of his kennel, emitting a deep growl. As we took a step closer, he flung himself at the door, baring teeth that looked like they belonged to a tiger from the Stone Age and barking abuse at the top of his voice. I swallowed hard.

The Manchester United Manager Sir Alex Ferguson is known as 'The Hairdryer' because when he dishes out a bollocking, it has the same blasting effect as being in front of a hairdryer. At that moment, I knew exactly how his players felt.

My knees trembled a little and my mouth went dry. Ali picked up some treats.

'What good are they?' I asked. 'Why would he want them when he can eat us?'

She didn't answer but instead got out her kennel key.

'Oh you're not serious . . .'

What happened next still haunts me to this day. She opened the kennel door and walked away!

I stood there, rooted to the spot, unable to move. Perhaps I should have listened to my mother all along; that office job seemed rather appealing from where I was now standing. Although frozen with fear, I remember being more than a little surprised when Satan immediately stopped barking. Actually, he looked as shocked as me and didn't really know what to do.

After a minute or so, he slowly and purposefully ventured out of the kennel, sniffing the floor but keeping a close eye on both of us. He walked over to me. Knowing that dogs can sense fear, I tried to maintain an air of casual nonchalance, which, believe me, at that moment in time wasn't easy. It really just constituted trying not to shake.

He sniffed my legs, never taking his eyes off mine. I think at that moment I broke wind, which was preferable to what else could have happened under the circumstances.

I looked over to Ali with a dual expression of 'Help' and 'If we ever get out of here alive, I'm going to kill you'. But she wasn't looking at me. She was kneeling down, side-on to Satan, looking at the floor with dog treats in her hand.

Nice, I thought, some friend you are. You got me into this mess and now you won't even look at me as I'm slowly devoured from toe to head. Thankfully Satan had finished with me and I was still intact. He had also become aware of Ali and was taking tentative steps towards her, sniffing the air, which was filled with the scent of Schmackos and fart.

She threw one over to him which he devoured. When no more were forthcoming he took a few more tentative steps over to her. Still avoiding eye contact, Ali held out her Schmacko-filled hand and to my utter amazement he gently took one. Still she wouldn't look him in the eye but instead slowly and gently stroked his chest as he took the treats.

She then began talking to him in a silly, high-pitched voice. Incredibly the tip of his tail started wagging. Ali asked him to sit, which he did, then she asked him for his paw, which he was also happy to extend. Within ten minutes they were rolling around the floor together like old pals.

Danger over, I started walking over to them, telling Ali that I was never really scared. Satan immediately caught my eye and growled, lowering his head and once again showing me those pearly whites. Open-mouthed I stopped dead in my tracks, and looked at Ali who casually put the lead on him, put him back in his kennel and said to me, 'Oh, stop being such a big girl's blouse.'

She then wrote on Satan's card, 'Rehab, for slow and careful socialising; any problems see Ali Taylor,' changed his name to Stan and waltzed off as though nothing more than a change of light bulb had just taken place.

The Rehab team dealt with up to 1,000 dogs every year and, frustratingly, many of the problems they faced were entirely avoidable. Many adult dogs came into Battersea displaying undesirable behaviours created during their puppy-hood. This was often due to the owner not providing the correct training or socialising during the dog's most formative weeks and months.

Grabbing people's trouser legs was endearing when their puppy was small and adorable. At that age it was easy to turn a blind eye but now that he was a full-grown adult Staffordshire bull terrier, this once-encouraged behaviour was a real problem. Jumping up, so often encouraged as a puppy, had become a worry now that their German shepherd was constantly leaping up to people's eye-level. Owners could not deal with these unacceptable behaviours so the dogs were dumped at Battersea.

The department also dealt with dogs that would be your friend one day and then bite you the next for no apparent reason, those lacking in social graces and those with attention-seeking or separation-related issues. Other wayward behaviours that formed part of the Rehabilitation team's day included aggression towards other dogs, and dogs with a high chase instinct. Chase could be a big problem, especially in London parks already overflowing with joggers, cyclists, kids and anything else that moves.

In fact, Rehab saw all manner of problems one might expect to find on the couch of any self-respecting canine psychiatrist.

Rehab's couch was well worn, so much so that Battersea offered another service to prevent it from becoming completely threadbare. This other vital amenity was known as the Behaviour Hotline. This telephone service advised fraught owners at the end of their tether how to deal with their uncontrollable pets and prevented many challenging dogs from becoming Battersea dogs and adding to Rehab's already overwhelming task. The Hotline received thousands of calls every year and the behaviourists who manned the phones sent out tailor-made programmes for owners – and their dogs – to follow.

The majority of dogs that spent time in the Rehab department went on to lead full, happy, non-aggressive lives with their new owners, most of whom were experienced with dogs. Some dogs were not so lucky and during my time at Battersea, the one thing I never got used to was the sight of an abused dog.

Always on their guard, tense and nervous, they were easy to spot. They squatted in their kennel, shaking, up on their claws, rigid with fear, ready to take flight from violence and abuse. Usually underweight, their sunken eyes seemed larger from the extreme fear that had become part of their daily lives. Too petrified to sleep, they shook all day and all night. Even in the height of summer, when temperatures soared, they shook. It was a pitiful sight.

How could anyone do this to a living creature? How could someone entrusted with the life of a defenceless animal inflict such terror upon it? For me, the hardest part was not being able to make these dogs understand that it was okay now, that they were safe.

Their rehabilitation could never be rushed; more than anything they needed time and patience. Too much pressure and they withdrew even further into themselves. Sometimes just sitting at the opposite end of a kennel from an abused dog was more than they could take.

Given time and careful, gentle socialising the majority of these dogs made it. Some, however, were too broken to ever lead a normal life again and it was kinder to end their desperately sad existence.

We were short staffed the day that Monty came in. I was working in two places at once; manning my kennel block and receiving dogs into the Home. It was as busy as ever on intake – my dogs would just have to cope without me for another half an hour.

An RSPCA inspector had brought in a small black-and-white dog she had just rescued from a shed in north London. The RSPCA had been called by a neighbour who'd heard Monty whimpering but hadn't seen his owner for a week. When the inspector went to investigate, she found Monty with string tied around his neck so tight that it was cutting into his skin. The other end of the string was tied to the inside of the shed door. If Monty stretched, he could just about reach a bowl of water but this resulted in the string cutting even further into his neck. There was no sign of food.

Knowing Battersea had the expertise and facilities to take care of Monty, the RSPCA brought him into the Home. When the inspector opened the back door of her van, I instantly knew there would be no guarantees that this one would make it.

Monty had squashed himself into the back of the small kennel, trying desperately hard to make himself invisible. He was emaciated, had overgrown claws and trembled uncontrollably.

I didn't want to distress him any further but there was no way I could get him out of the van without going in and invading his space. Like Monty, I tried to make myself as small as possible. As I approached him, he backed even further into the cage, his eyes grew bigger and he shook so violently his claws clacked rhythmically against the van's metal floor. I slowly reached out to stroke his chest. The sheer terror of this moment was more than Monty could take and he urinated where he stood.

Expecting to be hit, he sank low. I talked to him

in hushed tones, reassuring him it was okay. When he'd finished I slowly put my arm under his chest and picked him up. He was rigid with fear, front legs sticking straight out in front of him, eyes bulging. I took him straight to the veterinary department.

Shaun the vet checked Monty over. As I held him, I could feel his heart pounding. He squatted on the table, leaning slightly into me and allowed a full examination. He didn't try to get away, he didn't try to bite; he just had this vacant expression on his face. Oddly enough, perhaps from sheer exhaustion, he had stopped shaking. Initially, I took this as a good sign but as I looked into his big brown eyes and saw that he was just staring into space, it was clear something was missing; I just knew he'd sort of given up. Monty was as severe a case as any of us, or the RSPCA, had ever seen.

I took Monty to Rehab so that they could start helping him straight away. He was technically a stray but I was not going to let his rehabilitation be delayed by a week while he waited in the stray section to be claimed. And if his owner had the nerve to try and claim Monty, we'd have a few choice things to say.

Physically Monty was okay. The wound on his neck would heal and given the right diet he'd put weight back on. And that is exactly what happened. Within a month Monty looked as good as new. But that was on the outside. In his head, Monty was no better than the day he was rescued.

The days turned into weeks and the weeks turned into months but Monry wasn't improving. He was always tense and could never relax. Whether he was in a kennel at Battersea or in his foster home, Monty would take himself off into a corner and just stare at the ground. He was scared of everything and everyone. As hard as it was for us to witness this behaviour, we could be sure that living it was ten times worse.

Like all of us, the Rehab team was devastated. No one tried harder than them to put this tortured little dog back together but they couldn't. No one could.

In retrospect, the decision to put Monty out of his misery after three months should have been made sooner but we kept telling ourselves he'd show some improvement tomorrow. But he never did.

Every day was a struggle for Monty: he was a broken dog, an empty shell. Anyone could see that putting him down was the kindest thing to do.

Monty was about 18 months old. His short life had been one of misery and fear and it made me wonder why someone would have a dog if all they wanted to do was make its life hell. All I could think of was finding that person but they had disappeared into thin air and the police and RSPCA could do nothing to bring Monty's owner to justice. It was a double blow, one that took me a long time to come to terms with.

*　　*　　*

For all the Montys there were, the Rehab team experienced hundreds of happier, more successful outcomes. Their work was complex, painstaking and delicate but they took a great deal of pride in it. The rewards from their successes spoke for themselves but it was the ones they lost that made the biggest impact. No one at Battersea was immune from heartbreak.

# CHAPTER 7

# GIVE A DOG A HOME

I was as happy as Larry looking after the dogs in my rehoming block and although it was hard when the rehomers came for them, I gladly waved them off to begin their new lives. I could have stayed there for ever but the powers that be had noticed I got on well with the people I dealt with on Intake and Claims and decreed it was time for something a little more mentally challenging. I didn't want to be challenged, mentally or otherwise. Mental stimulation was for Border collies, not for me.

And so it transpired that halfway through bathing a particularly wriggly spaniel, I was told by a stern-faced Dot that I'd been promoted; I was now a rehomer. I knew better than to argue with her when she had that look on her face.

'Oh, right-o, thank you,' I said weakly.

With that, she gave the dog a no-nonsense pat on the head, turned and marched off. I stood there a little bewildered, not knowing how to feel. The spaniel seemed a little shocked too and for the first time during his bath, stood quite still. He looked at me intently with his big spaniel eyes as if to say, 'Well, what are you going to do?'

I looked back at him and thought about it for a while. I knew it would mean less contact with the dogs and more contact with humans and I wasn't sure about that. At least you knew where you were with dogs; people on the other hand were a whole different ball game. I liked the sound of promotion though; I'd never had one before. I would be a rehomer at the world-famous Battersea Dogs Home. It had a certain ring to it and would be something to tell my mother over the shepherd's pie that night. I decided to run with it (not that I had much choice).

I didn't know how she would react. My mother was still waiting for me to come to my senses and leave Battersea to embark on a 'proper career'. I knew this wasn't exactly the job she had always dreamed I'd do but at least I was being promoted. I was climbing the ladder and if nothing else she would surely be proud of me for that.

I'd had the whole afternoon for the idea to sink in and as I poured the gravy over my dinner that evening, my excitement brimmed over.

'I've been promoted,' I blurted out. 'I'm going to be a rehomer.' I sat on the edge of my seat and waited. You could have heard a pin drop.

My mother stood up and walked over to the fridge. She pulled out another bottle of wine. I took this as a sign of celebration but as she poured it into her glass, I realised it was more to steady her nerves.

The fourth and final 'R' (and in my somewhat biased opinion, having been involved in this department for most of my time at Battersea, the best 'R') was Rehoming.

If Battersea could not reunite a dog with its owner, its sole purpose would be to rehome it. That was what everyone – kennel hands, veterinary staff, ambulance drivers, office staff and of course rehomers – worked so hard towards.

To be able to successfully rehome a Battersea dog, we needed to know as much about it as possible, so every four-legged member of Battersea's family received a temperament assessment.

Although the information given to Battersea by owners handing in their own dogs was helpful, there were no guarantees it was truthful so both the strays (who entered Battersea life devoid of notes) and Gifts to the Home received the same assessment.

The assessing rooms were designed to replicate a normal home environment. They were equipped with sofas, TVs, chairs, tables and most other household items. There was even a bicycle, used to see whether the dog was prone to chasing.

The assessing team was made up of highly experienced kennel staff and rehomers and in pairs they tried to ascertain what the dog's motivation was. This magical item could be used as a very effective training tool. No prizes for guessing that the number one motivator was food, closely followed by squeaky toys.

The dog would be tested with other dogs, not only to see if it could live with another dog, but also to check its tolerance levels. London parks are teeming with dogs and any new owner would need to be aware of how their new charge might react towards them.

The decision whether the dog should live with children or not was also made during this assessment. Rest assured, Battersea did not wheel out a live toddler to dangle in front of every mutt, rather the decision was based on how the dog reacted to being handled, whether it might be possessive over toys or food, and its general tolerance levels.

Some behavioural problems were similar but no two dogs were ever the same and often behaved differently from one day to the next. For this reason multiple assessments took place and were always thorough. Alternative opinions were canvassed in complicated cases and the staff recognised that just like people, dogs could have off days too.

If the dog was a straightforward kind of hound, a sale card would be written and the dog would move to the rehoming section. Each dog was an individual, though, and report cards would reflect this. For example, the rehoming criteria for a ten-year-old dachshund would probably be very different from those of a ten-month-old golden retriever. The old fellow's sale card might read: 'WANTED: Quiet, retirement home without children, to spend twilight years in peace and comfort, taking gentle strolls and sipping tea.'

Whereas the retriever's card would probably say: 'WANTED: Active, energetic family with GSOH. Eats anything (and everything) but is yet to master the subtle art of housetraining. Patient types only need apply.'

Most of the dogs sailed through their assessment and went off to the rehoming block to await that special someone.

The rehoming block I was responsible for as a kennel maid (which was one of five such blocks) was a rickety one-storey affair, housing about 40 shivering mutts. During my tenure, the 200 or so dogs waiting patiently to be rehomed graduated from draughty dwellings to the Kent building, named after Battersea's president, Prince Michael of Kent. The Kent building was an all mod cons, three-storey construction, in which the dogs not only had under-floor heating in the winter and air-conditioning in the summer, but they also enjoyed a room with a view, overlooking south-west London's iconic Power Station.

Once a dog was deemed medically and behaviourally fit to move into the rehoming section, it would remain there whilst the staff set about finding it the right home, however long that took.

★   ★   ★

Everything was done to ensure each individual dog went to the environment best suited to its needs. In the vast majority of cases this meant rehoming a dog straight from the Kent building into a typical home, to live as a family pet, but it could also mean rehoming a Border collie to live as a working dog on a farm.

To ensure that the dogs needing more specialised homes were well catered for, Battersea Dogs Home dealt with many different external organisations ranging from the prison service and Hearing Dogs for Deaf People, to breed-specific rescues and the police.

Some spaniels and Labradors that came into Battersea would go stir-crazy as family pets. Many had such a high work instinct that they required far more mental and physical stimulation than the average family could provide. Perhaps this was why so many of them ended up at Battersea. The Home also received hundreds of ex-guarding German shepherds every year, many of whom had been trained to be aggressive and therefore could not safely be rehomed into society. Enter Her Majesty's Armed Forces, an organisation with whom Battersea had a lengthy history.

In 1918 during the Great War, an ex-Battersea Airedale named Jack died in France on the frontline after delivering a vital plea for reinforcements. His battalion was saved and Jack posthumously received the Victoria Cross.

During the Second World War, German shepherds

and Airedales were recruited by the Red Cross to track parachutists, carry ammunition and lay wires under fire. Battersea also provided a temporary home for soldiers' pets whilst they were away on active service.

The Defence Animal Centre (DAC) in Melton Mowbray was the central point in the UK where animals were trained for military service. The DAC visited Battersea once a week to look at dogs earmarked by experienced Battersea staff who believed they would do better as working dogs than as pets. These dogs were typically spaniels and Labradors that could be trained to sniff out drugs and explosives and ex-guarding German shepherds, useful for security work.

Every external organisation that Battersea dealt with was subject to stringent checks to make sure the dogs received the best care and the kindest training. The DAC was no exception and when the arrangement first began, they were more than happy (and a little amused) for Battersea to give them the once over. In fact they were so proud of their establishment, they invited a group of Battersea staff to drive up to Leicestershire, stay overnight and watch a typical day's training.

Not wanting to miss out on spending the night at an army barracks, ten giggling kennel maids piled into the Battersea minibus and set off. After we had driven for what seemed like an eternity the natives became restless.

'Bloody hell, where is this place? I hate the

country; this had better be worth it,' whined Jacky and Ali in unison. Ali had never been north of Watford before and Jacky thought her 20-minute commute to work was pushing the envelope.

When we arrived, we were warmly greeted by Dale, one of the men that came to Battersea every week to collect dogs. Wearing army fatigues and with a buzz-cut hairstyle and an impossibly square jaw, he looked like Action Man. Dale was delighted to see us and showed us to our quarters. The dormitory was exactly as I imagined it to be: tidy, sparse and functional, with hard beds and horse-hair blankets. Dale then took us to the canteen where we were given Lancashire Hot Pot for dinner, washed down with tea so strong it could have walked out of the cup. By this time it was late and there was no one there but us. Dale sensed our disappointment and informed us the soldiers were all in their quarters and we'd meet them the next day.

Crestfallen, we headed back to our dorm where things only got worse. In the comfort stakes, our beds were just one step up from concrete and as far as the horsehair blankets were concerned, we might as well have been sleeping next to a horse, so smelly and itchy were they. But put ten girls in a room together (or even two for that matter) and the gossiping, giggling and goofing around soon begins, and we were no exception.

We were having the time of our lives until halfway through the pyjama party, when an alarm suddenly screamed through our dormitory. We looked around at each other, stunned (for the first time that night) into silence. Was this a fire drill? I glanced at my watch. It was 6 o'clock. To my horror I realised that this was our wake-up tannoy. We hadn't even been to sleep yet and now it was time to get up!

Heavy eye-lidded, we showered, dressed and met Dale in the canteen at 6.30 a.m. 'Blimey, you lot look rough. I suppose you were up all night giggling and gossiping?' Dale enquired. How did he know? Thank God there was a full English breakfast on offer. It perked us up no end and at 7 a.m. we began our guided tour.

The place was huge and had the best facilities money could buy. Dale took us to the equine section first. We walked towards what looked like an aeroplane hangar and Dale swung the massive doors back and we were hit by the heat. We were in the farriery and even though this was the twentieth century, the methods they employed dated back hundreds of years. The soldiers were stripped to their waists, wearing heavy leather aprons and standing in front of open kilns, shoeing horses just as they might have done a century before. We were told that it took four years to become a qualified farrier, each of these men having learned their trade in the army.

Next, Dale took us to the veterinary section, which looked like it should have been in the next century with its state-of-the-art equipment. There was even a horse anaesthetic room, which constituted a massive area, totally padded to protect the horse from injury when succumbing to the anaesthetic.

After lunch, we were taken to the dog section. We'd been waiting all day for this and could hardly contain our excitement at the prospect of seeing some much-loved Battersea dogs again. The kennels were well built and the dogs well cared for and happy. Not all of them had come from Battersea but those that had recognised some of us and let out excited yelps, willing us over with their hyperactive tails. We looked at Dale imploringly. A nod from him said it was okay and all of a sudden it was a mini Battersea reunion. The scene was a mix of squealing, jumping up and burrowing noses, and that was just the kennel maids.

After our Battersea dog fix, Dale took us to see how they trained the dogs. Once again, we recognised some of the hounds that had come from Battersea; one in particular catching our attention. The last time we'd seen Stan the German shepherd (aka Satan), he was in a kennel at Battersea, lunging at everyone who walked past. He was desperately unhappy and although he had improved greatly under Rehab's guidance, they decided he was too great a risk to rehome to the general public. Two weeks on, he was looking a million dollars and responding well to his handler. I could see how it would take someone with command and experience to deal with an animal of Stan's size and strength.

We walked to another building to watch the sniffer dogs in training. I had watched Dale at Battersea, as he tested young spaniels and Labradors for explosives work. They only really needed one quality to make the grade: toy motivation. In my next life, I want to come back as a sniffer dog. Their whole day is based around play. All they have to do is sniff out a particular substance whilst their handler excitedly encourages them. When they find it, they are immediately rewarded with their favourite thing in the world: a game with a squeaky toy.

The soldiers have to keep the dogs' motivation high and they do this by running around like high-pitched lunatics. We watched open-mouthed as these big burly soldiers rolled around the floor, squeaking like excited schoolgirls. As we caught each other's eye, it took all of our willpower to suppress a major fit of the giggles.

While we were there, Dale and his colleagues said they had a treat for us. Clyde, a young Labrador from Battersea, was in training to be a sniffer dog, and with our help they'd like to test how he was progressing. Dale asked us to line up in single file. He then placed Jacky two-thirds of the way down the line and planted some drugs on her. Dale told us that even though we knew Clyde, we mustn't greet him as this would distract him from his work.

We all took our places and Clyde walked in with his handler. Speaking words of encouragement, she guided him down the line. It took a great deal of self-control not to reach out to this adolescent Andrex puppy with the happy face and 'pat me' eyes but we somehow managed to restrain ourselves.

Clyde wandered down the line at his own measured pace, taking great care to sniff each and every one of us. When he came to Jacky, he had a much more pronounced sniff and proceeded to go bonkers. There was no doubt about it, our Battersea boy had found the planted drugs, solved the case and made us proud.

We'd had a full day at the DAC and left content in the knowledge that, like Clyde, any Battersea dog with a military career ahead of him was a lucky dog. We said our goodbyes to Dale and wished Clyde the best of luck even though it was obvious that luck was the last thing he needed. This was one dog that clearly had a nose for it.

Whatever the most suitable environment for a dog might be, the staff did all they could to place them as quickly and effectively as possible but it sometimes took a little extra help from our friends in high places to pull it off.

In the early nineties, new clothes were the order of the day and I was measured up for my shiny new rehomer's uniform. It consisted of black shoes, black jeans, and a bright red polo shirt and sweatshirt. I also received my very own name badge with the word 'Rehomer' underneath my name. As I was being kitted out, so too a quiet mongrel called Marcus was handed a brand-new wardrobe.

The Queen had been on a state visit to Africa and knowing Her Majesty was potty about all things canine, her hosts presented her with six beautiful dog collars for her corgis, each artistically embroidered in typical African style. As Patron of Battersea Dogs Home, Her Majesty decided to donate these unusual gifts to dogs less fortunate than her own.

The collars were gratefully accepted and immediately adorned the most deserving cases. The first collar went on one of Battersea's many black-and-tan mongrels, whom the public usually bypassed in favour of less run-of-the-mill hounds.

Marcus had sat at the front of the same kennel for almost a year watching people go by. They rarely stopped to talk to him. Why would they? He was average-sized, short-haired, had brown eyes and was the same colour as so many of Battersea Dogs Home's homeless. But thanks to Queen Elizabeth II, Marcus the ordinary mongrel was about to become extraordinary.

In front of the press, his tatty old collar was taken off and replaced with one of the smart new ones from Africa. The cameras flashed all around Marcus who sat wide-eyed and anxious, blinking in time with the flashes. He couldn't have known what all the fuss was about but the day one of the Queen's collars was put on Marcus, his life changed for ever.

That day people didn't just walk by, they stopped and looked at him. His colourful and unusual new garb attracted much attention from the public and on reading where the collar came from, Marcus the mongrel drew a crowd. In return, he wagged for all he was worth and exactly three hours after donning his new clothes, Marcus went home.

Often a little help goes a long way when rehoming Battersea's long-stay dogs. Viva, a black-and-tan mongrel came in as a shell-shocked youngster. She needed extremely careful and painstakingly slow rehabilitation and was at Battersea for two years before finding the right home. In Viva's case it wasn't that people didn't choose her, it was that she needed an incredibly experienced new owner who could continue Rehab's good efforts, rather than going to a home that would unwittingly undo all that hard work.

As a result of being mistreated, Viva had a few different behavioural issues, one of which was choosing the fight response rather than flight when meeting strangers. It took the Rehab team a long time to train the nervous aggression out of her and Viva's new owners would need to react confidently if faced with any remnants of this behaviour. If her owners became spooked by any signs of aggression or if they unwittingly reinforced it by

131

telling her she was a good girl, all of Rehab's work would be undone very quickly.

We knew Viva's ideal home was out there somewhere but needed help reaching a wider audience. It was a bit of a long shot but we had nothing to lose. We phoned a few national newspapers and the very next day she was posing on the front page of the *Daily Mail*. Battersea was besieged with calls and two days later Viva found her perfect home.

Many Battersea dogs were fortunate enough to have the power of the press backing their bid to find a new home. Not all of us were so lucky. At around the same time Viva left the Home, I too felt it was time to bite the bullet and leave home.

This was going to be hard and without the press behind me, it would be a struggle to find as comfortable digs to rent as my parents' place. Where else could I get all my meals cooked, my washing done and have a cleaning lady thrown into the bargain? And why do parents insist on telling you not to treat the place like a hotel when that's exactly what hotels offer?

Thankfully, I found a fine substitute second home in a studio flat in Prince of Wales Drive, just around the corner from Battersea Dogs Home. It only had two downsides. The first, it was too small to keep a dog, and the second, it was on the fifth floor with no lift. What doesn't kill you makes you stronger, I repeated to myself as I lugged all my stuff to the very top floor. Twenty trips later my knees were buggered but I was in.

I returned home for the last time to pick up the remaining few items and as I packed them into my battered green car, I prepared myself for the emotional goodbye. Holding back the tears, my mother hugged me, kissed me on the forehead and said, 'Now remember, if things don't work out you can always come home. But try your best to make them work out.' Luckily they did, so everyone was happy.

It took my mother 22 years to rehome me. The average stay for a dog at Battersea was far less at just 22 days. This usually consisted of a week in the stray kennels waiting to be claimed, a week getting over kennel cough and a week in the rehoming section displaying best sits, puffed out chests and generally trying one's best to score a new home.

If all that trying paid off and a pooch was picked by a member of the public, they had to complete Battersea's rehoming procedure before entertaining the idea of Lassie coming home. The process was lengthy because it had to be thorough. First came the interview.

Although I received some heartfelt slaps on the back from my colleagues when my promotion was made public, it didn't make the national or local news unlike another announcement made on exactly the same day. From the Houses of Parliament, the Prime Minister, John Major, announced that Prince Charles and Princess Diana had split.

They'd obviously been having serious doubts; they weren't the only ones. I was having an attack of the collywobbles. I hadn't come to Battersea Dogs Home to work with humans; if that was the case I could have taken that office job my mother was so keen on. I came here to work with dogs – what was I doing? How does this promotion thing work exactly? Can one demote oneself if one isn't happy?

But before I had time to change my mind, I was bundled off to Mickey who was to train me in the fine art of rehoming. I said goodbye to the dogs in my kennel block, promising them I would visit regularly, and handed them over into Steph's capable hands. Although relatively new to the Battersea family, Steph was a rising star within the organisation and, with four dogs of her own, all right by us.

Mickey sat me down and gave me some sanguine pieces of advice, explaining to me that rehoming was a cross between being a detective, a used-car salesman and a dating agent. When interviewing prospective new owners, I should dig deep and ask plenty of questions, always be polite and professional and never lose my cool. She also told me that here at Battersea, the customer is not necessarily always right.

For a week, I watched Mickey conduct interviews.

134

She was very good – confident, knowledgeable and had a natural ease with people. I knew the dreaded moment when I'd have to do my very first interview wasn't far away.

Sure enough, Mickey called in the next customer, whispering to me that this one was mine as we took our seats. I was absolutely terrified and had to hold the form flat on the desk so that my first interviewee couldn't tell I was shaking.

I steadied myself and looked up to see a young lady with tattoos on her arms and a love bite on her neck. Before I'd even had a chance to say hello, she proudly informed me she'd had five dogs before: a Rottweiler, an English bull terrier, a Staffordshire bull terrier, a Dobermann and a pit bull.

When I enquired as to what had become of them, she told me she had lost the first one: the Rottweiler. In this instance the dog had been lost as in misplaced, not lost as in deceased. This confusing euphemism was to catch me out on more than one occasion during my rehoming career. The scene would go something like this:

Customer: I've lost my dog.
Me: Well, have you looked for it?
Customer: No, it died.

Lots of tears (them) and profuse apologies (me). It sounds like that joke, 'My dog's got no nose.'
'How does he smell?'
'Terrible.'

Anyway, in this case the young woman had

misplaced the Rottweiler, not an easy thing to do. She went on to tell me that the English bull had been stolen, the Staffie run over and that she'd given the Dobermann away.

'And what,' I enquired, 'happened to the pit bull?'

'Slasher? He was shot by the Old Bill.'

I looked desperately at Mickey who kindly took over, informing the young lady that her dog-owning history was not stable enough for us to be able to offer a potentially unstable rescue dog.

Hmm, if I thought dealing with dogs had been tricky, I was in for a bumpy ride on rehoming. I learned very quickly that where interviews were concerned, I should expect the unexpected.

One very nice family had a house rabbit. This was a high-risk situation. If the match between Battersea dog and house rabbit wasn't exactly right, there'd be more than just a chewed carpet at stake. I'd hazard a guess that most Battersea dogs, especially the ex-racing greyhounds, would see Thumper as dinner or at the very least an appetiser.

The family's previous dog, a large mastiff who had recently passed away, loved this bunny. His love was reciprocated and now the rabbit was pining for the dog. They showed me a photograph of the mastiff.

Being shown photos of dearly departed, much-loved dogs was extremely commonplace during interviews at Battersea. Owners, with a mixture of pride and sadness, regaled you with stories of their old dog. Some would dab the corners of their eyes whilst others sobbed uncontrollably.

I was offering words of comfort to the family of the late mastiff as I studied his photograph. I commented on what a handsome-looking dog he was. They replied matter of factly, 'Yes, he was, wasn't he? And that picture was taken after we'd had him stuffed.'

I tried my best not to flinch, to keep my gaze on the photo as constant as if those words were so common I'd heard them uttered a hundred times before. To this day I don't know if I pulled it off.

The interviews varied wildly and were a fascinating snapshot into people's lives. One minute I'd be interviewing Joe Bloggs of no fixed abode, the next royalty, but they all had one thing in common and that was my eternal envy. Envy that they were in a position to have their own dog and that, all being well, they were about to take one home.

Interviews can be a nerve-racking experience – not just for the interviewer – and being interviewed for a Battersea dog was no exception. The rehomers were trained to put people at ease, aiming for the interview to feel more like an informal chat. When people relax they become themselves rather than someone on edge, 'correctly' answering a set of questions on a form.

Amongst other things the interview form asked

about the person's previous dog-owning experience, their facilities at home, work hours, family members and other pets.

The interview could take up to 40 minutes and by the end the rehomer had three options to choose from. They were, quite simply put: yes, no or maybe.

The maybe constituted a home visit. Sometimes a home visit was necessary in order to see the size of someone's property or to check the fencing in their back garden. Alternatively it might be to take a look at local exercise facilities or perhaps because we felt in some way that the wool was being pulled and the situation required further investigation.

Later on in my career I performed a home visit on a houseboat in Chelsea. The owner already had one dog, prompting concerns about space. I needn't have worried; I had no idea houseboats could be so large and below deck found a cosy but spacious living area with the resident dog curled up in an armchair in front of a real fire.

Everyone who took home a Battersea dog received a follow-up home visit, regardless of whether they had had a home check previously or not. Follow-up home visits were part of Battersea's ongoing support to the new owners. Not only did they allow owners to receive help with any settling-in problems that might be occurring, they also gave Battersea the chance to make sure the animal was being properly cared for.

An outright no at the point of interview might

138

have been because the customer wanted the dog purely for guarding their commercial premises. It could also have been that, like our friend with Slasher the pit bull terrier, the interviewee just wasn't capable of properly caring for a dog. In such cases, the customer was told then and there. There was no point beating about the bush, arranging home visits and wasting charity time and money when the answer was no.

Another reason someone might be turned down for a Battersea dog was if they were out all day long, leaving the dog home alone. Rehomers spent much of their time trying to explain to people who worked all day that although they really wanted the cute puppy and were willing to pay over the odds to get it (sometimes in the shape of a bribe), they couldn't have it.

Some customers seemed to have real difficulty understanding the concept that it was not about the money or what they wanted for that matter; it was about what was best for the animal, which certainly wasn't leaving it on its own for ten hours a day.

Being told no could bring out the worst in people and many haughtily informed me that they would go and buy one from the pet shop instead so I had just lost Battersea Dogs Home £85. Some people just didn't get it. I often tried to pre-empt this response by getting in there first. 'Of course you are quite at liberty to go and buy a puppy from a pet shop but unless your circumstances change, please don't. Just think about the poor animal, spending the majority of its life in solitary confinement.'

Sometimes it worked, but other times I could tell by the look on their face that they just wanted me to finish talking, so they could get to the pet shop before it closed. The sad thing was, in most cases, that the puppy they raced out to buy would end up at Battersea after a couple of months anyway with behaviour problems relating to separation anxiety.

When necessary, the rehomers had no qualms about saying no. Actually, let me rephrase that because in truth qualms often played a big a part, especially when faced with a big brute sitting across the table from you. Thankfully, I never had to dodge a right hook, although sometimes I came close.

If the rehomer decided that the person in their interview room could provide a good home for a dog, the discussions about the type of dog would begin in earnest.

To a large extent rehomers had to rely on their experience and intuition but eventually the team benefited from the introduction of sophisticated computer software (not dissimilar to that used in computer dating) to match a homeless dog with a potential new owner. Battersea Dogs Home was a leader in its field and was the first rehoming centre to use this advanced form of technology for rehoming purposes.

From knowledge gained about the interviewee, the rehomer would type into the computer the answers to ten questions about them. These questions included whether they had a house or flat, garden or no garden, children, how many hours they were out for, whether they had other pets, if they were experienced dog owners and so on.

During each dog's behavioural assessment those same ten questions about the dog were fed into the computer: did it need a garden, could it live with children or cats, how long could it be left on its own, did it need an experienced owner, et cetera.

The rehomer hit the 'Match' button and, hey presto, a list of suitable dogs in the rehoming section came up on the screen. It was then down to the rehomer, in collaboration with the interviewee, to narrow down the choice and find the top three most suitable dogs on that list. We'd pick the top three because the more dogs a customer met, the more difficult they found it to choose just one.

Of course, it was important for the customer to see all of the dogs on offer with their own eyes but the rehoming software was there to provide a starting point of the most suitable. It was a more controlled way to proceed rather than haplessly trawling through hundreds of dogs, just hoping to pick the right one. This decision had 12-year implications so it was important to add a little science to the process in order to get the fundamentals right.

After the interview was over, the customer was at liberty to look around the kennels, paying particular attention to the dogs on their list. Even with the rehoming software streamlining the process to avoid unnecessary angst, rehoming a dog was an emotive business and people would often disregard suitable dogs on their list for the most inappropriate animal they could find.

People would take more time over choosing a car that they'd probably trade in three or four years down the line. If I were to go and buy a car, I'd take the salesman's advice. I've had plenty of them before but that doesn't make me an expert. Why is it when it comes to dogs everyone's an expert?

It is true one can't help whom one falls in love with, but if the chosen dog was unsuitable, the rehomer would carefully and sensitively explain the reasons why. This usually resulted in being yelled at but if the match wasn't right, the dog would be returned to Battersea and both family and dog would end up twice as upset (especially the dog, having been abandoned for a second time).

One could understand why people became frustrated when there were up to 200 dogs in the rehoming section alone, but their success or failure in walking out with a dog depended on how stringent their criteria were.

They might have required a dog that could be left for a few hours without wrecking the house or howling the street down. They could have six cats (or a house bunny) that the new dog had to get along with. Maybe they had a child with special needs. They might have been elderly and needed a small, quiet dog, which were few and far between at Battersea. The family might have been first-time owners who needed a dog that wouldn't run rings around them. Let's not forget, the dogs that came into Battersea could sometimes be a little on the wayward side.

Many of these people were genuine dog lovers that would give a fabulous home to any hound but whose circumstances made finding the right dog a real challenge. In order not to lose these people altogether, the rehomers endeavoured to personally find them a dog over the following days and weeks and I was no exception. Every other day I'd set aside some time to walk around the kennels and see if anything had come in that might suit someone on my list. Invariably I'd find a dog for everyone, and it would turn out to be the perfect match for the now delighted owner.

When dog and owner were introduced, they were given time to get to know each other over a packet of Schmackos and a squeaky toy. The dog's history, behavioural traits and assessment were all explained in detail to the new owner so that they knew exactly what to expect. Everything was revealed, warts (sometimes literally) and all.

This part of the rehoming process was as satisfying as it was rewarding and the excitement in both parties was utterly contagious. At that moment there really was no better job in the whole world than that of rehomer at Battersea Dogs Home. Seeing a Battersea dog trot off with its new owner to begin a fresh start with a family that already loved it was truly special.

And as the edges of that picture went misty, I'd say under my breath, 'Now for crying out loud, bloody well behave yourself so you don't end up coming back.'

One shameless trick of the rehoming trade was to bring dogs down from the kennels and have them in the interview rooms during business hours. If the customer could meet an individual dog, touch it, give it a treat and look into its eyes, they would usually fall hook, line and sinker before they even got as far as the other 200 or so in the rehoming kennels. These prime positions were reserved for dogs finding kennel life hard or those that no one seemed to want.

I first witnessed this brilliant sales strategy in action earlier on in my career. I was in the staff canteen eating breakfast with Kirsty, Battersea's newest recruit. After having cleaned out and fed a hundred lost hounds, she had the same expression I had on my first day. Mickey came in and asked if I had a special dog that needed extra help finding a home. Did I ever, and shoving the last of my breakfast into my mouth I raced up to find Roscoe.

It may have been his size that was putting people off or the fact that he was just a plain black dog. Whatever it was, two months after Roscoe and his hat moved into the rehoming section, he was still there.

I found him sitting at the front of the kennel watching the world go by. I clipped a leash on his collar and began to lead him out of the kennel but for some reason he decided he wasn't going anywhere and put his brakes on.

'Come on, boy, we're going to get you a home today,' I said, tugging on the lead. Nothing doing, he was adamant and too strong for me. I slackened the lead and he dragged me back into the kennel. This reluctance wasn't from stage fright; Roscoe (or rather I) had forgotten his hat. He gently picked it up in his mouth and then dragged me in the opposite direction out of the kennel block at 100mph, nearly pulling my arm out of its socket.

It was a busy Saturday and the rehoming reception was thronging with expectant faces. I walked Roscoe through the crowd and over to Mickey's interview room. He must have thought I was taking him out for a walk and when he realised I wasn't, he threw himself into the dog bed like a petulant teenager and heaved an exaggerated sigh.

'Oh stop your moaning; this'll be better than walkies,' I said as I kissed him and returned to my kennel block.

At lunchtime, I went to see how Roscoe was

getting on. As predicted, Mickey's first few customers fell in love with him but for one reason or another were not quite right. Others wanted small- to medium-sized dogs or had young children that were intimidated by Roscoe's size and clumsiness.

Mickey told me she thought she'd cracked it at one point. A man had come in wanting a large dog. He'd had big dogs before and wanted another but as Mickey dug deeper it became apparent that he was no more suitable for Roscoe than my mother would have been. He had produced a photo of where the new dog would sleep. The duvet looked very comfortable but the trouble was it was inside a kennel that had a large chain attached to it and was located in what looked like a breaker's yard. Deflated and disillusioned, Mickey sent the man off with a flea in his ear – dispensed by her, not Roscoe.

I took Roscoe for a walk to compensate for his unsuccessful morning. He trotted along beside me with the hat firmly in his mouth. I sat on a bench inside Battersea's grounds and opened up my lunch. After five minutes of hound-dog eyes boring into my sandwich and saliva strands reaching from his mouth to the floor, I could stand it no longer.

'Sit, Roscoe,' I said. He sat.

'Where's your paw?' I asked. He showed me.

When I offered him some sandwich, he spat the hat out, swallowed the food without it touching the sides and picked the hat straight up again.

In this ridiculous fashion, Roscoe and I finished my lunch and began to head back inside – me to my other charges, him to the interview room.

We hadn't got very far when a couple approached us. They had been watching Roscoe's strange eating habit and wanted to know what was with the hat. I told them Roscoe's story and watched as they knelt down to him, talking softly and offering him their hands for a stroke. They seemed very nice and when they expressed their interest in him I could barely contain my excitement. I told them to follow me and walked them at top speed to Mickey's interview room.

After introducing James and Sarah to Mickey, I turned to leave but knowing how attached I was to Roscoe, Mickey invited me to stay. As the interview began I watched in amazement as Roscoe picked up his hat and deposited it in James's lap. He'd never done this before, not even for me or Pauline or Ann or anyone else he knew. He wasn't possessive of the hat; he just preferred to keep hold of it himself.

I could tell that James and Sarah were genuine dog lovers and during the interview James's hand rested absentmindedly on Roscoe's head, occasionally massaging his ears. They told Mickey and me that their much-loved Belgian shepherd cross, Sheba, had recently died of old age. James showed me photos of Sheba, a handsome beast with a beautiful soft face and a huge grin that matched the size of her ears. They rescued her from a local farm where she had been kept in appalling conditions.

Sarah worked at the local school and James was a writer who worked from home. James had had the closest relationship with Sheba because he spent all day, every day with her and several times during the interview he had to compose himself before going on. He was holding on to her old lead, rubbing it as though trying to stay close to her, refusing to let her become just a memory. James understood why Roscoe could not be parted from his old master's hat. He too had not been able to relinquish Sheba's effects since she died.

James and Sarah had no kids and lived out in Suffolk in a large house with a four-acre garden; in short, they were perfect for Roscoe. The interview came to a close and I was aware of the growing bond between Roscoe and them.

Mickey explained that they were more than welcome to look at all the dogs before deciding if Roscoe was definitely the one. Secretly I hoped they didn't want to and as luck would have it, Sarah said she would rather not look at all those dogs knowing she could only take one home.

Fantastic! One-year-old black Labrador cross, one previous owner, good condition, sold as seen.

All up, Roscoe had been at Battersea for three months but to me it felt much longer. I'd had many favourites but I'd fallen harder for Roscoe than all the others put together. I had become more attached to him than I realised and watching him walk away to a new life, albeit a better life, was extremely hard. As much as I tried, I just couldn't stop my tears from spilling over.

James clipped Sheba's lead on to Roscoe's collar and then donned the Trilby hat Roscoe was so attached to. Roscoe couldn't take his eyes off James – that was except for one last look back at me – and then the three of them left Battersea, having filled a gaping hole in each other's lives.

Most of the dogs that came into Battersea were happy-go-lucky types, just looking for someone with love in their heart and food in their pantry. During my 15-year service, approximately a quarter of a million dogs passed through Battersea, which was 250,000 too many.

Battersea successfully rehomes thousands of dogs every year. Roscoe was just one of them. Although Battersea Dogs Home is a fantastic institution, which I hold very dear, nothing would make me happier than to see it become redundant. No Battersea Dogs Home would mean no unwanted dogs.

# CHAPTER 8

# THE BACKBONE OF BATTERSEA DOGS HOME

I had come a long way since my interview with Mr Wadman Taylor five years ago. I was now conducting my own rehoming interviews and, having built up confidence, even pictured myself as a chat-show host one day, skilfully teasing out tasty morsels of information from unsuspecting celebrities under my spotlight.

The interviews were only one half of the rehoming process and although I found them fascinating, my true passion was introducing dogs to their new owners because it meant that once again I had a hound by my side.

Just as the dogs that came into Battersea were all individual, so too were the staff that formed its backbone. They were 100 per cent committed to what they did and worked hard, day in day out, for little thanks and even less pay. Their reward came from a very different place, far more satisfying than money could buy.

Throughout my entire time at Battersea Dogs Home, I never really felt as though I was at work.

As far as I was concerned, I was spending the day surrounded by the creatures I adored, whilst hanging out with my mates and doing some good at the same time. If asked, I probably would have done the job for free.

Luckily, the boss hadn't asked and now it seemed he never would. Much to our collective sadness Mr Wadman Taylor announced his retirement. He and his wife had been more like our grandparents than our bosses and with their departure, I felt like a little piece of Battersea Dogs Home had gone for ever.

Not long after the Wadman Taylors left, so did Dot and Fred. It was all change at Britain's best-loved dog's home and my radar for impending doom began to twitch.

One rainy Thursday in the middle of our lunch hour, a meeting of all staff was hastily convened. As each department shuffled into the boardroom and the anticipation built, I looked around at this old room I'd only been in a handful of times before. It was like stepping back in time to another century. A huge antique wooden desk about 25 feet by 12, with a green leather surface, stood in the middle of the boardroom. An enormous painting from the eighteenth century depicting horses, hounds and a fat fellow hung from the wall at the far end. The walls to the sides carried both photographs and paintings of Battersea's royal patrons, past and present, as well as some framed letters written by Queen

Victoria pertaining to Battersea Dogs Home business.

I was halfway through reading one when in strode a man in his fifties and an attractive woman in her early thirties, both tall, both standing ram-rod straight, both ex-army. Blimey, I thought, what had we done that made it necessary for our new bosses to be trained in armed combat?

Lieutenant Colonel Duncan Green had served in Northern Ireland, which I suppose qualified him for the role of director general at Battersea Dogs Home. Quintessentially English, with a Sid James laugh and greased-down hair, he cut a distinguished figure (paunch aside) and epit-omised the ex-army type. He had two Springer spaniels – so far so good.

Nichola Vickers had had a successful army career too, reaching the rank of captain – no mean feat for a woman, and was to become Battersea's manager. Even though she didn't have a dog, I liked her from the off. She seemed charismatic, energetic and dynamic. I didn't know it then, but of all the bosses I'd had before or since, she was to be far and away my favourite.

Introductions over, and hidden from their view but not mine, Jacky gave a sharp salute to which I burst out laughing and had to pretend I was having a coughing fit. Great – singled out as a troublemaker straight away. Memories of school came flooding back. I was waiting for the order to drop to the floor and give them 50 press-ups each but thankfully it never came and the meeting ended. Jacky, Ali, Steph, Kirsty and I returned to the staff canteen to finish our lunch. There wasn't much to finish; two Labradors and a curlycoated retriever had seen to that.

'So what do you reckon?' I asked the others, salvaging a bar of chocolate that was too high up for the dogs to reach.

'Hmm, not sure. I can't see either of them with a poop scoop in their hand,' said Steph.

'I heard they have to spend a day in every department. Can't wait to see them in kennels,' said Kirsty.

'I've got just the dog for them to clean out,' said Ali with a mischievous look in her eye. 'And what's with the whole army thing?'

'You watch; we'll all be square-bashing before you know it,' Jacky said, taking a long drag on her cigarette.

I adored Jacky; she was funny and smart and extremely naughty, which ensured we would be great friends from the start. Jacky was partial to the hairless members of the canine world, reflected in the three dogs she owned. Shaggy, her Mexican hairless, Curly, her Chinese crested and Mouse, her Chinese crested-chihuahua cross. All three dogs were as bald as coots and for protection against the elements had to wear woolly jumpers in the winter and sunscreen in the summer.

Chinese cresteds were originally bred to act as hot water bottles and, as I found out, they work like a charm. I was dog-sitting Curly one weekend and he insisted on getting under the duvet with me. Within half an hour I was sweating and had to throw the covers off.

Like most of the staff at Battersea, Jacky was far braver than me and one afternoon, having failed to find anyone else to help her, foolishly asked for my assistance. It was my last day at work before going on a well-earned two-week holiday to Greece. I was always careful not to get bitten, but even more so just before a holiday. According to sod's law, if you're going to be bitten it'll be right before your holiday, ensuring your must-have accessories that year are bandages and a sling; not really a good look with a bikini.

When the Dangerous Dogs Act came into effect in the early nineties, all pit bull terriers were required by law to be neutered, microchipped and tattooed. Needless to say most were not, but one had come in that morning with a tattoo on the inside of its back leg. For identification purposes, we needed to be able to read and log the tattoo. My job was to lift the beast up whilst Jacky got underneath and wrote down the exact letters and numbers of the tattoo.

We reached the kennel to find a big brute wearing a huge studded collar. Jacky must have read my mind because before I had time to bolt, she had grabbed me, unlocked the kennel door and dragged me inside, slamming the door behind us.

154

'The sooner we get on with it, the sooner we're out,' she said.

I looked down at the dog and swallowed hard. Even if I had wanted to (which I didn't) the dog was so big I wouldn't have been able to lift it completely off the floor so I gingerly put my hands under its armpits, hoping to God it wasn't ticklish, and raised it up as best I could.

We were in a rather compromising position, Jacky underneath the dog and me holding it up by the armpits, when just at that moment it burped. Thinking the burp was a growl, I let go and hotfooted it out of the kennel. The dog landed on Jacky's head but luckily it was a friendly type, and although it must have thought this kind of carry-on more than a little strange, happily wagged its tail whilst licking Jacky's face.

Jacky found me at the other end of the kennel block peering around the door. She gave me a despairing shake of the head and a mild telling off. My reputation for cowardice didn't improve as the years progressed: if anything it deteriorated. The lowest point came when I was cast as the cowardly lion in *The Wizard of Dogs*, Battersea's third Christmas pantomime.

Some might say performing in panto was going above and beyond the call of duty – not so the staff at Battersea, who were happy to make fools of themselves once a year and embrace the Christmas spirit. In fact, trying to get them out of costume was the difficult part.

During the dark days of difficult customers, abandoned dogs and overcrowding, Steve Lynn, Battersea's kennel manager, was my sanity. He and I kept each other's spirits up and we giggled, guffawed and grinned the grim days away.

At six feet two inches tall and with killer looks and snake hips, Steve was a born performer and made a handsome pantomime dame. Everything he did, from starring in *Cinderella Mongrel and the Three Ugly Bitches*, *Snowy White the Westie and the Seven Done Dogs* and *The Wizard of Dogs*, to having a fire extinguisher thrown at him by an irate customer, had us in stitches. He was one of those people who was funny even when he was serious.

Steve had three dogs, Daisy-May and Henry – his two cocker spaniels – and Bertie, his British bulldog. All three were completely untrained and wild, even after he'd had them for years. After driving all the way from his home in Gillingham to Battersea, a two-hour journey each way, Steve would often arrive at work in a state of high harassment and with a slightly green tinge to him. This was not due to the rush-hour traffic, but more to Bertie having crapped in the back of the car, with Daisy-May and Henry helpfully trampling it in for the duration of the journey.

There were many times when I thought Steve would gather his three hounds and go directly from his car to the waiting room where unwanted pets were handed in. He never did, which should tell you a lot about his character. Lesser men would have, I'm sure.

Steve and I got into all sorts of ridiculous situations together, the pinnacle of which was being invited on to the BBC television show, *Style Challenge*. *Style Challenge* was a *bit* of daytime fluff where life's rejects were rescued and given a complete makeover: hair, clothes, make-up, the lot. The two of us – beleaguered and bedraggled animal charity workers whose uniform consisted of jeans, a sweatshirt and wellies – were perfect fodder for a makeover.

Actually we both scrubbed up quite well and were delighted to be allowed to keep our new clothes, which were the only decent things in our wardrobe. They made multiple appearances at weddings, funerals and bar mitzvahs for many years to come.

Steve and his dogs never failed to attend the weekly meeting of The Battersea Flyers, the Home's very own agility team, consisting entirely of Battersea employees and their ex-Battersea dogs.

Dog agility is a bit like equestrian show jumping, only on a smaller but more intricate scale. A course is designed and set up involving jumps, tunnels, a see-saw, a suspended hoop, a steep A-frame for the dogs to scale and descend, and anything else one might have to hand. The handler runs beside their unleashed hound, whilst expertly dishing out commands. The aim is for the dog to successfully

157

negotiate the course without knocking anything over, including its handler, in as little time as possible.

When performed by experts, dog agility is a mesmerising and thrilling sport to watch, prompting cries of excitement from the audience. When performed by The Battersea Flyers the audience just wanted to cry. Nowhere on earth would you find a more motley-looking bunch than The Battersea Flyers – and that was just the handlers. The only dog that flew anywhere was a little sable-coloured terrier cross called Tootsie, owned by June, who during her turn would, without warning, fly into the crowd to bite small children.

The other dogs weren't much better. Daisy-May, Steve's cocker spaniel, preferred to jump on top of the tunnel and run its length rather than through it. Pip, a little Tibetan terrier cross (on loan to me), always started well, then depending on her mood would either complete the course at 100mph without direction from me, or just exit stage left after the first jump never to be seen again. Holloway, a German shepherd (named after the district he was found in), was a natural-born singer and would yodel his way around the course, occasionally hurling himself at the odd jump or two, thinking the idea was to knock them down rather than elegantly skip over them.

The others whose report cards read 'tries hard', were Louie the ex-racing greyhound who just kept looking for the rabbit, Pippin the chihuahua who was more attitude than agility and Steve's other dog, Bertie the bulldog, who always liked to stop for a crap right in the middle of the course. Finally there was Jacky's bald dog, Shaggy, whose name was not an attempt at irony; it was more a description of what he liked to do to his teammates.

Thank heaven then for our showpiece, Tessa the Border collie (had to be, didn't it?). Owned and trained by Ali Taylor, Tessa would, with minimal instruction, complete the course at break-neck speed, incurring zero penalties along the way. Sometime later, Ali would reach the finish line, red-faced, huffing and puffing, where she'd find Tessa waiting patiently for her as if to say, 'This is all so beneath me, for God's sake, someone get me *The Times* crossword to do.' Ali's response was to light up a fag to aid recovery.

Needless to say, we never won any awards, but all members of The Battersea Flyers, both two-legged and four, had lots of laughs. Our audiences always enjoyed themselves too and actually preferred it when the dogs endearingly buggered up. That worked out well then.

Besides Tessa the Border collie, Ali was also partial to the small antiques of the canine world, most of whom were on their way out and needed that extra little bit of love. She took them home and with the help of her dad ensured their final weeks were full of love and happiness. The trouble was they really were on their last legs so when the inevitable happened, Mr Taylor was left bereft. Things didn't improve for the poor man either; after 15 years, Ali still brings home Battersea's geriatrics. It's hardly surprising her dad is an emotional wreck.

Ali's favourite antique (and the one that lasted the longest) was Ruby Long Legs, a sort of terrier cum chihuahua. Classed as a small dog, she had ridiculously long legs and lived to be a staggering 19 years old before turning up her toes.

These old-age pensioners were usually pointed in Ali's direction by Shaun, who took over from Mr Wadman Taylor as Battersea's head vet. In his professional capacity, Shaun had to remove some strange foreign bodies from dogs over the years, the most unlikely being a toy London bus, swallowed by an over-zealous spaniel called Howard. Realising the double-decker wasn't going to come out of the depot the way nature intended, Shaun knew that surgery was the only option. The operation was a great success and I am happy to report that both patient and bus lived to run another day.

But it wasn't always a happy ending and as head vet at Battersea Dogs Home, Shaun had to make some unenviable decisions. Shaun is a gifted vet who continues to work at the Home after approximately 20 years and I can only imagine how many thousands of canine lives he has improved and saved over the years.

★　　★　　★

It was not just Shaun and Ali who had clocked up many years' service at Battersea. Pauline, Jacky, Ann and many of the other staff were as much a part of the Home as the dogs and cats they looked after.

Jade was another Battersea stalwart and after rehoming Marley (the shortest lurcher in the world) during my early years, she too decided there was no other place on earth she'd rather work. She was the poshest kennel maid ever to have cleaned out a Battersea kennel – perhaps with the exception of me, and like many of the breeds she adored, Jade came from good country stock and was hard-working and loyal.

She and Ali became great friends and one weekend when Jade was returning home to visit her parents, she decided to invite Ali along. Jade's parents lived in a large country house in Wiltshire and as Jade and Ali neared the house, Jade pulled the car over to the side of the road.

'What's wrong?' Ali asked.

'Look . . .' Jade said, shifting uneasily in her seat, 'I just wanted you to know that my mum and dad live on an estate.'

Ali looked at her sympathetically and said, 'Don't be so silly, Jade. There's no need to worry. It's okay; I live on an estate too.'

Jade did not seem placated, in fact she turned a deep shade of pink, put the car in gear and drove on.

As the car wound up the impressive oak-lined

driveway, the ten-bedroom house set in 100 acres of stunning English countryside came into view.

'Oh,' Ali said with eyes as wide as saucers, '*that* kind of estate.'

Battersea Dogs Home was bursting with real people and one of my favourites was Margaret. She was the archetypal British tea lady, right down to her blue housecoat. She loved a natter, had a heart of gold and would do anything for anyone. But most of all Margaret loved a party.

Even though she was well into her seventies, Margaret had more energy than the rest of us put together and attended all of Battersea's parties, out-dancing everyone else. She was even known to party on long after the official shindig was over.

On one such occasion, we found ourselves moving on to a nightclub in Vauxhall, just a stone's throw from the Home. We walked in and to our delight a drag queen contest was just starting. Ten of them were up on stage bedecked in feathers, sequins, leotards and fishnets. The host asked for a volunteer from the audience to be the judge. There was no way I was volunteering; with all those claws out and handbags at 20 paces, it could have been a very dangerous undertaking. Margaret, however, had no such reservations and shot her hand up.

Lily the Pink stood at least seven feet tall in her six-inch stilettos, beehive hair-do and spectacular feathered tiara. She helped Margaret up onstage, stuck the microphone under her nose and asked her name and where she worked.

People were always intrigued to discover someone that worked at Battersea Dogs Home and their reaction rarely differed.

'Ahhh,' Lily replied, drawing the syllable out for an impossibly long time.

Once over their initial delight, they'd always go on to ask the same question and Lily the Pink was no exception.

''Ow many d'you put down then?' she asked Margaret.

Quick as a flash Margaret replied, 'Less than you've got holes in your tights, mate.'

The Battersea contingent gave a roar of approval, Margaret picked the winning drag queen and we all legged it out of there before the losers could get their claws into her.

Every member of Battersea staff had at least one dog and, in some cases, three or four. Margaret's was a black-and-tan mongrel called Butch, not endowed with much up top and hopeless at agility but, like his mistress, he had a heart of pure gold.

Having a heart of gold was a prerequisite for working at Battersea Dogs Home. The staff and volunteers demonstrated their kindness every single day – and some nights too. In fact, seeing them with dark circles under their eyes was commonplace at Battersea, as many would foster newborn puppies and kittens that required feeding every two hours through the night.

Some would take animals home that coughed and spluttered into the small hours, others took care of dogs with upset stomachs that demanded back doors be opened at 3 a.m. Then there were the youngsters that might have had any of the aforementioned afflictions, but funnily enough were never too sick to play with a squeaky toy at midnight.

The dogs that had trouble adapting to Battersea's kennel environment were also prime candidates for fostering because going home with a member of staff could go a long way towards helping them adjust to their new and unfamiliar life.

Fostering was an art form though and, depending on the reason the dog was being fostered, involved a fine balance between TLC and ground rules. Sometimes more harm than good could come from a stint in a foster home.

Feeding a dog tasty food in an attempt to get it to start eating again could result in it never wanting to go back to plain old dog food. Lavishing too much attention on a shy and introverted dog could result in it attention seeking once it came out of its shell and the foster carer's previous levels of attention naturally waned. Spoiling a despondent dog could result in it becoming possessive of its spoiler, in extreme cases not allowing another dog or human anywhere near that person.

The foster parent must be on their guard to prevent all of these potential pitfalls whilst at the same time helping the dog overcome its problems. The length of foster could vary from a few days to months but Battersea's behaviourists and vets were always on hand to offer advice and support.

Fostering was also an excellent way to monitor a dog's behaviour out of the somewhat unusual Battersea environment and it could give a more accurate insight into a dog's personality.

One such hound whose behaviour altered dramatically outside of the kennels was Morris the mongrel terrier. An eight-week-old puppy, Morris had bright, intelligent eyes, a scruffy black coat flecked with white, pointed ears, a bushy tail and could fit into the palm of your hand.

He was rehomed to a family with children but two weeks later was brought back to Battersea having bitten every member of his new family. Everyone at the Home fell about laughing at these preposterous allegations and the guinea pig-sized Morris was rehomed for a second time. On this occasion he went to an experienced terrier owner who, just in case the allegations were true, would be able to keep those big terrier traits in check. This time he was back within a week for the same reason.

During each assessment, Morris was the model dog, never once revealing his Mr Hyde side. Ann was curious to find out if there was actually any truth to these slanderous rumours and decided to foster him herself. As head of Rehabilitation, she felt she was more than a match for this little terrier terror. Sure enough, she came into work after having him at home for the weekend, revealing several plastered fingers.

'He's a little git!' she cried. We couldn't help but laugh. This was the person who tackled every size of unruly and rebellious dog for a living, and a guinea pig had got the better of her. She was not amused.

There were always one or two dogs that wormed their way so deep into your heart that you could not possibly give them up. Morris was Ann's little worm and ten years later she still had him. His face was now grey and he was a little arthritic but his temperament had improved significantly with age. Over the years, he had latched on to many members of Battersea staff (not in a good way) and even in my last days at Battersea, the miniature-sized Morris sporadically continued his campaign of terror.

Besides Battersea's own staff there was an army of external foster parents who usually had much more time to devote to their charges and were ready, willing and able to take up the cause. Dogs that went to external foster homes did not have to go into Battersea at all during their recuperation and could often be rehomed straight from there.

The only problem with external foster carers was

that they invariably fell in love with the first dog they fostered and were unable to give it back. This was of course excellent news for the hound but it meant that the next dog placed in this particular foster home had to be good with other dogs and not have a contagious lurgy that it might pass on to the newly installed dog. In the worst case scenario, if the now-resident dog became jealous about sharing the love, Battersea had lost a valuable foster home.

Much like the kennel maids that worked in the rehoming section, all foster carers became attached to their charges and the moment the dog was rehomed was truly bittersweet. There was a feeling of joy and satisfaction that their much-loved foster dog, whom they had nursed and nurtured, was now at the stage where it could go off to its new home. However, this euphoria was tinged with a sense of sadness and loss. Their canine companion, with whom they had built a strong bond, was about to set off on a new adventure alone.

If the dog was fostered by a member of Battersea staff, it would reside by day in one of Battersea's offices, in an attempt to replicate a more natural environment than that of a kennel. Time out of kennels in a quiet place with a human in constant attendance worked wonders. Battersea's offices offered all of this and more and this prime real estate was also used to help dogs convalesce from operations and general illness, as the recovery process was far speedier when the animal was un-stressed.

As the member of office staff tapped away on his or her computer, the dog snoozed on a blanket at their feet. The dogs improved dramatically; it was the poor unsuspecting office staff I felt sorry for. They really did deserve medals as they unwittingly opened their offices to unexpected bowel and bladder movements, vomit, chewed phones and furniture, and computer wires continually being pulled out of sockets. Work sometimes had to take a back seat. Oh, so that's why they did it . . .

Rebecca was a young, fresh-faced secretary straight out of Pitman's college. She applied for a position at Battersea and a week later found herself making the 90-minute journey from Billericay in Essex to Battersea for an interview, not giving a second thought to the fact she'd have to battle her way in and out of central London on tubes and buses ten times a week were she to be successful.

It was her dream to work for an animal charity so when she was accepted at Battersea Dogs Home to work as Nichola's secretary, she thought all her Christmases had come at once. Little did she know she would be played like a violin, by kennel staff wanting her premium office space for their sick and depressed hounds to recuperate in.

Enter a three-month-old, rather threadbare Scottie.

He had tufts of hair in some places but in others was completely bald with baby soft, pink skin. This made his snout look extra long. In fact with his little legs and long nose, he looked just like a baby aardvark and was christened Ardie.

Ardie was picked up from Paddington Green police station on a cold winter's morning by one of Battersea's animal ambulances. It is a well-known fact that Paddington Green police station holds category A terrorists but looking at Ardie, somehow I didn't think he quite fitted into that category, unless of course he was packed with Semtex, which seemed unlikely.

As soon as he set foot inside the Home, the bag of dog jumpers was wheeled out. These pullovers were knitted by an army of dog-loving old ladies who liked to do their bit for 'those poor unfortun-ates', as they called the dogs and cats at Battersea. They were expert knitters but sometimes their colour schemes were a bit off. It wasn't so bad for the pups but when ailing Rottweilers were wres-tled into pink pullovers insult was most definitely added to injury. Still, the most important thing was that the dogs were warm in winter, especially half-bald Scottie pups.

The next thing was to find Ardie a nice warm office to reside in until his tufts had evened out a bit and he could be put up for rehoming.

This was Rebecca's first day. She was trying to get to grips with the telephone system and the filing system, as well as breaking in her new ex-army boss. All was going more or less according to plan until a tufty little aardvark puppy, wearing a yellow-and-orange striped woolly jumper, padded in, squatted and peed right in the middle of Rebecca's floor.

That was it. The moment Rebecca set eyes on this rather peculiar apparition, the phones were switched to answer machine and the filing could wait. She scooped him up and squeezed him so tight he let out a noise that sounded more like it had come from a cow rather than a dog.

Ardie was an extremely friendly little chap. There were no signs of nervousness or maltreatment. On the contrary, his tail wagged furiously as he trotted from Rebecca to Nichola and back to Rebecca again introducing himself to his new landladies.

I imagine he was abandoned due to his skin condition. Perhaps his owner didn't know how to deal with it or couldn't afford to. They probably didn't know that there are organisations that treat animals belonging to people who cannot afford private veterinary fees. Of course, some owners just don't care, in which case the dog is better off starting life again with someone who does.

Rebecca adored Ardie; dogs like him were the reason she wanted so desperately to work at Battersea. Their love affair lasted for two months. His hair grew back and Scottie Rescue, who had already found him a wonderful new home, came to collect him.

Rebecca wept when they took him away. Poor

thing, how could she have known this was just the beginning – or what was coming next. The first one is always the hardest, though, and she wept for five hours before Buster was deposited over the baby gate and bulldozed his way into her heart.

Buster, a two-year-old, tri-colour Jack Russell terrier, had come into Battersea for fighting with the other dog in the household. On top of that he'd chewed his way through his owner's three-storey home, from bottom to top.

He'd been in Rebecca's office for one hour and in that time had managed to slam his way through the baby gate twice in order to terrorise Poppy, the office cat.

Poppy had come into Battersea as a feral kitten five years previously. The Home was all she had ever known and she strutted around like she owned the place. Over time, Poppy became less feral but remained as daunting to humans as the day she came in. She could usually be found snoozing on top of the photocopier, daring anyone to come and use it. As for dogs, Poppy had more dogs than hot dinners and I never saw one get the better of her.

The first two times Buster escaped on his errant mission he was brought back before any harm was done. The third time, Rebecca was on the phone dealing with a delicate situation involving an ex-Battersea dog, a cushion and the local vicar. The fledgling secretary was becoming more and more stressed as she watched Buster systematically

171

dismantle the baby gate. There was nothing in her Pitman's training about such occurrences and all she could think of to do was squeak a squeaky toy in a desperate effort to distract him.

'It really was awfully embarrassing, the vicar didn't know where to look. Are you listening to me, dear?' said the voice on the other end of the phone.

'Yes, madam,' Rebecca replied, her voice rising as she saw that the squeaks had only served to whip Buster up into a frenzy and increase his determination.

Suddenly, the baby gate was swinging from its one remaining hinge and Buster was out. Hearing screams a few seconds later, Rebecca dropped the phone and ran towards where they were coming from. She followed the trail of destruction Buster had left in his wake, until she reached the kitchen downstairs where she found him lying belly up, cowering, with an imperious Poppy standing majestically over him, ears back, one paw on his chest, claws out.

After that, reinforcements were called in to strengthen Rebecca's baby gate. They came in the form of Nigel and his maintenance team whose jobs ranged from painting kennel blocks and unblocking unpleasant drains, to fixing kennel locks and cutting dogs out of choke chains. These choke chains were often put on dogs when they were young and still growing. Sometimes owners never bothered to take them

172

off, resulting in the chain slicing into the now adult dog's neck. If the dog was large and aggressive, it would have to be held at bay with graspers whilst the maintenance team used bolt cutters to free it from its torturous appendage, taking care to cut the choke chain, not the grasper which was the only thing keeping the maintenance man from the jaws of the dog. A nerve-racking task for which they were not paid danger money.

Once Buster was back in Rebecca's office, safely contained behind his reinforced baby gate, I set about finding him a home. His needs were pretty specific and it took a while. Weekends were the busiest time and therefore the best opportunity for the dogs and cats to find new homes. This being the case, the dogs that were in an office by day resided back in their kennel on view to the public at weekends.

Every Friday evening, Rebecca put Buster into a kennel in the rehoming section, said goodbye and wished him luck, and on Monday morning she'd go straight back up to Buster's kennel hoping to find that someone had picked him and he had gone home. For six Mondays though, there he was, sitting patiently, waiting for her to take him back up to her office. On the seventh Monday, however, Buster was gone.

Once again Rebecca buckled up for another emotional roller-coaster ride. She was sad that she wouldn't see Buster again, but delighted he had found a new home. She returned to her office,

173

wondering which needy case would be brought to her next.

She didn't realise Buster hadn't gone home. I waited until she'd had her morning caffeine before breaking the news to her. Buster had been stolen from his kennel on the Sunday. Someone had forced the lock and smuggled him off the premises.

Jack Russells are good ratters and the concern was that he'd been stolen by insalubrious characters to go down holes and catch rats. This is a dangerous pastime, often ending with the dog becoming stuck down a deep hole, never to be seen again.

Rebecca spent the next two hours sobbing. Nichola was very understanding to begin with but as the in-tray piled up, her patience began to wear thin.

Three days went by with no news on Buster. Then on the fourth, Pauline phoned me to say that a dog fitting Buster's description was at Eltham police station and she was on her way to pick him up.

An anxious wait ensued and as soon as Pauline returned, Rebecca and I raced down to meet her. When Pauline opened the back of her van, there was Buster, looking a bit bedraggled and muddy but none the worse for his adventure. When he saw Rebecca, Buster let out a howl of delight and threw himself at her.

We decided that whoever had pinched him had

got more than they bargained for. Buster probably ate their home and if they had a cat, chances were he would have tried to snack on that too.

No one knew what Buster had been through but from that moment on, he behaved impeccably. So much so, I managed to find him a home within a week of his return. He now resides in Cheshire and remains the best-behaved dog in the village.

Rebecca's time at Battersea continued to be an emotional yo-yo. All those tearful goodbyes were counterbalanced by truly seeing the difference she was making unfold before her eyes. Doe-eyed dogs, happy in their new homes, adorned her office pinboard – a testament to all the good she had done.

Lieutenant Colonel Duncan Green had been at Battersea for six months. He seemed like a pleasant-enough fellow and as yet hadn't caused too many ripples in the Battersea millpond. He'd even opened up his home to a Battersea dog, although I sometimes wondered if he wished he hadn't. Too late now – it wouldn't do for the director general to be returning his Battersea dog. Ginny was a maniacal adolescent chocolate Labrador whose manners left something to be desired. She resided in Colonel Green's office, held in place by a baby gate, but would screech her head off whenever anyone walked by, driving the other office staff to distraction. Those that entered did so at their peril.

One morning he called me up to his office. Uh oh, I thought; the fear of being in trouble and getting mugged by Ginny filled me with equal dread. I fought my way through Ginny much like a person might fight their way through a swimming pool filled with molasses. I was making a supreme effort but getting nowhere fast.

After 60 seconds of what felt like trying to fight off a love-sick grizzly bear, I pulled up a chair, exhausted.

'Er, you've got some . . . on your face,' Colonel Green said apologetically.

I put my hand up to my face and felt warm, wet dog saliva. I wiped it off.

'. . . and some . . . in your hair,' he said, this time looking down at the floor a little embarrassed. I reached up and felt my hair. I pulled out some carpet that Ginny had been chewing as I entered the office.

'Thanks,' I said, an awkward smile passing between us.

Colonel Green was due to give a talk at the Shepperton Townswomen's Guild but had double-booked himself (or so he said) and asked if I could take his place. Frankly, I was relieved I wasn't being fired – or, heaven forbid, promoted again. Could be worse, I thought, and loaded the car up with Battersea literature, Battersea slides and Battersea dog.

I hadn't given a talk about the Home before but thankfully had no problems with public speaking.

In fact, in the sixth form at school I had to do all the Head Girl's speeches because faced with an audience, she'd go to pieces.

I was thrilled to be asked to represent Battersea and spread the good word. My talk to the Townswomen's Guild was a great success although I think the women were more taken with Katie the scruffy mongrel than me, the scruffy rehomer. At the end of the talk, the chief Townswoman publicly thanked Katie and me and presented us with a large donation to take back to Battersea.

'Thank you so much, that was wonderful,' she said to me as I packed up the last of my things. 'I'm so glad it was you that gave the talk instead of some stuffy old colonel.'

When I got back to Battersea, Colonel Green asked me how it went. I couldn't help telling him what the lady had said. He guffawed, saying he didn't mind being called stuffy, it was the old he didn't like!

Colonel Green settled into Battersea life and became a great asset to the Home. He even made numerous guest appearances in Battersea's Christmas pantomimes. He had that rare ability to mix with all types of people and without exception remembered everyone's name. On any given Friday evening he could be found down the pub, wearing his red socks and chatting amiably with the kennel staff and rehomers. Subjects ranged from the state of the England cricket team and politics to which was the best curry house in south-west London, the coolest bands around and of course everyone's favourite topic, our four-legged friends.

Part of Colonel Green's job was to meet with Battersea's Council of Trustees once every six weeks to assess the big picture. Under the watchful gaze of Her Majesty's portrait, this diverse group of 16 sat around the boardroom table and made decisions for the greater good of Battersea Dogs Home.

Amongst them were the mayor of Wandsworth, the commissioner of the Metropolitan Police, a celebrity yet, several eminent businessmen, a TV presenter and a member of the landed gentry.

The Earl of Buchan, now vice president, was a regular face at Battersea and over the years I built up a good rapport with him. His wife, Lady Buchan, was one of the warmest people I'd ever met and I adored her.

When the time was right for them to open their home to a Battersea hound, Colonel Green passed them to me. I found them a very lucky dog that went off to live on their country estate, only disgracing himself occasionally when the odd pheasant came too close.

In the early years when I was a kennel maid, Lord Buchan only knew me by sight from his six-weekly visits to Battersea. Take me out of situ and he might understandably struggle to place me, especially were we to cross paths somewhere altogether unlikely.

My mother has been a member of the Royal

Enclosure at Ascot since the age of 18; the privilege passed down from her father, and now passed down to me. The Royal Enclosure has a strict dress code and is one of the few times in the calendar year when I have to dress up. It is a whole hog kind of occasion, one that even demands headgear be included in one's ensemble.

My mother and I usually had a flutter at Ascot. She'd win something almost every time and I was always left wondering if it was possible to bet on who would come last, the only way I could see of ever recouping my losses. Dressed up to the nines, we were patiently waiting in the queue at the Royal Enclosure bookies, when who should be in front of us but Lord and Lady Buchan.

'Lord Buchan!' I blurted out before I could stop myself.

Tall and lean and looking more suave than Fred Astaire could ever have hoped to look in his top hat and tails, Lord Buchan spun around.

He greeted me warmly, shaking my hand and with all his breeding it took a keen eye to detect that he actually didn't have a clue who the hell I was. I reminded him as subtly as I could at which point he looked me up and down openmouthed, stammering for words. Poor chap; he'd only ever seen me in jeans, a sweatshirt and wellies, usually with some soppy hound slung over my shoulders, and now there I was in all my finery, complete with lipstick, mascara, feathered hat and high-heeled sling backs.

To give him time to compose himself, I introduced him and Lady Buchan to my mother, who sounds a little like the Queen, and as Lord Buchan raised an eyebrow, I could see what a curiosity I must have been to him. On the one hand, shovelling up after London's unwanted dogs, and on the other enjoying a day in the Royal Enclosure at Ascot.

At the introduction of Lord and Lady Buchan, my mother perked up. If I was moving in these circles, maybe my career at Battersea Dogs Home wasn't such a bad thing after all. Whatever she was feeling, I just felt relieved. At least my double life was out in the open now – Lord Buchan knew my secret, too.

Working at Battersea was a vocation and although the wages were modest, they did pay the bills and buy a pint or two in the pub on a Friday night. How wonderful, then, that Battersea Dogs Home had a 210-strong army of dedicated volunteers who put in a massive amount of time and effort with no financial reward whatsoever. The best thing was that the man hours they expended went directly on the dogs and cats.

Each year approximately 10,000 volunteer dog walks took place. The volunteers also spent 10,000 hours socialising the dogs, and the cat volunteers spent 16,000 hours socialising the cats.

As with Battersea's dogs, staff and customers, the volunteers came from wide-ranging backgrounds, all brought together by their passion for dogs.

Battersea Dogs Home's first-ever volunteer was a retired judge called Lawrence. I don't think his former career of dealing with two-legged beasts helped him in any way with his new-found career, as I watched him continually dragged off to Battersea Park by beasts of the four-legged variety.

Battersea's second volunteer was a King's Road inhabitant with a high-powered husband, a good heart and time on her hands. She knew this spare time had to be put to better use than shopping and lunching.

Carolyn adored dogs but couldn't have one because her cat hated them. One day she came into Battersea and enquired about becoming a volunteer dog walker. I gave her all the information she needed and a week later bumped into her taking a beautiful lurcher for a walk; she'd signed up!

Come rain or shine, Carolyn walked the dogs every day. It was one of those rare situations in life where everyone wins: Carolyn, the frazzled staff that didn't have time to walk every dog and of course the dogs who benefited from long rambles in the park.

It was during one of these long walks that disaster struck. Carolyn was walking one of her beloved greyhounds and had the dog on an extendable lead in order to give it a much-needed, if somewhat restricted run around. But as the dog took off, the lead became entangled around Carolyn's forefinger and when the lead came to its natural end, it sheared most of her finger off as efficiently as a meat slicer at the delicatessen. Whilst in great pain, Carolyn managed to get herself and the dog safely back to Battersea Dogs Home where an ambulance was promptly called. The dog was fine but due to her extreme pain, Carolyn was close to passing out.

Although badly shaken by the experience and with a permanently disfigured finger, Carolyn returned to volunteering at Battersea within a month of her ordeal – a testament to her abiding love for the dogs.

Carolyn and I struck up a friendship that lasted many years and I was sad when she told me she was leaving London to move to France. Sure, I would miss her but I knew Battersea's greyhounds and lurchers would miss her more. We stayed in touch and a year after she left, Carolyn kindly invited me to spend a couple of weeks at her beautiful St Tropez home, where she now lives permanently with her golden retriever, Diablo.

Of all the wonderful staff that worked at Battersea Dogs Home, it was hard not to be particularly fond of one's own team. There were 15 of us on the rehoming team and we predominantly dealt with the public. Our duties, however, extended beyond simply looking after our human customers and first thing every morning we could be found assisting the kennel staff with the monumental 'full clean out' of our canine customers.

Although this was hard physical work, dirty, smelly and pretty unsavoury, most rehomers threw themselves into it with gusto because this was real one-to-one dog time which was, after all, the reason we were all there in the first place. Our career paths within Battersea may have taken some of us away from dealing directly with the dogs, the rehomers toward the public, the drivers to their vans and the office staff to their desks, but ultimately we all relished the chance to remind ourselves what it was all about; being covered first-hand in dog slobber.

Over the years, my team members came and went. Some stayed for many years, others dipped their toe in and realised the stressful demands of both an emotional public and a never-ending stream of abandoned and mistreated dogs wasn't for them.

In any team there are some people that you natur-ally gravitate more towards than others and for me, Marilyn was one of those people. She was kind, caring, sensitive and good fun. She had a passion for all things canine and the naughtiest giggle in town.

Her greatest love was lurchers and whenever a decrepit one came into the Home, Marilyn was hot on the case. It wouldn't be long before she'd plundered the laundry on the dog's behalf and he'd be lying on a mountain of soft blankets, like in the story 'The Princess and the Pea'.

Marilyn was a natural with the dogs that needed a little extra love and care and she fostered many a destitute mutt who always came back looking a million dollars.

Before agreeing to foster any dog, Marilyn had the consideration to phone her husband, Piers, and run the request by him. Piers worked from home so it meant the dog could be with him during the day. In the relative normality of a home, the dog would come on quite literally in leaps and bounds.

With the amount of wee, vomit and worse that poor man had to clean up, not to mention the wreckage to his house, Piers should have been on the Battersea payroll. He obviously didn't mind too much; either that or he knew how much it meant to Marilyn because they took in many dogs, all of whom benefited immensely under their care.

When the time came for her to rehome her foster dogs, Marilyn stoically wiped away the tears and got on with the job in hand. She went to great lengths to find the perfect home for her dogs and if necessary travelled the length and breadth of the country to hand-deliver them.

I'd often walk through the kennels and find her comforting shell-shocked and bewildered dogs. Marilyn took those that were struggling most under her wing and did everything in her power to make sure each dog received the very best Battersea had to offer.

Marilyn worked as a rehomer for three years. She loved Battersea Dogs Home and Battersea Dogs Home loved her. Her other great passion was Piers and it was inevitable that this bright, beautiful young woman would leave the Battersea family one day to start a family of her own.

After Piers and Marilyn had their first child, Marilyn proudly brought Georgie into Battersea to show her off. She told us how good Georgie was, always smiling, never grizzly and already sleeping through the night, no doubt due to Marilyn's parenting skills. Marilyn looked so well and happy, as did Georgie who was the spitting image of her and obviously her pride and joy. Marilyn made having children look so effortless, we all wanted to instantly rush out and have babies!

We were delighted for Marilyn when she phoned a couple of years later to tell us she was expecting her second child. She had it all, a beautiful daughter, a wonderful husband who adored her and another baby on the way. No one deserved it more than Marilyn.

That is why to this day I still cannot believe she has gone.

Marilyn gave birth to William Elvis, a healthy baby boy. She and Piers were ecstatic. He kissed his wife goodbye and said he would bring Georgie in to see her and Elvis the next day but no sooner had he arrived home than the telephone rang. It was the hospital saying that there had been complications and Piers should get back to the hospital as quickly as he could.

He rushed back to find an army of doctors surrounding Marilyn. They were frantically shouting instructions to each other as they battled to save her life. Piers couldn't understand what he was seeing. Only an hour ago he had left his beautiful, smiling wife holding their newborn son and now she was unconscious, hooked up to machines and drips, fighting for her life.

Ten minutes later, a doctor came to tell Piers that Marilyn had died.

He didn't quite take it in when the doctor explained what had gone wrong. In the end they were just words. The tragic fact was that this beautiful young woman, the love of his life, had been taken from him at the worst possible time, in the worst possible way.

With the unimaginable enormity of what had happened bearing down on him like a ton of steel, Piers held his newborn son and began to make the most impossible phone calls of his life.

Marilyn was a sweetheart; she was one of life's good people. She was intelligent and down to earth, charming and funny. She was easy to get along with and extremely likeable – I can still hear that naughty giggle.

Although her children will not be fortunate enough to have her around in a physical sense, I know she will always be watching over them, loving them from wherever she is.

I visited Piers after Marilyn's death. We sat in his garden and talked about Marilyn, the kids, how he was coping and life in general. I was aware of a robin redbreast sitting on a wall a few feet away; a rarity these days, especially in east London. It was completely still and stayed there for such a long time that I began to wonder if it might be one of the kids' toys.

It was so extraordinary that I pointed it out to Piers who said it had been a regular visitor to the garden over the past few months. I'm not one of life's 'believers' and can be pretty sceptical, but at that moment in time I had this overwhelming feeling.

Could it be? The robin was certainly beautiful enough to be Marilyn.

# CHAPTER 9

# BATTERSEA'S COLOURFUL CLIENTELE

The world was in shock; Princess Diana was dead. As we tried to go about our daily routine at Battersea, it seemed somehow surreal that the dogs were still bounding around, demanding to be fed and played with. Thank God they were, otherwise the collective grief of a nation (which was snowballing out of control), threatened to take over. It was the dogs that kept us focused on the job in hand.

Under normal circumstances there is nothing better to coax one from self-pity, misery and doom than a wagging tail and a cold wet nose. These were far from normal circumstances, however, and on the day of Diana's funeral we all sat in a reception devoid of customers and sobbed into our dogs.

Princess Diana mixed with celebrity and the glitterati but she also knew what was important in life. In that respect, the world's most famous woman and the world's most famous dogs' home had plenty in common.

Although the rich and famous have patronised

Battersea, it is far from a place where celebrities pick up a pet. Indeed, the likes of Kenneth Branagh, Kevin Spacey and Robbie Williams have all come looking for love, but Battersea Dogs Home is much more about real life than fame and fortune. This reality is reflected in the everyday, extraordinary people that make up Battersea's colourful clientele.

At the opposite end of the spectrum to Battersea's better-known clientele was a septuagenarian named Bill Turner. Bill was a tall man with broad shoulders. He had short hair, which was grey and thinning but slicked down with Brylcreem nonetheless. His face was handsome but lined, and from the constant expression of worry etched across it, I could tell he'd had a tough life. His clothes were frayed and his shoes worn out.

Even though Bill clearly didn't have much in the way of material possessions, his manners were impeccable and when we walked into the inter-view room together, he pulled my chair out for me to sit down, the only time that happened during my 15 years at Battersea.

Bill had come to Battersea to find a new dog because his beloved Staffordshire bull terrier, Beauty, had just passed away after 16 years. Battling to control his emotions – and losing – Bill sat in my interview room and sobbed his heart out.

After a minute or so, Bill gave me his form and

I realised why he was so uneasy about handing it over. He hadn't filled it in. Apologising profusely, he looked at the floor as he explained to me that he couldn't read or write. Before we'd even got to question number one I had more time for this man than any rock star, actor or celebrity.

When Mickey trained me as a rehomer, she taught me never to judge a book by its cover. Although frighteningly easy to do, I learned time and time again what an inaccurate assessment first impressions give.

We went through his form together. Bill lived in a ground-floor council flat in south-east London. He was retired so was at home all day. He used to be a labourer, working for the same man for most of his life. The company belonged to a friend of Bill's dad who had taken him on as a 16-year-old apprentice. I imagined Bill was very good at his job; even now he looked fit and strong.

Bill was permitted to take his dog to work with him and over the years, his dogs became the unofficial company mascots. Bill told me how the other men became attached to the dogs and, as each got old and died, were inconsolable at the loss. I pictured the scene: 20 burly labourers perched on scaffolding, weeping into their handkerchiefs. When Bill was good and ready to have another dog, all of his workmates took an active part in training the new pup.

Bill had always had dogs, four in total, all living to ripe old ages. He showed me photos of them and they all looked happy and healthy but I was more interested in Bill, standing proudly next to them. Some of the photos were really old; sepia and faded. From these five photos in front of me, I could see this man's whole life at a glance; every decade from his twenties to his sixties, with the present-day Bill sitting before me.

In the first two photos Bill had that look of youthful invincibility on his face. In the third, I could see the first signs of age creeping in and in the last two he looked older and wiser; more comfortable as though he'd finally worked out what life was all about.

As I looked at the photos of the young Bill, I wondered if he'd ever thought about what he would be like as an old man. Did he now feel as if those pictures had been taken yesterday and wonder where his life had gone? Whatever the answer, one thing was glaringly obvious: Bill adored his dogs as much as they adored him.

The photo of Beauty was the best. She was a petite Staffie – although a little on the portly side – mainly white with a big black splodge on her head and a broad grin. She and Bill were at the seaside, it looked like Southend, and I was immediately transported back to my twenty-first birthday.

Bill's parents were big fans of the Staffordshire bull terrier and he had inherited their love for this stalwart breed that has become almost more synonymous with the British character than the bulldog. Loyal, dependable, strong and courageous, the Staffie has become one of the most popular breeds in the country.

In my experience, people whose parents were responsible dog owners usually go on to adopt those same ethics and standards themselves. In direct contrast, those that grow up in a world where a living, breathing, dependent animal can be disposed of like yesterday's bath water, find it hard to understand the concept of responsibility.

When asked about their previous dog experience, they'd explain how they had a dog for a couple of years as a child, but their parents gave it away. They'd then go on to repeat almost verbatim, that the same fate had befallen their own dog a year or so ago as they themselves didn't have the time or the inclination to look after it. Thankfully their honesty (or stupidity), meant we could ensure they didn't repeat history with a Battersea dog.

Bill knew the score and he talked effusively about all four of his beloved dogs, taking great pains to do each of their characters justice. His dogs went almost everywhere with him and he'd trained them all to a high level, using kindness and rewards.

One of his dogs, Rocky, was a bit wayward with other dogs but with time, patience and careful socialising, Bill overcame the problem. By the end of his life, Rocky allowed puppies and even the odd kitten to clamber over him.

But when Bill spoke about Beauty, his eyes filled up again and he couldn't speak. He seemed empty, as if there wasn't much point to anything without her. His voice broke and he gave a gruff cough in an attempt to correct it as he explained how they'd shared the same routine for 16 years and that he just missed her so much.

It had been three weeks since he'd had to make the heart-breaking decision to have her put to sleep. Her back legs had given out four days before that and Bill had carried her everywhere. Then for the first time ever, she hadn't wanted to go to the park. Three weeks and two days ago she'd stopped eating. Bill knew at this point she simply didn't want to go on; she'd had enough. So he did the decent thing and made the hardest decision a dog owner ever has to make.

When Bill was ready, we continued the interview. We discussed costs involved in keeping a dog, to which he told me in no uncertain terms that if he was short one week it was him that went without, never Beauty or the new dog. Bill had registered Beauty with the PDSA and she had been fully vaccinated, as had all of his four dogs.

I organised Bill's home visit and explained he was welcome to look around at the dogs for sale, with the impossible caveat that he was not to fall in love with a dog until he had had his home visit. Battersea did not reserve dogs pending a home visit because if the person were not approved, the dog would have been held back unnecessarily.

Bill's home visit report came back a few days later much as I'd expected. His housework left a bit to be desired, but the Home Visitor felt that Bill would love and care for any Battersea dog lucky enough to end up with him.

Bill chose an eight-year-old male Staffie called Tom who'd come to be at Battersea in much the same way that Roscoe had. His previous owner had died and, with no living relatives, Tom was left all alone in the world.

He had been well trained and was calm and sedate. He was knocking on a bit and was a little rough around the edges; not dissimilar to Bill. They looked remarkably similar, like a pair of old gits that would get on famously together.

A month later, Bill sent me a letter with a photo of Tom attached. He was sitting in the park under the shade of an oak tree surrounded by daffodils.

Bill came to every single Battersea event, proudly showing Tom off. He never failed to put a coin in Battersea's donation box. Even though he had very little, he would still give whatever he could in order to help those dogs down on their luck.

A few years later, Tom won Best Veteran at the Battersea Reunion, or was it 'Dog that Most Resembles its Owner'? Whatever it was, Battersea had brought these two lonely souls together and neither one ever looked back.

The BBC happened to be filming the TV series on Battersea Dogs Home at the time and captured Bill's story in glorious Technicolor. However, when Bill's episode went to air, we had a few complaint calls, asking how we could have rehomed a dog to a tramp that lived in a dirty house.

I asked the switchboard to take names and numbers of the disgruntled few and give them to me to deal with. I took great satisfaction in asking the callers if they knew anything about Bill's situation, the previous dogs he'd had, how much he'd loved them, that fact that his dog would always be with him and never want for anything. I asked the callers if they thought the dog minded if the hoovering hadn't been done. I told them that many wealthy people, whose homes were spick and span, had brought their dogs into Battersea because they had messed on the carpet or chewed the expensive furniture. In one mind-boggling case, a dog was brought into Battersea because it didn't match the colour scheme.

I told them not only had Bill met all of Battersea's criteria for offering a stable, loving, permanent home to a dog, but that he'd passed with flying colours.

Before climbing down from my soap box, I finished by saying that given the choice, if I were a dog, I'd like nothing more than to go and live with Bill and that six months on, Tom is one of the happiest dogs with one of the proudest owners I had ever had the pleasure of knowing. Good day!

One of the many highlights of being a rehomer was receiving letters, thank-you cards and photos from new owners delighted with the furry addition to their family. Some of the letters were written in the shaky hand of the elderly, some were typed and others were penned by kids, with interesting illustrations attached. If you held the picture at a certain angle, in a dimly lit room, then sometimes the illustration sort of resembled a dog, but mostly they just looked like fat babies.

Whoever wrote the thank-you letters, they were all filled with love, gratitude and emotions so profound and genuine that in many cases they could have qualified for a literary prize. It wasn't always fan mail we received, however, and a few of these letters would describe in great detail how the dog had systematically destroyed the house from top to bottom, terrorised the neighbour's cat and dug up Granny's prize roses. Getting it off their chest must have somehow been cathartic as once Fido's misdemeanours were out of the way, they'd go on to say how dearly they loved him, how it was as though he'd always lived there and how they couldn't imagine life without him. With a crime sheet like that, I certainly could.

If a problem sounded serious, I'd pass the letter on to the Behaviour Hotline for a follow-up call, which the owner was usually surprised, but always delighted, to receive.

Most letters and cards came with photos numbering anywhere from one to literally a whole album. The photos never failed to bring a smile to my face, as countless dogs I'd rehomed looked back at me from their garden, armchair, bed, field, muddy puddle, the beach or on top of the cat. All blissfully happy dogs – what more could I possibly have asked for?

Actually, I have always felt it important to have a mechanic, a solicitor and a plumber in one's family. You never know when you might need their services. My family consisted of none of the above so the best I could hope for was to make their close acquaintances. I went one better and when a magistrate found me, I was delighted because you just never know.

Val was sent to Battersea by the Border Terrier Rescue Society after we had phoned them requesting a special person be found for a rather special little dog.

Dusty was about four years old, housetrained and past the destructive stage, she was small, pretty and extremely friendly to every person and dog she met. In short, she was the perfect dog.

This was a rarity at Battersea Dogs Home and word soon got round. The staff came to gawp at her like kids at the zoo. Dusty should have had a sign on her kennel saying 'Canine Perfectus – extremely rare worldwide, almost extinct in SW8'.

Astoundingly, she was a stray but I was convinced she'd just been mislaid and that her owner was on their way in to claim her. It was a dead cert. I hadn't had time to start a book and give odds on her being claimed, which was just as well really because to our collective bewilderment, no one came for her. The Lost Dog Department made dozens of calls and followed up every lead but to no avail. Of the quarter of a million dogs that came into Battersea during my time, if I had to put money on one stray never needing the services of Battersea's rehoming department, it would have gone on Dusty. We'll never know how or why she came to Battersea but astonishingly she wasn't claimed, so on the eighth day, with the help of Border Terrier Rescue, we set about finding her a new home.

Val had come highly recommended by Border Terrier Rescue, but as always Battersea carried out its own checks. During her interview, Val explained that Samson, her last Border, had lived to a ripe old age but he'd never liked other dogs so she always had to be one step ahead of him on the Common. She wouldn't have that problem with Dusty.

Val had a large house and garden and sometimes worked from home, but if not, she could take the dog to work as she had done with Samson. I wondered if the dog had the final say on whether a guilty or innocent verdict was passed. If Dusty wagged her tail at the defendant would they go free? This was a worrying thought – if this was the case, the streets of south-west London would be overrun with criminals.

We were delighted with Val who fitted the bill

perfectly, and I brought Dusty in so the two could meet. It was love at first sight, for both parties. Dusty jumped straight into Val's lap and planted a big wet kiss, right on her nose. That was that; sold.

If only they were all this easy.

Like Val, most of the customers I dealt with were a joy but it wasn't all hearts and flowers, and I sometimes spent a large portion of my day battling with people that couldn't have picked a more unsuitable dog if they'd tried.

Mick and his wife already had an elderly female boxer, Penny, and they'd chosen a bossy ten-year-old female mongrel as their second dog. The golden rule when matching dogs together is that opposites attract. Mixing like for like to live together is often a recipe for disaster. That's not to say it would never work, but the dog they chose had come into Battersea for dominant behaviour with other dogs so it was a bad idea from the outset.

I tried to explain this to Mick. I told him there was a high possibility that the new dog would try to dominate Penny and that I didn't think this was fair. He had a great home to offer and I asked him if there were any other dogs he liked but he had his heart set on this one and wouldn't entertain anything else. I wouldn't entertain that particular match so it was stalemate. Before he left, I said I'd look out for a dog for him and call him when one came in. He wasn't impressed and stormed off.

I asked Kirsty if she'd had any nice new arrivals in the stray block, preferably male and good with other dogs.

'Walk this way,' she confidently said as she led me to the very last kennel in Unders. I peered in and looking back at me was a small, white, scruffy, middle-aged male. He was kennelled with a youngster that was bouncing mercilessly on his head. Hmm, tolerant with other dogs, I noted to myself.

I unlocked the door and entered the kennel. Holding the young Duracell bunny at arm's length, I bent down to get a better look at Kirsty's suggestion.

'Hello there. And what's your story?' I asked and he tilted his head to the left. He had good manners and immediately got out of bed and padded over to greet me. He sat at my feet looking up, blinking, no doubt wondering what came next. I gave him a stroke and he wagged his tail.

'You'll do,' I said and named him Benny. Benny still had to complete his seven days as a stray and then be assessed before I could contact Mick. I needed to be really sure Benny was good with other dogs. A week later I was in luck – Benny had his assessment and not only was he good with other dogs, he loved them.

That afternoon I called Mick and although he was a little reluctant, he and his wife came back to Battersea to meet Benny. They instantly fell for him but even better than that, it was love at first sight for Penny and Benny. Mick was ecstatic. He thanked me profusely and apologised for his behaviour the previous week.

He told me he also worked with animals and invited me to come and visit his domain. Accepting his invitation before he had even told me where he worked, I suddenly had the terrible thought it might be with sharks. Panic over – Mick worked in the primate section at London Zoo.

The next week, not really knowing what to expect, I set off for the zoo. I hadn't been there since I was a kid.

Mick met me at the gate and we headed straight for the monkeys. Because I was with Mick, I was able to get extremely close to some of them, perhaps a little closer than I would have liked. The chimpanzees that look so cute as babies were terrifying as adults. They were in their indoor enclosures (not accessible to the public) when we arrived and as we approached, they let out blood-curdling screams and beat their chests with formidable fists. Even though they were behind heavy bars, I felt extremely intimidated.

I was glad to get out of there and into the staff area. One of Mick's colleagues was bottle-feeding an eight-week-old chimp. She asked if I'd like to have a go. This was a little more my style and I was struck by how human he seemed. Mick told me that chimpanzees are man's closest relatives, sharing 98 per cent DNA and I could see why as I held the baby and he looked back at me with almost human eyes.

This little imp was adorable, but my favourites were the gorillas. I could have watched them all day. They seemed so regal, as they chomped their vegetables. The silverback was gigantic and had an impressive physique, with huge biceps; not someone you'd want to meet on a dark night. Mick told me he could rip my arms right off if he wanted to. Thankfully he seemed more taken with his banana.

Mick asked me if there was anything else I'd like to see at the zoo. The big cats, please.

As we headed towards this section, he told me how Benny was getting on. He and Penny played together, ate together and slept together; in short they were inseparable. Being middle-aged, Benny was completely housetrained and hadn't had any accidents; neither had he chewed anything in the house when left alone. Mick and his wife were delighted with him.

We entered the staff-only area in the big cat section. One of the Bengal tigers was caged inside because he was due to see the vet. Mick asked if I'd like to see him close up. We went through a couple of security doors, turned a corner and all of a sudden I was standing a few inches away from a magnificent, pacing tiger.

On television tigers seem so much smaller but, close up, this formidable beast was absolutely enormous. I imagined being attacked by him. No human would stand a chance. As he paced, he roared his disapproval at being confined. Even his roar was enough to scare the living daylights out of me.

Being so close to these wild animals and seeing their raw power and strength was a real eye-opener. If faced with a silverback gorilla, a Bengal tiger or a pit bull terrier, I knew which one I'd rather take my chances with and vowed to stop being such a big coward.

A few months before I met Mick, a timely but massive rebuild of Battersea Dogs Home had just been completed. For a year and a half, the staff and dogs alike experienced an immense amount of disruption as the ancient and draughty kennels were ripped out in favour of a multi-storey, state-of-the-art building with all mod cons. The last time the diggers had come to the Home was back in 1991 when a shiny new three-storey kennel block had been unveiled by Her Majesty the Queen, but now, seven years later, Battersea's newest building easily eclipsed its predecessor.

The Kent building was a triumph and became the new rehoming and veterinary section. Both rehomers and veterinary staff were bowled over by their new facilities and the dogs had no complaints either.

★　★　★

Although not quite up to the standards of the Kent building with its under-floor heating, air conditioning and piped classical music, my digs suited me just fine and living away from home definitely agreed with me. However, as much as I loved my independence, when I could no longer look at another baked bean, I'd go back to see my mum and have some real food again.

Having some distance between us alleviated the career issue enormously; so much so I was stunned during one dinner when my mother said she wanted me to find a dog for a friend of hers.

'Why all these people have to have dogs, I'll never know,' she said. 'And this lady is so . . . so normal.' She still didn't understand and I had given up trying to make her.

'Anyway, she's a very dear friend of mine and when her dog died, I told her about you and she wants to come and meet you as soon as possible,' said my mother.

Two days later, Carol, the Battersea receptionist, let me know that Lady Weatherall was waiting to see me. I walked into an empty reception (it was five minutes until opening time) to find a small woman who ever-so-slightly resembled the Queen. Lady Jean Weatherall leapt up, gave me a surprisingly strong bear-hug and told me how much I looked like my mother. I didn't mention my theory that I'm adopted and Barbara Woodhouse is my real mother.

Lady Weatherall was lovely – warm, friendly and

down to earth, and we hit it off straight away. The first thing that struck me during the interview was that she was passionate about dogs. She had always had them and really knew her stuff without being a know-it-all. She knew exactly what type of dog she wanted and was looking for a female, semi-long haired, middle-aged and manageable; perhaps something like a Cavalier King Charles spaniel or a Sheltie.

Her equally charming husband was Marshall of the Diplomatic Corps and they lived in a house that came with the job. That house was St James's Palace, just off the Mall.

The interview went swimmingly and Lady Weatherall and her husband wandered up to the kennels to have a look around. Finding one she thought 'might fit the bill', Lady Weatherall picked up the dog's sale card and came back to find me.

This was going to be one dog's very lucky day but as I stood outside kennel number 43 of the Kent building and stared at the chosen hound, I was a little confused to say the least. I double-checked the sale card Lady Weatherall had handed me and looked again at the dog. Staring back at me was the complete opposite of what she had said she wanted during the interview.

Nelson was the biggest, scruffiest, hairiest, one-eyed male mongrel I'd ever seen! I picked up his notes and went back downstairs to make sure he was the right dog. Lady Weatherall saw my confused expression and we both burst out laughing.

Someone at Battersea had named him Nelson because he only had one eye and due to her husband's significant connections with the Royal Navy, Lady Weatherall told me that his name was the first thing that had attracted her to him.

I read out Nelson's résumé. A member of the public had found him straying in north London and took him to the police station from where Battersea had collected him.

His assessment read: 'Nelson knows no commands but is willing to learn for treats. He is extremely gentle and very friendly. He loves toys but has no idea what to do with them and is scared of cats. Will make a great companion with kind training and lots of patience.' (A Battersea euphemism for 'not too bright'.)

Lady Weatherall said he sounded like he was 'just the job' so I brought him out to meet her. Nelson put a great deal of effort into selling himself, and what a good job he did. He must have been having an off day when he was assessed because far from not knowing what to do with a ball, he picked one up and dropped it straight into Lady Weatherall's lap. He proceeded to give her his paw, roll over for a tummy tickle and then lay his head on her lap, looking up at her soulfully while she groomed him. I'd say he was one of the most intelligent dogs around and knew exactly what he had to do in order to be taken home.

Jean Weatherall had come in for Lady and was walking out with The Tramp but he was hers and she was most definitely his. Nelson moved straight into St James's Palace and never put a foot wrong.

During the follow-up home visit, the Home Visitor was a little surprised, not to mention overwhelmed, to be knocking on the door of St James's Palace. Needless to say, she found the care given to Nelson and the facilities he now enjoyed quite acceptable for a Battersea dog.

And with his new parents being so well connected, Nelson went on to meet the Queen, Princes William and Harry and even Nelson Mandela. Lady Weatherall later told me that when Mandela met Nelson he winked at her and asked if the dog had been named after him. What could she say but 'Yes, of course!'

Nelson proved to be the most wonderfully loyal and loving canine companion Lady Weatherall had ever had. When he died aged 15, she was inconsolable. When they were ready, her husband called and asked me to find them another dog. I found them Fred. They loved Fred dearly but no dog before or since has ever meant as much to her as Nelson.

It was through meeting Lady Weatherall at Battersea that I later found myself at a party for diplomats and ambassadors, held in Prince Charles's private offices at St James's Palace.

I'm not sure how or why I was included on the guest list but I distinctly remember walking into those grand premises and thinking, oh my God, what am I doing here? I felt a little intimidated so I grabbed a drink for Dutch courage and started chatting to a lady who looked like she was on her own too.

The small talk was a little stilted to begin with until she asked me what I did. When I said I worked at Battersea Dogs Home, the transformation in her was incredible. Her whole face lit up, she beamed a huge smile, seemed to grow by about five inches and instantly looked ten years younger.

It transpired she had a deerhound, a whippet and an ex-Battersea mongrel, whom she took great delight in informing me was her favourite. Jack, the Battersea dog, had chewed his way through £800 worth of antique furniture but she didn't care, he was her pride and joy.

She was so enthusiastic that others started drifting away from their own staid conversations to come and join us. I'd say about 80 per cent of the people there had at least one dog. They were asking me a million and one questions about Battersea in rapid succession. I answered all of their questions and went on to tell them (a group of about 20 by now) that apart from seeing a dog go off to a wonderful new home, one of the best parts of my job was seeing a lost dog reunited with its owner.

I began by telling them how the dogs are rather shell-shocked when they first come into Battersea, usually staying at the back of their kennel and peeping out nervously every now and then to see what is happening. Then the owners come in, usually distraught, desperately worried that their beloved dog might still be roaming the streets, dodging cars or worse, but hoping against hope that it is there in the safety of Battersea.

At that point, you could have heard a pin drop.

I went on to describe how the owner scours row after row of kennels, anxiously looking and listening for their dog, frantically calling its name. Then finally, the moment they see each other. The owner shouts the dog's name and as the realisation slowly sinks in, the bedraggled and frightened animal sitting at the back of the kennel bursts to the front, squealing with excitement, up on its hind feet.

Then I stopped speaking because a strange sensation had washed over me. I was having some sort of weird, out of body experience. There I was in Prince Charles's private office holding court, telling ambassadors, diplomats, lords and ladies all about my world at Battersea Dogs Home, and to my amazement they were hanging on my every word.

By this point in my story, the dog was howling with joy, the owner was crying tears of delight and relief, and three of the ambassadors' wives were wiping away their own tears.

They all agreed what a wonderful job it must be and they were right. I felt very proud to work at Battersea Dogs Home and knew just how lucky I was.

I hadn't gone there canvassing for donations but as the cheque books came out, Lady Weatherall gave me a sly wink; the reason for my invitation revealed.

# CHAPTER 10

# BATTERSEA'S
# BROADCASTING BONANZA

In my early days, before Battersea had a PR department, there was no one specifically tasked to deal with the media. The pleasure fell to whoever fancied it. The trouble was, no one did. People came to work at Battersea to care for the animals, not to mess about on the television.

In the end, the person who recoiled least in horror at the very thought of appearing on TV was shoved in front of the camera. In my wide-eyed, youthful innocence and in the name of trying anything once, this turned out to be me. Without realising it, the die had been cast and I'd practically been offered up as the face of Battersea. 'Miss Battersea Dogs Home' – you can imagine my mother's expression.

In some way, be it directly or indirectly, dogs figure somewhere in most people's lives, therefore the television programmes that featured Battersea Dogs Home were as diverse as the people they targeted.

Over the years my repertoire varied from live and recorded interviews on regional and national news, to lifestyle programmes, children's programmes and debate shows.

One minute I'd be joining in with a group sing-along on the *Tweenies* (and dying a thousand deaths) and the next I'd be on *Kilroy* having a verbal Sumo wrestle with some politician that wanted to implement anti-dog laws left, right and centre.

From my many on-screen escapades, I discovered that TV was one big 24-inch illusion. Take *Kilroy*, for example. You saw a shiny set with its slick host who professionally kept control of what was supposed to be a fired-up, passionate rabble, all of whom had something controversial to say. In reality these people constituted about 60 per cent of the audience. The remainder was made up of *Kilroy*'s canteen staff and cleaners.

Once the genuine audience had been seated along with those of us brought in to comment on a particular topic, there were about 30 vacant seats left. Not to worry. Enter stage left the army of Mrs Mops and Greasy Spoons who were called upon to make up the numbers.

As I was being seated and fitted with a microphone, I watched a researcher haul one poor tea lady out of the audience, saying she'd seen her in yesterday's show and she couldn't appear twice or the viewers would think there was something fishy going on. There *was* something fishy going on.

The very next week I found myself sitting in the green room at *GMTV*, tucking into the complimentary croissants. As the newsreader informed us that Nelson Mandela had become president of South Africa, I was hurriedly ushered, mouth full, on to the sofa where Eamonn and Fiona were waiting for me.

I was there to answer the usual general questions about Battersea Dogs Home and also to try and find a home for a particular dog. I'm not sure whether the dog I'd brought along was a little star-struck or if it was the prospect of appearing on national TV, but with less than a minute before the cameras swung back to the sofa, he became so excited that his manhood – or should I say doghood – threatened to steal the show. Not wanting to reduce his chances of finding a home, especially if the elderly were watching, I attempted to get him to lie down. He wasn't playing ball so the entire interview was conducted with me blushing, him frothing at the mouth and Eamonn and Fiona in fits of giggles.

My very first taste of television came in the shape of a kids' Saturday morning show called *Motormouth*. The producers had phoned Battersea wanting to run a piece on responsible dog ownership.

I'd only been at Battersea for a few months when Dot asked Jacky and me to take four dogs to Maidstone, where the show was filmed, and be interviewed live for ten minutes. Due to the extremely early start, the network would pay for us to stay overnight in a five-star hotel.

All we heard was 'five-star hotel' and we were in. But which dogs to take? Two pairs would make the most sense and reduce the risk of any scrapping on live TV. Occasionally Battersea received pairs of dogs that had been brought up together or acquired at similar times. I instantly knew which pair was coming to Maidstone with me.

Fraggle and Rock were brothers: two inseparable middle-aged Labrador crosses that had come into Battersea because their owner had been sent to prison. Whilst their old master languished at Her Majesty's pleasure, Fraggle and Rock were about to spend a night in decidedly different digs.

Jacky chose to take Pebbles and Lucy, two collie-cross sisters. Pebbles was a white and brown spotty mongrel and Lucy, her older sister, was fat, black and the laziest dog ever to have collie blood running through its veins. Their owner had died and her son, who worked full-time, couldn't keep them so he brought them into Battersea. Pebbles and Lucy were used to the good life and in their previous home I'm sure they had tea and cucumber sandwiches every day at four o'clock, served in fine bone china, complete with doilies.

Battersea took some getting used to for each pair and after spending six months in kennels, their housetraining had severely lapsed. When we came into work at 8 a.m. every day, it looked as though they'd redecorated in the night, pebbledash being their favoured design style. Our main concern, therefore, was not appearing on live telly, but what the dogs would do to the hotel room. But the TV studio put a lot of business the hotel's way and they were more than happy to have four Battersea dogs stay with them. They probably hadn't considered the worst-case scenario and just thought how delightful it would be to have dogs in residence.

The night before our broadcast, Jacky and I turned up at the Maidstone Grand, checked in and took turns using every facility the hotel had to offer. Not wanting to risk leaving the dogs alone, we ordered room service for dinner and then took them for a last wee before settling down for the night.

This being my first foray into TV, I was a bit nervous and couldn't sleep. After what seemed like an eternity, I finally dropped off only to be woken half an hour later by foghorn snoring. It wasn't just one snore either: Fraggle, Lucy and Jacky were all at it. Great. I'd be making my screen debut in front of friends, family and the child population of the United Kingdom with dirty great bags under my eyes. Things went from bad to worse. After a while all five were snoring and two were farting. I managed a total of two hour's sleep that night.

The alarm went off at 6 a.m. but I didn't dare open my eyes. I was terrified I'd find room No. 19 at the Maidstone Grand completely redecorated in a delightful shade of brown. I used my other senses to give me a clue. My nose detected no suspicious aromas, my ears fell upon silence – except snoring, so I opened one eye. Jacky was doing her hair, looking extremely nervous and all four dogs were still sound asleep. To think, we were terrified of them crapping all over The Grand when in reality we had to drag them outside into the cold morning air in order for them to do their ablutions.

The cab came to pick us up and we arrived at the studio at 7 a.m. I was amazed at how big the entire set was compared to the tiny bit that appears on television. The lights, cameras and all the other equipment were overwhelming and suddenly I was petrified. If I thought I was nervous, I just had to look over at Jacky who had, in the words of Procol Harum, turned a whiter shade of pale.

An hour later, with two minutes to air, the crew were rushing around frantically, but as soon as the five-second countdown commenced, a calm calculated control descended upon the set.

Jacky and I were not on for an hour, which in my book was a bad thing. We'd already been there for 60 minutes and had another 60 ahead of us in which to work ourselves into a frenzy. Half an hour later, a young pigtailed lady of about 20, wearing pink jeans, yellow leg-warmers and a green top with 'wicked' on it, came and introduced herself to us. Milly Molly gave us both clip-on microphones and, speaking to us as though we were five-year-olds, told us the questions the presenter would ask and in what order. She then trod on Rock's tail prompting a banshee-like scream. Everyone looked over. I'm not sure how the presenter explained that one away.

It was now about five minutes until our turn. A cartoon was being shown so the make-up artists were touching up the presenters (I'm assured this is legal within the industry) whilst they went over their lines. Milly Molly showed us to the sofa where we took our seats in front of the cameras and settled the dogs down.

'Two minutes!' Milly Molly shouted.

The make-up lady dabbed us and the presenter flashed his best TV smile and patted the dogs. My mouth went dry and I could hear my heart pounding.

'And on in five, four, three, two . . .'

'Welcome back. Today we're lucky enough to have six beautiful Battersea dogs on the sofa . . .'

Maybe you don't have to be able to count to be a children's TV presenter. I didn't know about Jacky but that was the first time I'd ever been called a beautiful Battersea dog.

After that smooth introduction, the presenter asked his first question. The cameras swung around to Jacky whose mouth opened and closed like a prize koi carp and whose eyes resembled frisbees. There was a pregnant pause.

I took the initiative and answered, which must have looked extremely odd to the viewers as the reply came from off camera. The producer up in the gallery must have been having a fit. By the time he'd screamed instructions and the camera was on me, I'd already given my reply. The presenter switched back to Jacky for the next question. She hadn't rehearsed this one as it was supposed to be my question and looked like she was going to throw up so I took that question too.

The producer, deciding to play it safe, left the camera on the dogs for the remainder of the interview. They behaved impeccably and stole the show. By the end of the interview I'd answered all but one of the questions and earned the moniker 'Motormouth' from the Battersea rabble who were all watching back at base.

The interview was over and we couldn't get out of there fast enough but everyone wanted to meet the dogs. Not wanting to rob them of their well-deserved attention, we hung around for as long as we had to before heading back to the hotel and straight for the mini bar.

Back at Battersea, Pebbles and Lucy, Fraggle and Rock were greeted as heroes; never mind Jacky and I who had aged about 20 years each. The best news was that the switchboard had been jammed with people wanting to rehome the dogs. They stayed in their pairs and after six long months at Battersea and five short minutes on television they went home, our abject terror a small price to pay for 15 minutes of fame and four dogs rehomed.

Over the years, my various TV appearances had given me an insight into the power of television but I never experienced its full force until one fine spring day in 1999 when Battersea Dogs Home decided to open its doors to the BBC.

Although the media had an ongoing love affair with Battersea and the odd reporter could usually be found hanging around the Home, nothing of this size or depth had ever been undertaken before. No one was sure how it would turn out but the decision was made to proceed and when Colonel Green announced the news to the staff, a Mexican wave of excitement rippled around the boardroom.

'This is it! This is when I get discovered,' Steve announced, and then mumbled something about getting his drag gear out of the cleaners. We looked at him a little dubiously but long before the Reality TV gold rush of gardening, cooking, interior design and tantrum-throwing toddlers, I knew the everyday happenings at the world's most famous dogs' home would make for compelling viewing. How could it not when we had dogs, drama and a drag queen to offer?

The BBC arrived at Battersea Dogs Home bringing with them expensive-looking equipment. They seemed like an extraordinarily happy bunch, but I later discovered that it was landing a job at Battersea Dogs Home that had brought about this continual state of euphoria. Every member of the BBC crew was a dog lover and many had grown up with family hounds. They learned very quickly, however, that their dream job of playing with puppies all day long was in fact a pipe dream and the reality could be a whole lot more dangerous. Most learned the hard way that not all dogs were as friendly as the docile family mutt they grew up with and that a cautious approach was the best way to keep all digits intact.

The Battersea gang and the BBC crew hit it off straight away. Bob, the show's producer, was an amiable, patient chap although his patience was sorely tested by Steve suggesting on more than one occasion that they change their plans from making a documentary, to making *Battersea: The Musical*. Next in line was Sarah, the assistant producer, a feisty TV type who knew what she wanted and usually got it. Then, amongst others there was Harriet, a tall, serious-looking camerawoman, Daniel, the sweet but dopey audio lad, and Sharon, a keen young researcher.

Shauna Lowry was chosen to present the series. I'd seen her on TV before as one of the roving reporters on *Rolf Harris's Animal Hospital*. She obviously loved animals, which was a good start. It turned out to be better than that. She was fun, down to earth, and real – not one of those stick insects you normally see on television.

The Beeb and their equipment became part and parcel of daily life at Battersea. Some of the Home's staff were more comfortable in front of the camera than others and, to begin with, everyone was self-conscious about how their 15 minutes of fame would turn out. After a few weeks, though, the Battersea staff completely relaxed and went about their daily business without even noticing the cameras trailing them. It was slightly different for the BBC crew who had much more to get to grips with than we had.

The vans were just starting to come back from their morning rounds. Pauline made it back to base first and the BBC crew was ready to capture the offloading of her van. I was also in attendance and opened the back of the animal ambulance to find three mongrels, two terrier types, a Tibetan spaniel and a Japanese Akita staring back at me. Akitas are powerfully built beasts, traditionally used for hunting and fighting. Physically they are extremely strong and usually have formidable temperaments to match. This one was no exception. He had given the police a tough time whilst in their care and, on his arrival at Battersea, looked set to dish out more of the same.

Once all the other dogs were safely offloaded, it was time to tackle our oriental friend. I'd never seen Pauline appear nervous around any dog until now. She asked Martin, her burly van-driving husband, to accompany us up to the kennels in case the Akita decided he didn't like his new accommodation.

We coaxed the dog up the stairs of the stray block with an apprehensive BBC crew filming as we went. Just as we rounded the corner and prepared to enter the kennel block where an empty kennel had been made ready, our group almost collided with Rebecca who was walking Buster. Buster decided to have a crack at the Japanese Akita (ten times his size) who in response went berserk, rearing up on his back legs, snarling and lunging at Buster. At full height he was taller than Pauline and she was having trouble holding him. The Akita would have killed Buster if he'd reached him but in an automatic reaction (had I had time to think, I might not have been so fearless), I grabbed him and pulled him back. The dog then rounded on me but Martin intervened and the Akita lunged at him, missing his crown jewels by centimetres.

Pauline threw the dog into the empty kennel, slamming the door behind him. We all stood there catching our breath, nerves jangling, a pale-looking BBC crew trembling beside us.

Pauline looked at me.

'Impressive,' she said, nodding. 'I remember the days when you would have run a mile.'

A compliment like that, from my dog-handling hero, made me feel as though I'd finally made it; as though I was running with the big dogs.

After months of filming, the first programme was about to go to air. There was great excitement and anticipation amongst Battersea's staff. It was a daytime show so was scheduled to go out at 12.30 p.m. on BBC1; excellent timing as most of the staff were on their lunch break. Crowds flocked around the Home's two TVs, one rickety television in the staff quarters and the other in rehoming reception, where the looped public information video was tossed out in favour of the Beeb's far more exciting offering.

Twelve-thirty p.m. arrived; the BBC announcer did his bit and the opening credits rolled. These alone were enough to thrill us. It was a montage of dogs barking to the song 'Perfect Day' by Lou Reed. Extremely clever and highly amusing, especially as we all knew every single dog that was singing.

We were glued for half an hour, watching our friends, our colleagues and our dogs. The show was informative, moving, realistic and funny, and we loved it.

As it ended, the BBC crew looked tentatively around at us for some kind of approval. They need not have worried: a spontaneous round of applause broke out, their sternest critics satisfied.

Battersea Dogs Home was a dream for the BBC. Everyday extraordinary events, which to the staff were just another day at the office, delighted and thrilled them and their TV audience. I understood their glee; years before the BBC ever came to Battersea, I often felt I was living in a television show.

The series went on to be a huge success, drawing the largest number of viewers ever for a daytime show. We were delighted the programme was reaching such a huge audience and that so many unfair and incorrect myths about the place we all loved so much were being dispelled.

What none of us could ever have predicted, however, was just how much of a victim of its own success Battersea Dogs Home was about to become. As soon as the public saw Battersea as an organisation that genuinely cared about its charges, they had no qualms about bringing their unwanted pets in by the truckload. Once they realised Battersea was not the dungeon they thought it was, but rather a place of hope and happiness, their guilt was assuaged.

I imagine before the programme aired, people that were having problems with their pets persevered rather than bringing them into Battersea Dogs Home where they 'were sure to be put to sleep'. Now, however, they felt that they could bring their dogs and cats in with impunity, safe in the knowledge they'd be looked after extremely well and given every chance of finding a better life.

For the first time in Battersea's 140-year history, the gifts outnumbered the strays and they were arriving in droves. Of course, we would rather people brought their dog directly into Battersea than throw it out on the street – at least that way the dog was safe and the owner could provide Battersea with valuable information about its history and personality. However, the sheer numbers being brought in were verging on the ridiculous.

At the other end of the Battersea see-saw, rehoming went through the roof as hundreds of people descended upon the Home every day. This was excellent news and many more dogs than usual were rehomed, which at least helped to balance out the numbers of dogs coming in. But no one could have predicted just how many people would converge on Battersea and as numbers skyrocketed uncontrollably, staffing levels that had previously been sufficient were suddenly woefully inadequate.

Each rehomer was doing the work of four, whilst being on the receiving end of a bad-tempered public, frustrated at having to wait at least five hours to be seen. Usually, there was a slow, steady stream of public and the rehomers would finish up at 4 p.m. Now we were dealing with an unrelenting horde from 10.30 a.m. until 7 p.m. every day. The rehomers were overworked and exhausted.

Timing has never been my strong point and during the furore of dealing with what felt like the whole world and his wife descending on Battersea Dogs Home, I was in the midst of attempting to buy my first home.

I had outgrown the little studio flat in Prince of Wales Drive and decided it was time to expand into a one-bedroom place. Yes, it was time to grow up and get a mortgage. If I'd known what was in store, I probably wouldn't have bothered.

This was a depressing time to say the least as I was shown the miserable accommodation within my price range. Smiling estate agents showed me cramped and dingy offerings described on their paperwork as bijou and cosy apartments. After the twentieth hovel, I had almost given up. We were on the twenty-first and as Mr Smiley agent walked me up the communal stairs of a house to show me the first-floor flat, I came within an inch of turning around and telling him not to bother. The communal area was awful: dusty, dirty, dark and with post strewn everywhere.

Now on auto-pilot, I followed him up and was rewarded as he unlocked the door and sunlight flooded into the communal hallway. I walked into a bright, airy, split-level flat with a big bay window. Now I was smiling. I loved the flat the moment I saw it and the communal area's imperfections were cosmetic and could soon be fixed up. I'd found my first home and breathed a huge sigh of relief, not realising the trauma was only just beginning.

I'd heard that death, divorce and moving were supposed to be the most stressful times in one's life. Try death, divorce and moving whilst Battersea Dogs Home is on national TV.

Between the never-ending throng of customers, I'd try to snatch five minutes here and ten minutes there to call the bank, solicitors, surveyors and estate agents who were becoming more frustrated by the minute at not being able to get hold of me.

It didn't help that we were still dealing with customers way past the time that my solicitor and the other players in my house move had all gone home. They couldn't possibly understand the beast I was battling so I didn't even bother trying to explain.

I was utterly drained and by the time I was handed the keys to my own home, I just wanted to crawl inside and collapse. Before one collapses, though, one must of course make the place habitable. I took one day off (grudgingly approved by Nichola) to move in and then had to wait another four days until the weekend before I could even think about where to place my furniture or what colour to paint the walls.

After the week from hell, came the weekend from hell. I didn't know which was worse: home or Battersea. I felt like frogmarching the entire BBC crew to my flat to do the painting and decorating; this was after all their fault. I worked so hard on my new flat that it was almost a rest to go back to work and greet the next onslaught of people wanting to rehome a dog. I say almost, because by this stage things at Battersea had become serious.

When Battersea was running under normal circumstances, there were enough rehomers and kennel staff to operate the rehoming department, man the kennels and assess the dogs. These, we very quickly found out, were far from normal circumstances and every rehomer available was dealing with prospective new owners, whilst every kennel hand that was not directly looking after the dogs in kennels was assigned to deal with the public bringing animals into the Home. This left no one to assess the dogs, which meant a serious bottleneck in the Battersea system.

Dogs were being rehomed at a rate of knots and the rehoming kennels were emptying out. This was the good news. The bad news was that because there was no one available to assess the dogs, there were no more coming up through the ranks and the kennels used to place new residents were over-flowing. In glorious Technicolor, television had unleashed all of its terrifying power on SW8. Something had to give.

Colonel Green called an emergency crisis meeting and it was agreed that unprecedented steps had to be taken. For the next two days the Home would close to all public except those bringing animals in. Staff would be assigned to this area and a skeleton staff would man the kennels, whilst everyone else that was trained to assess would deal with the backlog of dogs. This arrangement would also give everyone the chance to catch their breath.

The decision was also made to close the Home for rehoming and viewing every Thursday until further notice, in order to stay on top of assessing the new arrivals.

Action was taken just in time. With five million

daytime viewers, the BBC series was so successful it was about to be moved to an evening prime-time slot. The second onslaught was just around the corner.

Success went straight to the heads of the BBC powers that be and in their infinite wisdom they decided that the programme needed a more high-profile presenter. It mattered not one jot that Shauna Lowry had helped to make the programme such a success, or the fact that she was an articulate and experienced presenter who over two series had demonstrated a genuine love of animals. Why have all that when you can have someone fresh out of *EastEnders* like Patsy Palmer, aka Bianca, who is best known for screeching 'Rickaaaay' at the top of her Cockney voice around Albert Square. She was brought in to present the third and final series of *Battersea Dogs Home*.

I thought she was awful and she insisted on bringing in her young son who spent the day wreaking havoc on his scooter. As well as some viewers complaining about her voice and her accent, she didn't seem to be a natural presenter and often had to do numerous takes.

When I left school an academic failure, I remember telling my teachers in dramatic fashion that one day I'd be back and probably with a film crew trailing behind me. Well, bugger me if that's not exactly what happened. It might not have been quite what I had in mind – *This Is Your Life* was nearer the mark – but I guess you've got to take what you can get.

I had a sneaking suspicion my headmistress thought I would never amount to anything. She only had eyes for the academics, but so what if I wasn't one of them? We can't all be Albert Einsteins, and with hair like that who'd want to be?

Once I'd got my first Battersea talk under my belt at the Shepperton Townswomen's Guild, I became quite a dab hand. School talks on responsible dog ownership were part of Battersea's plan to educate the dog owners of tomorrow and every year I returned to my old school to do just that. I never kidded myself that the first years at Streatham Hill and Clapham High School were interested in me; it was the bundle of fluff I'd bring along that had them queuing in the aisles to attend my lecture. I'm sure the free pencils, rubbers and stickers helped but I was under no illusion who was the star of the show.

My educational half hour took place in the gym, usually attended by about 40 girls, with one harassed teacher to control them. One year this harassment fell to Mrs Smith, my old English teacher, who announced to the kids that she used to teach me before they were born. I laughed out loud thinking no wonder she teaches English, maths obviously isn't her strong point, until I did a quick calculation and was horrified to find she was right.

Mrs Hooper, who was the first point of contact when arranging the annual Battersea talk, was also my old biology and careers teacher. She was my favourite: fun, happy and mad about Bruce Springsteen. She was a great teacher too – either that or it was a fluke that I came second with 82 per cent in a biology exam one year. I'm not sure who was more amazed, she or I.

I remained in contact with Mrs Hooper and her husband after my schooldays came to an end and a few years after I began working at Battersea, they came to offer their home to a Battersea dog.

Although Ann Hooper worked full-time at school, Alan's job allowed him to be at home for a large part of the day. They were true dog lovers and had grown up with dogs, as well as owning their own. Ann had a mongrel called Rio who had expired some years ago aged 14 and Alan had always had German shepherds with his family.

Having known them for years, their dog-owning credentials were academic. The home visit was definitely surplus to requirement in this case too, as I'd been to their house several times before. I knew they had a fully fenced garden and room for a small- to medium-sized mutt. They were specifically after a puppy and, having none available on that day, I promised to keep an eye out.

A couple of days later I walked into the nursery, where the puppies were housed, and as soon as I saw him I knew he was the one. Eight weeks old, white with black splodges, long ears and short legs, he was found in Surrey and was the cutest thing ever to have come out of East Molesey. I think he was some kind of spaniel crossed with dachshund, which might explain the long body, big ears and little legs. No one came to claim Shorty and by the time his seven days were up, he had picked up a bad case of kennel cough.

Nevertheless, I called Ann and Alan up to come and have a look at him and within ten minutes they were sitting in reception. From Tooting to Battersea, that must be some kind of land-speed record.

I took them to the sick bay and opened up Shorty's kennel. He was feeling a mite sorry for himself. His eyes were droopy like a bloodhound's, his chest rattled like a 40-a-day smoker and he had BGBs (veterinary term for big green bogies) running from his nose. I picked him up and plonked him in Alan's arms.

From that moment on – with his snotty nose and wheezy cough – Floyd, as he was christened, had secured his place in their lives.

As soon as Floyd was over his kennel cough, he went home. He marked his first day by pooing in Alan's shoe. What aim for one so young. I looked after Floyd when Ann and Alan went on holiday and we spent many a happy day in Richmond Park together. I especially loved autumn, when he'd gambol through piles of leaves becoming totally submerged, which didn't take much with those legs. Every now and then he'd spring up like a gazelle, only to disappear again a second later.

I also took him to work with me which he loved. I suppose, for him, it was a bit like going home. His dog days at Battersea obviously hadn't done him any harm whatsoever. Occasionally Ann took Floyd to school as a special treat for the kids. They loved him and turned him into the best-socialised dog in town.

Now here I was many years later, returning to my old school to give my annual talk. This year was different though. This year the BBC was filming at Battersea and I was returning with that film crew I promised I'd be back with all those years ago. My school was going to be on prime-time national TV and it was all down to me. I was greeted at the gates like a celebrity, like I was somebody. So, my learned old teachers, which would you rather I had now: a dozen O levels or a BBC film crew?

To some, being on the Box is a big deal but you'd have thought royalty was coming to the school. The kids had been scrubbed to within an inch of their lives, green uniforms pressed, egg stains removed and shoes shined. I'd never seen the teachers looking so dapper either. And the talk wasn't in the gym with 40 unruly kids and one harassed teacher. No, this time it was in the main hall with the whole school, and the headmistress to introduce me.

The BBC signalled that they were ready to start

and after my modest introduction from the head-mistress, I stood up. On my way out of Battersea, I had ducked into the nursery to pick up a puppy to bring along with me. The only one available happened to be a rather cute ten-week-old cocker spaniel. She and I walked on to a rapturous and elongated 'Aahhh'.

I usually took some slides with me on school talks which contained a mixture of cute animals and historical photos, as well as Battersea branded stuff to give away. Seeing as I was addressing 600 people (which I was unprepared for), I decided to dispense with all of that and wing it.

I think I pulled it off because throughout the talk, the kids sat very still and it was only the puppy that fidgeted. The Q&A session afterwards was going extremely well too, with lots of inter-ested little hands shooting up. That was until one kid called out, 'My family came to Battersea to get a dog and you interviewed us and wouldn't let us have one.'

There was some sniggering amongst the older girls, the teachers shifted uneasily in their seats but, worst of all, the cameras were still rolling. How was I going to get out of this one? I took a gamble and guessed that her parents worked full-time. Thankfully I guessed right. My blushes were saved as I went on to explain how just like us, dogs were social creatures that needed company for at least some of the day. How would we feel if we were left on our own for nine hours a day, five days a week with nothing to do but stare at the walls? I gave the camera a cheesy grin. Danger averted.

Other questions came thick and fast and in the end the headmistress had to bring the proceedings to a close. I hoped the abundance of questions was due to genuine interest and not one of my old tactics – keeping the speaker talking to delay going back to lessons.

That day, the BBC got what they wanted but more importantly so did I. Recognition from an establishment which always placed academia at the top of its list, that there's more to life than just passing exams. Life is about having fun and doing some good along the way, which is why my love affair with Battersea lasted for 15 years. And it never hurts to have the BBC in tow either.

My new flat was taking shape. I'd cleaned it, painted it and almost furnished it. Everything was in place except my new sofa.

'We recommend you measure any doorways or passageways the sofa might have to travel through,' said the Ikea sales assistant.

'Nah, it'll be fine,' I said, throwing a cursory scan over the sofa whilst trying to remember roughly how big my doorway looked.

I'd opted for a three-seater – a must for falling asleep in front of the telly, and a week later the delivery men turned up at my front door. I raced down to greet them as best I could; my back was a little worse for wear from weeks of trying to stretch out on a beanbag. I signed the paperwork and they heaved the monster out of the van.

I cried when they couldn't get it through the door. Ridiculous I know, but after many exhausting televised weeks at Battersea, this was more than I could take.

'Don't worry, love,' one of the men said, 'it's not the end of the world.' He was right. I pulled myself together and said goodbye to my sofa as they took it back to the depot.

The most important thing was I had my own place and of all the things that meant to me, none was as precious as knowing that for the first time in my life, I could have my own dog.

The media played a huge part in helping us to rescue and rehome thousands of dogs. Their assistance might have come from rival channels, but that could only be good for business and as the ratings war took hold, Channel 4's *Pet Rescue* edged in front.

*Pet Rescue* was one programme that was as successful for its TV station as it was for the animal-welfare organisations it featured. Every weekday, it pulled in a huge number of viewers, both curious animal lovers and those who could genuinely offer their home to one of the many animals featured on the show.

*Pet Rescue* visited shelters across the country, showing the cruelty this nation of supposed animal lovers is capable of inflicting. It also highlighted the plight of individual dogs, which for us rescuers was the business end of the proceedings.

The segments that made up the rest of the daily half-hour programme were all too familiar to us. Great TV it may have been but why go home and watch it when we lived it every day? Love it or hate it, *Pet Rescue* was a lifeline to many animals and animal rescues across the length and breadth of the country.

Now a senior rehomer, the researchers called me once a month to organise days to come and film at Battersea. They featured many other rescues, from John O'Groats to Land's End and although they tried to be fair with the allocation of slots, I think Battersea did slightly better than the others. I put this entirely down to geography; being a London-based organisation, we were a mere stone's throw from their headquarters compared to many of the other rescue centres.

Sometimes they requested a type of dog to feature or, to be more accurate, not to feature. This was because they wanted to show their viewers a range. If, for example, four black mongrels with separation anxiety were being featured that week, they felt viewers would lose interest.

At first this made me bristle. Battersea was not here to make great TV, rather to find homes for the dogs that needed them most. But as with most things in life, it was all about compromise. If the viewers lost interest, the ratings would fall and the plug would be pulled on the show. We scratch their back and they scratch ours. And besides, Battersea had all of the colours in all of the sizes with every behavioural problem under the sun, so there was never any trouble finding one to fit the bill.

The bigger problem was finding a member of staff willing to appear with the dog. Someone had to start the ball rolling so I volunteered my services when the very first Battersea dog went on *Pet Rescue*. Urcher the lurcher wasn't kennelling well and needed to find a home as quickly as possible. The trouble was the camera crew took so long to film the five-minute slot that although Urcher was a youngster when we started filming, by the time the crew had finished both he and I were ready to draw our pensions.

There was so much hanging about on those filming days: testing of lights, changing of tapes, reviewing what had been shot and, of course, many bloopers. That old adage, never work with children or animals, is good advice. Time had to be added on to every shoot to account for little episodes such as the dog eating the furry microphone, slobbering on the camera lens and crapping at the most inappropriate times. Not only did these interruptions slow things down, we had the added complication of trains to and from Victoria station going overhead every couple of minutes. Battersea is also on the flight path to Heathrow so, by the end of filming, the poor sound man was apoplectic.

Once a staff member had been begged and bribed into appearing on telly, they would spend as much time with the selected dog in the run-up to filming as possible. This was especially important so that the pair could form a bond because subconsciously the dog's interaction with the handler is what attracts the viewer more than anything. They can imagine themselves being the one it runs to, the one it fetches a stick for and the one whose lap it lays its head in.

A combination of the dog's bond with the handler and its winning looks, coupled with the millions of viewers that tuned in to *Pet Rescue*, guaranteed a healthy interest in any featured dog. Each dog regularly pulled in between 300 and 500 interested callers. Not bad, considering we only needed one to be the right home. The rest were a bonus, many of whom we rehomed other dogs to.

One dog blew those figures out of the water, reeling in over a thousand calls, the most for any animal featured on *Pet Rescue*. He had come into Battersea 12 months earlier, a shell-shocked year-old guard dog. It must have been his breed and size that attracted his owner to the guarding potential because it couldn't have been his temperament.

A 30-kilogram black-and-tan Rottweiler cross, he certainly looked the part, but he was scared of his own shadow. If it came down to the fight or flight response, he would have chosen flight every time. And if the choice were fight, flight or fart, he definitely would have gone for the last of the three.

Due to his lack of job skills, this dog was never going to be claimed and for most of his first week at Battersea he stayed in the back of his kennel in Unders, shaking constantly like the cowardly lion from *The Wizard of Oz* – a dog after my own heart. Unders was now run by Kirsty and Jade who took him for walks, fed him treats, sat and talked to him, groomed him and used all of their expertise to settle him down. None of it worked. He was too tense to even think about enjoying any of the attention.

Ali and I assessed him but decided to keep it brief as we didn't want to stress him out. Even though he was huge, I didn't feel intimidated by him: I just felt desperately sad to see this majestic beast struggling with everyday life. Ali identified that he was in no way aggressive, not from her many years' experience, more from the fact I wasn't hiding in the filing cabinet.

This poor dog was completely under-socialised, which is where our assumption of a guarding background came from. It was as if he'd been kept in a yard all his life, never coming in contact with anything from the outside world. Everything freaked him out: people, bikes, cars, trains, other dogs. He acted like he was seeing everything for the first time. We named him Desmond and marked him up to go to the Rehabilitation department.

Ann worked with Desmond for weeks which eventually turned into months, socialising him little by little, never wanting to push him too fast. Walks in the park allowed him to become familiar with people and other dogs, trips up the road got him used to traffic, and time spent at Battersea Park station eating sausages helped him overcome his fear of trains.

Desmond was beginning to relax, and slowly but surely Ann and her team were acclimatising him to modern, everyday life.

He spent the main part of his day in Nichola's office. About six months earlier; Nichola had taken on a ten-week-old puppy from Battersea whom she named Frankie. Frankie had scarring all the way around her muzzle where her previous owner had placed a tight elastic band, in an attempt to stop her chewing the furniture when they were out.

Nichola continued Rehab's good work but it was probably Frankie that played the biggest part in Desmond's rehabilitation. Through her natural puppy ways, she taught him how to relax, how to play and how to be a dog. Most importantly she taught him that life could be good and if you were lucky enough to have people around you that cared – you'd made it.

Desmond had made it. He was utterly at home on the first floor of the office block. Everyone loved having him around. They didn't even mind the farting. Maybe they'd become immune to it.

I'd sometimes go up to see Nichola and be greeted by this overpowering smell of rotten eggs, whilst the office staff happily typed away, completely oblivious.

'Seriously? None of you can smell it?' I'd asked in disbelief to which they all shook their heads in genuine surprise.

Desmond had fallen in love with Nichola and the only downside to his newfound love of life was when she said good-night to him. At 6 p.m. every night, Desmond's tail would drop as low as the hangdog expression on his face. We thought that by not returning him to his kennel at night but instead allowing him to hang out with Charlie, the night security man and his big dopey dog Toby, Desmond would be happy. But Desmond only had eyes for Nichola.

At 9 a.m. when she came in to work, he'd spring up vertically in the air like a kangaroo, tail thumping everything around him, licking her to death and play fighting with Frankie. But when she left at night and that face dropped again, we knew what we had to do.

How could we have lost sight of our goal? Of his goal? Perhaps it was because his rehabilitation had taken so long, perhaps it was because we had got so used to having him around. Whatever it was, we realised that now we had turned him into this happy, sociable, well-balanced dog, we'd be failing him if we kept him at Battersea. We had to complete the job.

Nichola couldn't keep him as her flat wasn't big enough, besides which she never planned on having two dogs. We knew Desmond needed a special home, one that understood him, his past, his personality, his needs and the fact that letting him go would break our hearts. Through *Pet Rescue* the search began.

Needless to say it was Nichola who appeared on TV with him. She was a natural and to see how much he adored her was poetry in motion. It was a stunning piece, but we could never have imagined that more than a thousand people would agree.

Their calls went to a special number Channel 4 had set up. They in turn emailed them to our PR department who passed them on to me. We had to deploy at least ten members of staff to return the calls but taking ten rehomers away from dealing with Battersea's public would have had a catastrophic effect on the running of the Home. Steph, now a rehomer, and I volunteered our services and anyone that was not directly customer-facing staff was dragged from their office to help. Director-general, manager, heads of departments and admin staff all donned their best telephone manners and got to work.

I gave everyone a template to work from, which included the basics such as if the caller had kids, other pets, a garden, what their previous dog-owning experience was and how long they were out for on an average day.

By the time we had eliminated those that were unsuitable for Desmond, we had cut the list by two-thirds. Of the remaining third, about 10 per cent were serious contenders for Desmond. The other 90 per cent, although not quite right for him, were identified as good homes for other individual dogs and were invited to come to Battersea.

That was the great thing about *Pet Rescue*. Not only did the programme find a fantastic home for the featured dog, but it also unearthed dozens more that were perfect for other dogs in need of a special home. Although disappointed Desmond wasn't going to live with them, they'd be flattered that we wanted them to take one of our other dogs. We would shamelessly stroke their egos if it meant them stroking one of our dogs in front of their roaring fire at home.

One might think that from the original thousand-plus homes that called up wanting Desmond, it would be impossible to decide exactly which would be the best one for him. Actually it wasn't. The shortlist of about 30 was whittled down to three, the rest having been persuaded to take other dogs.

I called the three numbers and immediately identified that they were, indeed, great homes. But there was only one Desmond and a decision had to be made. Maybe it was a sixth sense or just experience I'd gained over the years from having to make swift character assessments during interviews. Whatever it was, it helped me make my decision.

I chose a couple from Canterbury who fitted the specifications perfectly. No kids, plenty of space – 40 acres to be precise – and they worked from home. The icing on the cake was that they had a middle-aged female mastiff; a dog large enough to deal with Desmond's size and matriarchal enough to be a guiding influence for him. Desmond was devoted to Frankie and living with another dog would help fill the gap she would undoubtedly leave.

We invited Robert and Francis to Battersea to meet our boy and bring their dog, Delores Delargo the Toast of Chicago (DD for short), in to meet Desmond. Often the decision boils down not to whether the people like the dog, but whether the two dogs like each other. As with human beings, dogs sometimes take an instant dislike to one another, resulting in the rehomer having to wade in and split them up. Thankfully this rarely happens with opposite sexes and definitely didn't happen in this case; quite the opposite in fact.

Formally interviewing Desmond's prospective new owners at Battersea was academic as we'd spoken to them at length over the phone. It was more to get a three-dimensional perspective of them and see how they interacted with their dog. You may think this strange, but I've had folk in my interview room hitting their own dog, whilst hoping to get one from Battersea. No such concerns with Robert and Francis who obviously adored DD and I could see why.

DD was tremendous: a real beauty, big for a female, with an impressive bark and plenty of slobber. Saliva wasn't something they would have to worry about with Desmond: his problem came more from the other end.

Robert and Francis had rescued DD from a breakers' yard where for the first three years of her life, she was kept as a guard dog in squalid conditions. They'd walked past the yard every day and witnessed the men shouting at her, probably in an attempt to make her aggressive. It hadn't worked and instead she just withdrew into herself. Her kennel barely had a roof and her food bowl was usually empty. Robert and Francis had called the RSPCA but because she had food (albeit irregularly), water and shelter, there was nothing they could do.

Robert and Francis befriended DD through the wire fence and fed her treats when no one was around. This proved she didn't have the guarding instinct. One day they could stand it no longer and went into the yard, offering her owner £300 for DD. He agreed on £500 and they took her home.

As with Desmond, DD's rehabilitation was slow but with time and patience they had turned DD into what I saw before me that day: a happy, well-balanced giant of a dog who was as gentle as a lamb – sound familiar?

We introduced these two bears outside where there was plenty of room so that neither would feel intimidated by the other. The meeting rooms in the rehoming building were a fair size but with these two enormous beasts cavorting around in them it would have been a squeeze.

We walked the two dogs down to the play area on their leads and as we humans chatted, the two dogs sniffed the ground and wagged their tails, taking absolutely no notice of one another. Not love at first sight, then.

When we entered the compound, the dogs sniffed each other's back ends. Charming creatures. The leads were still on just in case, but tails were wagging furiously so we let them loose. Desmond immediately went into a play bow which DD took him up on and both galloped around chasing each other, bowing and wagging.

Then trust the boy to lower the tone. Desmond became over-excited and tried to get amorous with DD. She gave him a short sharp telling off and like a naughty schoolboy he submitted straight away – a good sign.

After 30 minutes of exuberant play the dogs were exhausted and Robert, Francis and I were delighted at the outcome of the meeting. I arranged to take Desmond up to their house the following week, in order to do the home inspection and, all being well, drop Desmond off with them for good.

By now, Desmond was part of Battersea's fabric

and before he left, everyone said their own personal goodbyes to him. He of course didn't realise what was happening, but we did – none more so than Nichola who, in the weeks preceding Desmond's departure, would come into work with the same hangdog expression that Desmond used to have when she left him at night. Although he was going to leave a cavernous void in Battersea life, we all knew this was the right thing for Desmond.

The home visit could not have gone better. When the two dogs saw each other again, they galloped the length of the lawn to greet one another, like long-lost lovers rekindling a timeless love affair.

The house was amazing and the grounds even better. Robert and Francis had a big lawn surrounded by trees and bushes just begging to be explored and they even had a small lake at the bottom of the garden. Desmond charged down to investigate, sending ducks quacking in every direction. He thought that was hilarious until he tried it with a swan.

I was thrilled with the whole set-up; so much so I thought it was wasted on Desmond and would suit me far better. After lunch, I said my goodbyes to Desmond and left, happy in the knowledge he had struck gold.

We kept in regular contact with Robert and Francis to offer advice and support, not that they needed it. Desmond was in their words 'the perfect dog'. We already knew that.

A year later I had an invitation to lunch and to see how Desmond was getting on. I gladly accepted, and this time Nichola came with me.

When we arrived, Desmond went crazy. He greeted us with boundless enthusiasm and then let rip with one of his best-ever farts. He'd put on a bit of weight, his eyes were bright and his coat shiny. He sat by Nichola the whole afternoon, eventually falling asleep with his head on her feet.

In the house there were photos of Desmond and DD everywhere, as well as a trophy for Best Rescue Dog that Desmond had won the week before at the village show. I'd never seen him so happy but I knew the acid test would come when Nichola said goodbye to him.

The moment arrived but I needn't have worried. As Nichola bawled into her hanky and kissed him on the head, Desmond finished his rawhide chew, let out a burp and trotted off to find DD.

Nichola and I couldn't have wished for more and as we said our final goodbyes and drove off, I looked in my rearview mirror to see our boy lying on the lawn with his girlfriend, just as though they had always done. *Pet Rescue*, for Desmond's happiness, we owe you one.

# CHAPTER 11

# FINDING ONE FOR ME

'Can Melissa Wareham please go to Colonel Green's office,' screeched the tannoy announcement. Why did I feel like I was being summoned to the headmaster's office? My mind raced through every possible reason he might have to want to see me. To give a talk? To discreetly rehome his crazy Labrador? To go on the telly? To get fired?

I was in the middle of a delicate introduction involving a Pyrenean mountain dog belonging to my customer and a young Battersea mongrel about the size of a poodle. I had just bought young Joey into the meeting room and when he saw the size of the other dog, he quite literally screamed. Talk about amateur dramatics – I know the Pyrenean was big but Joey's reaction was a little over the top.

The big fella was quite taken aback and flung himself into the corner, refusing to go near the small screamer. We waited patiently for their curiosity to get the better of them and just as they were beginning to take tentative steps towards one another, my tannoy announcement came screeching through the speaker system, making them both jump out of their skin.

It was the end of the century and the second hand nonchalantly ticked from 1999 into the year 2000 without incident, not that Battersea Dogs Home was worried. It had, after all, survived for most of its life without the help of computers. If the Millennium Bug had wormed its way into Battersea, the good old-fashioned ledger system would have been re-commissioned to mark the entry and exit of each of our four-legged friends.

My Millennium New Year's Eve consisted of a cup of cocoa and an early night. I had never forgotten the words uttered to me over a decade ago by Mr Wadman Taylor: 'The dogs don't know or care that it might be a public holiday; they still need feeding and looking after.'

How true this was; somebody had to work on the very first day of the new century and one of those somebodies was me.

A month later it was my anniversary – I had been at Battersea for 12 glorious years; five spent in kennels looking after the dogs and the other seven finding them new homes. I was deliriously happy in my work and never wanted to do anything else.

Although Ginny, Colonel Green's Labrador, was a little older, she was no better behaved and as I fought my way through her to get to Colonel Green I vowed never to have a dog under the age of 14 years old. Ali had the right idea with all of her antiques.

Colonel Green sat behind his desk with a big smile on his face and told me I'd been promoted. Here we go again, I thought, why can't they leave me alone?

I was now the Rehoming Manager and with this promotion came a team of 15 rehomers and 10 home visitors – more responsibility, more stress and even less contact with the dogs. But it also meant a pay rise, which would ease the pressure of my new monthly mortgage repayments.

I sought advice from my wise old dad and before I knew it I was sitting behind my brand-new desk in my very own office, trying to turn on a computer I didn't know how to work.

Although I missed the direct contact with the dogs, it didn't take me long to realise that from this position I could make a difference in other ways, far more substantial ways.

My office was the first floor (one up one down) of Battersea's original cat-house, designed by Clough Williams-Ellis of Portmeirion fame and built in 1906. Directly before becoming my office, it housed the Behaviour Hotline and Lolly, a brindle mongrel. Lolly came with my office and belonged to one of my colleagues. She was temperamental to say the least; suffice it to say that no one ever entered the room. She was used to those that manned the Behaviour Hotline and would usually give them a free pass but to those she didn't know so well, she was a tiger in dog's clothing.

This was going to be interesting. The first eight times I tried to enter, she chased me out again. This is ridiculous, I said to myself, it's your office. Pull yourself together and show no fear. I remembered back to the day I was interviewed by Mr Wadman Taylor and had to overcome his Cairn terriers. Where was Mrs Wadman Taylor when I needed her?

I stood outside the door and thought for a while, mustering up all my years of experience and know-how. A light bulb came on and, feeling rather pleased with myself, I walked to the canteen and ordered sausages. That afternoon, Lolly and I became friends.

Of all the staff that worked at Battersea, I was the only one who didn't have a dog. Aside from the environmental restrictions of living with my parents and then rented accommodation, I wanted to make sure the time was right. I'd witnessed, day in, day out, the misery caused to both dog and owner when something goes wrong and the dog has to be rehomed.

But now I was in my own home, I could have the dog in my office with me during the day (luckily Lolly liked dogs far more than people) and I could walk to and from work across Clapham Common. Everything was perfect.

Although I had the pick of 500, looking for a

dog didn't become the focus of my day. When the right one came along, I knew our eyes would meet across a crowded kennel block and that would be that.

Working at Battersea for all those years had taught me a thing or two and I only had one stipulation – I knew I wanted a dog that had already been trained. I wanted one that someone else had done all the hard work with, a nice calm dog that I'd get the companionship from without having my house wrecked.

Cute, cuddly puppies are all very well but they are extremely hard work. Depending on how young they are, they might need feeding through the night and they will certainly need house-training as well as almost constant care and attention. I take my hat off to those that bring dogs up from puppy-hood. Not only is it hard work, if the owner is serious, it is also an extremely long-term commitment. None of this sounded like me.

Puppies were definitely out, as were the youngsters. Two-thirds of the dogs that came into Battersea were under the age of two, probably because they are even harder work than puppies. They poo more, chew more and run around like bulls in china shops. Although this age group is great fun, their behaviour is only hilarious within the four walls of Battersea where it doesn't matter if blankets are chewed into a thousand pieces, newspaper shredded into a million and beds systematically destroyed. It also doesn't matter if the floor is peppered with poo.

By the time dogs reach middle age, they are a much more appealing proposition – to me anyway. They are housetrained, have grown out of being destructive and don't require such vast amounts of exercise.

Easiest of all are the dogs that are drawing their pensions. They sleep for much of the day, only ask to go out when necessary and still offer all the companionship of their younger counterparts. People think that once a dog is middle-aged or older it is set in its ways. It probably is a little, but these ways include being housetrained and obedience trained plus half a lifetime of learned manners.

All things considered, I resolved to get an oldie. Wandsworth Common, Clapham Common and Battersea Park were my local parks, all brimming over with dogs, many of them from Battersea. As such, I thought I'd probably end up choosing a female, seeing as they get into fewer scrapes, tend to be less problematic behaviourally, don't stray as much and are generally a bit less up for it than the boys. Most dogs brought into Battersea are male which says it all.

Walking through the kennels one afternoon, my eye was caught by a little beagle sort of thing. She was middle-aged, shorthaired, a practical size and attractive-looking. I opened the kennel door and she immediately came to me.

I asked her to sit and she gave me what I could tell was her very best sit; chest puffed out, nose in the air and ears dangling down in perfect symmetry. She looked at me earnestly with her big round eyes, waiting for the next command. So far so good – I put a tentative reserve on her whilst we got to know each other better.

She was in good condition and even though I half expected her to be claimed, no one came forward. On her seventh day, I decided to take the newly named Jessie for a walk in Battersea Park after work. Jessie plodded along right by my side, nose to the ground, not pulling at all. Dogs from the kennels were not to be let off the lead during walks in the park, a rule that applied to both staff and volunteers and was simply due to the fact that in most cases, given the opportunity, the dog would bolt.

Although Jessie wasn't technically mine yet, Battersea Park was pretty safe and seeing as rules are made to be broken, I let her off. I wasn't worried; I had 12 years of experience – I knew dogs. I could tell just by looking at them which ones could be let off the lead and those that would make a run for it and I knew Jessie would be fine.

I unclipped the lead.

The phrase 'Bat out of Hell' immediately sprang to mind. Gone was the docile, middle-aged, ladylike plodder. Jessie was off, nose still planted firmly to the ground. I could see the staff newsletter headlines: 'Rehoming Manager Loses Dog' or maybe even 'Rehoming Manager Loses Job'.

Jessie was zig-zagging fast in all directions like a greyhound on speed. I was never going to catch her but as luck would have it she suddenly needed to stop for a poo. I guess when you've gotta go, you've gotta go. I raced towards her and while she was still concentrating on the job, lassoed her just before she tried to shoot off again. I casually pulled out a poo bag, trying to act as though my life hadn't just flashed before me.

Two days later, Jessie's owner came to claim her. It turned out she was a fully trained, retired hunt beagle.

'If she gets the scent of a fox, she'll never come back, that's how she went missing in the first place,' her owner said.

'Really,' I replied, 'how interesting,' and left it at that.

Undaunted by this experience, my search resumed.

Sometimes I'd walk through the kennels as an excuse just to see what had come in because as my Battersea years progressed, weirder and more wonderful breeds were coming through the door. Traditionally common breeds such as Labradors, spaniels, terriers and of course good old mongrels were being replaced by Chinese cresteds, New Zealand huntaways, Hungarian pulis and Italian spinones.

Whatever the breed, they all had different reactions to their new-found kennel life. It was sad to see very nervous dogs and I'd wonder what life they'd come from and hoped this was the start of a better one. Other dogs seemed ambivalent about the whole situation and some looked like they were positively enjoying the experience.

I walked past one kennel where a hairy, smelly, scruffy mongrel was up on his back legs at the front of the kennel, tail wagging, tongue hanging out. I gave him a Schmacko and looked further back into the kennel, mindful of giving to one and not the other, and saw a pristine, porcelain-white poodle. A Burberry diamante collar hung around its neck. Its posture was nothing less than regal, but it had a very intense look on its face. The look reminded me of someone (poodle) desperately trying to catch the eye of another (me) without alerting anyone else (hairy, smelly, scruffy mongrel).

It looked straight at me and seemed to be saying in the Queen's voice, 'Excuse me. I'm terribly sorry to bother you, but there seems to have been some sort of dreadful mistake. You see I shouldn't actually be in here. My owner is probably waiting for me outside in the Rolls. If you could just open the door and let me out, I'd be most grateful.'

I hoped the poodle's owner was waiting outside. But I knew from experience that, however well looked after and loved a dog appeared to be, sometimes that counted for nothing. If no one came for her, a good home would have been just around the corner. Fortunately, small breeds like poodles were always in demand. It was the older mongrels and cross-breeds that weren't so lucky and often had to wait much longer to feel wanted.

I continued my walk around the stray kennels and was enthusiastically greeted by just such a dog. About the size of a Border collie, he was black but with a grey face and had pointy ears that flopped over at the end and a big Basil Brush tail. He wagged this bushy tail so hard that his whole bum swayed from side to side.

I stopped outside his kennel for a closer look, prompting an even harder wag. I guessed there was Husky in there somewhere, maybe his grand-father twice removed.

I asked him to sit, which he did: excellent. Dogs, like children, are so much more appealing when they're well trained. I read his card and saw that he was neutered: excellent. Neutering sorts out so many unwanted behavioural problems in male dogs, not to mention unwanted pregnancies in females. This boy could be a serious contender for the starring role as my first dog.

I read on. His owner had been arrested and this poor hound happened to be in the car at the time of the arrest. The owner was taken to the big house and the dog to the Battersea dog house.

The dog had been at the Home for three days now, classed as Prisoner's Property. In cases where the owner of a dog is remanded in custody, the family of the prisoner were given 28 days to decide and make arrangements to either keep the dog or give it up for good.

The police didn't think to ask what the dog's name was, so when he arrived at Battersea devoid of any personal items including a name, my colleague, Erik, called him Gus; a very distinguished name, I thought.

Gus was given the once-over by Shaun who listened to his heart and diagnosed that he had a massive grade five heart-murmur, grade six being the worst. Coupled with his age, this didn't bode well for the future and to make matters worse, he was already coming down with kennel cough. If his kennel cough became serious it could be life-threatening due to his age and heart condition. How much bad news can a dog take in one day? There was nothing else for it; someone had to foster him. Seeing as though he was already a contender for my affections, I decided that someone would be me.

I took him to the pub in my lunch break that day and it became immediately evident he was a pub dog. He lay down at my feet as if this had always been his local and I had always been his owner, and caught every single peanut I threw to him.

Gus greeted everyone that came into the pub with the same enthusiasm and affection. Even with all his ailments, he was a happy and contented gentle dog.

We left work that evening armed with dog food and dog bed and when I opened the car door, Gus jumped straight in as though this was his car.

He was obviously a seasoned motor car passenger seeing as he was arrested in one.

We drove home together; it was St Valentine's Day. I didn't know it then, but this was to be the beginning of a beautiful relationship.

All things considered, Gus and I slept pretty well on our first night in each other's company. I don't think the dogs slept too well at Battersea; the barking, the night feeds for those that were underweight and the sheer anxiety of being in such a strange place must have kept them awake sporadically through the night. When some kind of normality returns and there are home comforts such as carpet under paw and peace and quiet, they must catch up on lost time.

When rehoming a Battersea dog, new parents were told by the rehomers not to allow their new charge to sleep in the bedroom and, heaven forbid, definitely not on the bed. Rescue dogs were notoriously insecure. Feeding that insecurity by allowing the dog to become overly attached in the first few months was fatal. Instead, new owners were told to try and settle their charges down somewhere like the kitchen, with easy-to-clean floors and not much to chew.

Inevitably the dog would whine and bark to begin with. In a strange new place, it would want to cling to its owner for security. The worst thing the owner could do was go to the dog when it was barking; the dog would think that its barking had brought the owner back.

If the owner were to leave the dog alone, it would learn that barking gets it nowhere. With some dogs the penny would drop after 15 minutes. With others it could take days, but when the penny did drop the dog settled down and the owner could remove their earplugs.

This may sound harsh but it was tough love. What owners didn't see was the distress their pet went through when it was left alone after having been allowed to over-bond.

Over the years, I had given this same advice to thousands of people.

On that first night, Gus slept on my bed.

In my defence, I wasn't necessarily going to keep him, so didn't need to set down any ground rules. I was only fostering him to prevent him catching kennel cough.

By day four, Gus was hacking away like a septu-agenarian on 60 Marlboro a day.

Shaun gave him some antibiotics and listened to his heart again. Vets are a strange breed; the most peculiar things excite them. He called over a couple of student vets and nurses to listen through his stethoscope to what he called 'a stonker of a heart murmur'. Before I knew it ten veterinary staff were crowding around Gus. He looked a little bewildered but didn't seem to mind as he lapped up the attention.

Another vet I once worked with at Battersea would insist upon opening the mouths of puppies brought to his attention, regardless of their ailment. He'd then take a good long sniff and say, 'Ah, puppy breath!' So effusive was he, I thought I'd see what all the fuss was about. Actually, puppy breath is really very good. It smells very distinctive; always the same regardless of individual pup and is sweet-smelling and warm – unlike Gus's breath which could turn milk.

Gus's cough got worse before it got better. I dread to think what my neighbours above and below must have thought of all the hacking and retching going on each night. They must have heard it; it certainly kept me awake. For seven nights in a row it kept me awake.

Lolly permitting, I had planned for Gus to stay in my office during the day. Gus had other ideas. My office was supposedly haunted but I'd never given it a second thought. Lolly seemed settled enough up there and nothing supernatural had ever transpired whilst I was seated at my desk.

When I first took Gus up the single flight of stairs and into the office he was immediately unsettled, panting and looking at the door. Natural behaviour, I deduced from being in a strange new place. Lolly gave him a cursory glance but seeing nothing worth getting out of bed for, went straight back to sleep. It was breakfast time so I left Gus in the office with Lolly and walked to the canteen for my bacon and egg roll, with a side order of sausages for the dogs.

On my return, I walked around to the front of my office and looked up to see Gus dangling halfway out of the first-floor window. He had a look of both determination and panic on his face.

Ali Taylor occupied the office below mine. Through her window, I began to mime that Gus was trying to commit suicide by jumping out of my office window. She was on the phone and gave me a blank look.

What followed next was like something out of the Keystone Cops. I heard myself telling Gus to 'Stop, go back' as if he could speak English, and holding my hands up (as best I could without dropping my bacon and egg roll), gesticulating for him to retreat.

He was far enough out that I couldn't decide whether to hang on and try and catch him, or race up the stairs and hope I'd be in time to grab him. Catching him would probably have resulted in injury to both of us so I raced up the stairs three at a time. I threw the door open to find his back legs paddling furiously in mid-air. He was now stuck between freedom outside and captivity with the ghosts he had clearly encountered inside.

I grabbed his back legs and pulled so that he was now more in than out and gently lifted him down. Was the thought of coming to live with me so bad he wanted to kill himself? I gave him his sausage which he wolfed down. I guess he decided it wasn't.

After that little incident, I asked the PR department if I could try Gus in their office. Gus loved other dogs so I knew there wouldn't be a problem with them continuing to look after poorly dogs from the kennels. Helen and the other PR girls said they'd be delighted to have him and he soon settled into the spectre-free office.

The 28 days that Gus's family had to come and claim him were ebbing away. He and I fell into a routine and I was becoming more and more attached to him.

On the twenty-eighth day I woke up a bag of nerves. If his family decided to keep him, he'd be going back to a kind of familiarity even though it wouldn't be to his jailbird master. If this were to be the case, I'd miss him terribly but if they didn't want him, I'd get to keep my buddy, I'd have my very first dog.

I had wanted a dog ever since I could talk. Could this be the moment I'd finally get my wish? Everything seemed so right, as though it was written in the stars – why then, did I have a massive wobble right at that moment? Dog ownership meant responsibility, that's why.

I knew my life would never be the same again and of course I mean that in a good way; the companionship, the love and the warm welcome whenever I came home but there were down sides to dog ownership too. Living in a flat with no garden would mean getting up and going to the park at 7 a.m. come rain or shine, even on days off. I would no longer be able to fall asleep on the sofa in front of the ten o'clock news because someone would need to go out for a last wee. The spontaneity of weekends away, clubbing till 3 a.m. or not even coming home at all would be gone.

Oh well, I suppose I already had a mortgage and, besides, I couldn't give Gus up now, not after spending the last month with him. We fitted together so well, plus I sort of loved him a bit. I tried not to get ahead of myself. I still didn't know, what the outcome would be.

Having each clocked up over a decade of service, my closest colleagues had risen through the ranks with me. Ali and Jacky now headed the behaviour department, Steph became my right-hand man on rehoming and Kirsty was now Steve's deputy kennel manager.

Kirsty was also in charge of Prisoner's Property dogs, a responsibility I didn't envy. It wasn't the dogs that were the problem; some of their owners were hardened criminals, nasty pieces of work who would do their best to intimidate Kirsty. She wasn't easily intimidated and always gave as good as she got.

That morning, Kirsty came into my office to tell me the decision Gus's family had made about his future. It wasn't until that very moment that I really knew which way I wanted the decision to go. I desperately wanted to keep him. She teased and tormented me for a few minutes until I threatened to set Gus's death breath on her.

The very thought of that made her crumble and Kirsty gave me the answer. His family didn't want him. In my head I could hear violins and the room went all misty around the edges.

'Gus, Gus,' I called to him, 'you're staving with me, boy.'

Bloody dog didn't even lift his head up, just continued snoring. At least one of us was happy.

That afternoon I took Gus to see Shaun to check on his kennel cough and have him microchipped in my name. Just for fun Shaun listened to his heart again and muttered, 'Amazing,' under his breath.

I told Shaun I was keeping Gus and his expression turned a little grave, just like a doctor's before bad news is announced.

He told me as gently as he could that such a serious heart murmur, coupled with Gus's great age, meant he probably only had about six months to live. Wow, that was hard to hear. On the bright side, I'd do my best to make sure it was the best six months of Gus's life. None of us could have known the little faker would go on for three and a half years!

The next hurdle was a behavioural one. During the last 28 days Gus had been with me morning, noon and night. Because I wasn't sure that I'd be keeping him, I'd broken all the settling-in rules. I had to do a test to find out exactly where we were in the over-bonding stakes.

I took him home and settled him down. I walked out through my front door closing it behind me, down the dusty flight of communal stairs (I still hadn't got round to cleaning them up) and closed the main front door behind me. I sat on the steps and chanted my mantra, 'Please don't bark, please don't bark.' It didn't work. Within 30 seconds Gus was barking his head off; sure enough, I had a dog that had overbonded with me.

After 20 minutes the barking stopped, so I went back up. I opened my front door, or at least I tried to. He'd pulled the carpet up and I couldn't get in. He was frantically trying to get to me and I was frantically trying to get into my flat. Just at that moment, my upstairs neighbour came in from work. We swapped pleasantries on the stairwell but God knows what he must have thought of this carry on. Gus and I had some work ahead of us. Luckily I was friends with Battersea's so-called top behaviourist, Ali Taylor.

One day I left Gus with Ali and her dad for a couple of hours. Mr Taylor was at work and Ali needed to nip out for cigarettes. She was aware of Gus's little neuroses but he was fast asleep and she decided she could make it out and back before he woke up.

She was wrong.

As soon as she shut the door he was awake. He ran the length and breadth of the house and, finding no one home, began to panic. He clawed at the front door, then pulled up the newly laid kitchen lino and finally, when all else failed, howled for help. When none came, he took a running jump at the closed first-floor window.

Had he learned nothing from that first day in my office?

In the mode of stunt dog, he hurled himself right through the window and landed not on ground level, thank goodness, but on the garage roof which was only a few feet below the window. Pleased with himself, Gus stood there, a free dog, barking with delight.

At that point Mr Taylor came home from work to find his window smashed out and Gus on top of his garage, attracting a crowd of impressed onlookers. Ali then rounded the corner and the cigarette that had been the root cause of this carnival fell from her stunned, open mouth.

Many weeks of behavioural work ensued but before the problem was fixed, things became a little strange. So serious was his separation anxiety, that if I went clubbing at the weekend I'd have to take Gus with me and leave him in the car. It was either that or have my flat wrecked and the neighbours complaining. Gus loved being in the car so as far as he was concerned it was fine, but my friends started thinking I was a little weird, bringing my dog clubbing.

This was ridiculous; the problem had to be resolved. By trial and error I found out that the key was ensuring Gus couldn't actually see me leaving the flat. I did a Baldrick and devised a cunning plan.

If I knew I was going out, I'd feed Gus just before I was ready to leave. Whilst he was happily stuffing his face, I'd take some clothes out of the dirty laundry basket and put them on the bathroom floor. I'd then grab my tape player, put it in the bathroom and play a cassette of me speaking (artfully taped from telephone conversations I'd had in previous weeks). Then I'd close the bathroom door and sneak out the front door.

When Gus finished his food, he'd automatically come looking for me. He'd see I wasn't in the kitchen, living room or bedroom. He'd probably think about panicking and ripping up the carpet or barking but just to make sure, he'd need to check the bathroom. This is where the genius of the plan came into action. He'd hear me talking, sniff at the bottom of the door to make sure I was definitely in there and thanks to the old clothes on the floor and the tape, would put two and two together and come up with five! It worked every time.

I did feel sorry for him when I came home though; the poor dog must have thought he was losing his mind. He'd watch me walk through the front door, then he'd look towards the bathroom and back to me again as if to say, 'Who the hell is in our bathroom then?'

Apart from his separation anxiety, which was fixed with shameless trickery, Gus's only other dislike was thunder, so I became an avid weather watcher. If I was due to go out and a storm was brewing, I simply didn't go. This was not only to prevent a wrecked flat, but also because I couldn't bear the thought of him facing his greatest fear alone.

For an hour before the storm hit, Gus would salivate, tremble and try to get into the smallest spaces. During one pre-storm, he upended my bedside table and all its contents, including a pint glass of water, trying to seek sanctuary from the impending tempest.

Fireworks had the same effect on Gus as storms so every November, he and I joined the Taylor bandwagon and headed for the coast. Ali's five dogs were all neurotic about fireworks too so she and her dad would clear out of London for the Guy Fawkes period. The fireworks in Herne Bay were altogether less violent than those in London, where all six dogs would shake and slobber for a whole fortnight of fear.

Gus's greatest love was the seaside and he thought he'd died and gone to heaven whenever I took him to see my grandmother in Eastbourne. I loved visiting her, not just because she'd make me a wonderful curry but because she was a joy to be around. At 80 years old Gran Gran was as fit as a fiddle, full of fun and as sprightly as a puppy. She was my kindred spirit, the only other member of my family that liked dogs, and she adored Gus as much as I adored her.

When she met Gus for the first time, Gran Gran flung her arms around him. This was exactly the reaction I was looking for, unlike that of my mother who, when introduced to a polished and buffed Gus and told she was a grandmother now, looked from me to Gus and then back to me and asked if I had finally gone completely mad.

When my brother first met Gus, he looked down at him in a rather superior manner and announced, 'Your dog has halitosis.'

Gran Gran took great pride in walking Gus up and down the main street, stopping to tell everyone about him and where he came from which inevitably led on to me. Although excruciatingly embarrassing, I'd smile and make all the right noises as she told random strangers all about my achievements, until I could gently steer her back home for tea and biscuits.

Once back at her little house, Gran Gran would always ask me if she could give Gus a biscuit. 'Just the one,' I'd say and then when she thought I wasn't looking she'd feed him about 20 more. These were some of the happiest days of my life, and I hope his too.

As the months went by I felt as though I'd struck gold. Gus was a dream; the perfect gentleman. When I first took him on, he already knew sit, lie down, and his best command: wait. Wanting to know what else my clever dog could do, I asked him for his paw. He looked at me with utter disdain. I never asked again.

Gus was also perfectly housetrained, in fact incredibly so. He had such an iron bladder that he'd quite happily hold himself until I'd had a good sleep in on my days off. In fact he was not a morning dog at all and was usually better at sleeping in than I was.

The only exception to this was if he'd eaten something that didn't agree with him. On one occasion the poor fellow had to wake me up several times during the night. It was a mark of how well trained he was that he took the trouble to wake me up rather than have an unfortunate accident indoors.

It was 2 a.m. when I felt a cold, wet nose nudging me. It took me a while to regain consciousness but when I saw the intense look on Gus's face I knew I needed to get my act together quickly.

I threw my clothes on over my pyjamas, grabbed the keys and we ran down the stairs. I opened the front door and Gus shot out like a greyhound from its trap. I assumed he'd make a run for the privacy of the bushes on Wandsworth Common, a minute's walk away and his preferred lavatory of choice.

I was wrong; he needed somewhere much, much closer. He darted into next-door's front garden and proceeded to squat. I whispered, as loudly as I could without waking the neighbours, for him to get out of there.

He turned to me from his squatting position, looked at me like some sort of crazed beast and let rip. The noise was deafening. I could have sworn it was going to wake the neighbours. I had visions of them pulling back their curtains to find this creature annihilating their garden, like some sort of canine crop sprayer.

Luckily we got away with it and, without CCTV, they couldn't prove a thing.

Wandsworth Common is a wonderful place, teeming with dogs of all shapes and sizes. Maybe the humble mongrel is becoming a thing of the past because mostly it teems with pedigrees. Gus was one of only two or three other mongrels; quite rare, I liked to think.

The common's top breeds were Labradors and spaniels, usually owned by town-country folk. You know the ones I mean – decked out in tweed clothing and Hunter wellies, they drive their bull-barred Chelsea tractors to Sainsbury's and back, clogging up London's roads. But they own dogs, so I don't suppose they're all bad.

On a couple of occasions I'd see a dog happily running around the park and think to myself, where have I seen that dog before? Then it would occur to me, I saw it a couple of weeks ago in a kennel at work. I got to know some of those dogs in the park; I had even rehomed some of them. Seeing ex-Battersea dogs running around the common never failed to warm my heart, especially when I saw how well looked after and happy they were.

When their owners saw Gus in his blue-and-white Battersea Dogs Home logo collar (often matching their own dog's) we'd strike up a conversation.

When they found out I actually worked at Battersea they'd become completely animated. Some might say having to talk about your place of work on a day off would be utterly tiresome but I never minded, especially when they talked with such passion and interest about the place. It made me feel so proud to be a part of it.

Gus loved the other dogs in the park and he would run up to investigate them with tail-wagging, bum-sniffing enthusiasm. Greeting over, he'd race back to me, tongue hanging out and with a wide smile planted firmly on his mush.

But as good as Gus was, he was by no means perfect. Blondes were his weakness. Any yellow Labrador or golden retriever would make him go weak at the knees. He'd forget himself and be straight on their back humping away as if his life depended on it, until he literally did go weak at his slightly arthritic knees. He was neutered so no harm done but oh, the embarrassment.

And do you think I could call him away when he was in shag mode? Unless the dog Gus was taking advantage of (male or female, by the way, he wasn't fussy) gave him a good telling off, I'd have to go and physically drag him off. It was shameful.

More often than not, his victims were Labradors, yellow, of course, owned by one of those town-country people. Not realising Gus was neutered, they'd run up to the melee, flapping their arms about, appalled that a mongrel might be impregnating their pedigree. Matters were only made worse when their extremely posh children would ask, 'Mummy, what's that dog doing to Rupert?'

Thankfully, Gus was always really good with the puppies and kittens at the Home and never tried to bonk them. He was so gentle that he was used many times to test how kittens would react to living with a dog.

The cat staff often came to ask me if they could use Gus for cat tests and I always complied with this request until one incident made me reconsider. A rather confident, feisty eight-week-old ginger Tom decided to take an instant dislike to poor old Gus. As Gus came over to give the kitten a gentle hello sniff, the youngster launched himself at Gus's nose, swiping with razor-sharp claws and cutting Gus's hooter in three places.

Gus yelped and went into reverse, whizzing around behind me for safety, avoiding any eye contact with the tiny eight-week-old. Imagine an old soldier like Gus being beaten up by a kitten the size of his paw. Needless to say, we didn't rehome that kitty within a ten-mile radius of any dogs – for their sakes!

Gus really did have that old soldier air about him. If he had been human, he would have fought in both World Wars and perhaps even reached the rank of General.

The persona of 'General Gus – war veteran', took off and was used in a fundraising campaign complete with suitably distinguished photograph.

Not only did the campaign raise £20,000 for the Home, Gus was also sent a fantastic letter and photo from a 'Private Gus', who bore an uncanny resemblance to the General. They looked so much alike, I'm sure they could have been related.

Always a little eccentric, I learned to take some of Gus's behaviour with a pinch of salt. One morning, for no apparent reason, he decided stairs weren't for him. Leaving home for work as usual, Gus and I walked down the 12 dusty communal stairs. He reached the halfway point and refused to go on. I walked on assuming he'd found something interesting to sniff. When I reached the bottom, I looked back to find a rather hesitant Gus looking down at me. All of a sudden he hurled himself all the way down to the bottom of the stairs and landed in a heap at my feet. After the third time he performed this act of lunacy, I booked him in with the psychiatrist.

In her infinite wisdom, Ali Taylor asked me if I'd had his eyesight checked lately. I hadn't. Next stop, the veterinary department. Sure enough, Gus's vision was on the wane.

After this diagnosis, every time we came down those dimly lit stairs, I held Gus's collar, gently persuading him to put a paw down on every step. This seemed to do the trick.

His eccentricities and infirmities only made me love him more and of the 500 I had to choose from, I knew I'd picked the one in a million.

# CHAPTER 12

# BATTERSEA ON TOUR

Battersea Dogs Home holds a special place within the hearts of the British people. This affection is similar to that held for the 1966 England World Cup-winning football team, Winston Churchill and even Battersea's present-day patron, the Queen.

Our patron had been on the throne for 50 years and in honour of this great achievement, Concorde, escorted by the Red Arrows, was due to fly over Buckingham Palace that evening. To allow this unusual convoy safe passage over London, Heathrow Airport would temporarily close down and all flights in and out of the world's busiest airport would cease for ten minutes.

The aircraft were to fly from Heathrow towards central London, up The Mall and then directly over Buckingham Palace's famous balcony where the Queen and other senior royals would be waiting. Before reaching Her Majesty, however, the airborne convoy would fly directly over Battersea Dogs Home, where I would be waiting.

I was not disappointed and from my seat on the roof of the Kent Kennels, at approximately 6 p.m.,

Concorde and nine Red Arrows flew at the incredibly low altitude of 1,500 feet, directly over my head.

I have always admired the Queen for her unswerving sense of duty and, of course, her love of dogs and felt proud that she was Battersea's Patron.

The next day as I tried to juggle the staff rota, I wondered whether the Queen ever had the kind of staffing problems I had. What would happen if three footmen phoned up sick on the same day? What if her Lady in Waiting slept through her alarm? What if the cook's train was cancelled?

Realising I didn't have enough rehomers to fill the necessary quota, I gave up. A Basset puppy had been deposited in my office for socialising and was making a deposit of his own. Lolly looked on unimpressed. I strode over to the steaming pile, poo bag in hand, wondering whether the Queen ever had to pick up after her corgis, when the phone rang.

I picked the phone up with one hand and the hot turd with the other. The dog looked at me sheepishly.

'Hello?' I muttered, gagging at the smell.

Nichola Vickers came on the line in her usual bright and breezy manner.

'How would you like to go to America for two months?'

I was speechless. I stood there open-mouthed, poo in hand.

'Excuse me?'

'North Shore Animal League wants to do a staff exchange programme and you've been selected from a cast of thousands. You'll spend six weeks in New York, a week in Miami and a week in Dallas.'

'Erm, all right then,' I heard myself saying.

'Great, we'll start making arrangements.'

I put the phone down and stared at the poo. It was a whole five minutes before the conversation registered. Swept away in the moment, I threw the poo bag out the window and the staff rota in the bin and whooped with joy.

If I was going away on holiday – albeit a working holiday – that meant Gus would be going away too. From a practical point of view, being in such a doggie community made going away easy because there was a huge support network for looking after each other's dogs. For the eight weeks I was away, Steph would have Gus for the first month and Ali for the second, so I knew he'd be well looked after and happy. There'd be no shortage of canine companions for Gus to hang out with; between them, Ali and Steph had nine dogs – unfortunately for him, none of them were yellow Labs.

From an emotional point of view, going away wasn't so easy – not for me anyway. This was the first time Gus and I would be properly apart since I got him. A little teary-eyed, I packed his suitcase containing food, a jumper, two bowls, one ball, one bed and a brush, and dropped him off at Steph's house. A week after receiving Nichola's call, I was on the Gatwick Express heading for New York with a suitcase the size of Manhattan.

Battersea Dogs Home might have been ancient within the realms of animal welfare, but its outlook was young and visionary. Staying at the cutting edge was extremely important and Battersea's position on staff development and training was second to none.

Animal behaviour is an inexact science and one that continues to evolve and develop. It was imperative that anyone working in the field kept abreast of new theories in order to try to understand what went on in an animal's mind.

At Battersea, the improvement of the human mind to better understand the canine mind ranged from day-long dog behaviour courses in the UK, to weeks at a time visiting dog rescues in far-flung countries with the aim of sharing knowledge, ideas and expertise.

Several times a year, staff were sent on week-long animal behaviour courses on the Yorkshire moors. These weeks resembled boot camp and I wondered if we were sent there by some kind of higher power as punishment for offences committed in a previous life.

Battersea's external behaviour consultant was John Rogerson. He and his family lived in the countryside a few miles outside Durham, with only Travellers for neighbours. It was a very rustic set-up geared around the needs of dogs rather than the comfort of humans. The ramshackle house was large and could accommodate guests for the week but if all the rooms were taken – or one required a little more creature comfort, there was a bed and breakfast up the road run by a rather large lady who bore an uncanny resemblance to Mrs Doubtfire.

I had the pleasure of sampling both hostelries; the difference between the two was like staying at an army barracks or staying at your mum's. Mrs Doubtfire's modest abode was cosy and, like most B&Bs, extremely chintzy but she cooked a mean full English.

John Rogerson and his wife Moira were wonderfully hospitable people and in my opinion Moira was nothing short of Superwoman. As well as bringing up three boys, nine Border collies and a horse, she opened up her house to all sorts of strange dog-obsessed types, cooked a fabulous banana curry and was an expert dog groomer. She also ran behaviour and training classes and the collies had all been trained to an extremely highly level, much like the men in Moira's life.

The courses were always varied and never dull. We might begin the week by listening to the latest ideas and theories on animal behaviour. By midway through the course we could be training John's pet rats to do a mini-agility course and at the week's culmination, training one of his collies to take the horse out for a trot!

John lectured all around the world and his courses gave Battersea's staff a deeper insight into the minds of the dogs they rehabilitated and rehomed every day.

Conferences were also an excellent way to share knowledge and meet like-minded people and, every 18 months, the International Conference on Companion Animal Welfare took place. The three conferences I was lucky enough to attend were held in Istanbul, Prague and Warsaw. They gave us a fascinating insight into the hardship faced by some shelters in poorer countries and a reality check of just how good life was at Battersea.

Big-hearted people who adored animals but had no money or business sense ran many of these rescues and after visiting some of them it was clear that loving animals and wanting to save them just wasn't enough. Many of these rescues had the additional hardship of being situated in countries where animal welfare was ridiculed, countries where it was the norm to show a dog aggression rather than affection. According to old records, that was how it was for Mary Tealby, Battersea's founder, back in 1860.

Most of these rescues did the best they could and if it was not in their country's culture to keep dogs as pets, they would simply trap, neuter and release them. At least this kept the street dog and cat population under some sort of control.

During the trip to Warsaw we visited a local rescue. The place was pretty grim. It consisted of a compound about half the size of a football pitch which was completely open plan. Sixty or so dogs were quite happily running around the compound together but around the edges there were about 50 extremely run-down kennels containing highly aggressive dogs. They were in extremely poor condition; some had weeping sores that were left untreated either due to lack of resources or the fact that no one could get near the dogs to treat them.

Two dogs kennelled next to each other spent the whole time snarling, trying to attack one another through the bars. It was a sad scene, one that brought some of my Battersea colleagues to tears.

Animal welfare walks an extremely fine line. Many people who are undeniably devoted to animals sometimes cannot see what is staring them in the face; that the option to put the animal to sleep might in fact be a better one.

The lady in charge refused to entertain the idea that the life those caged dogs were living was, in effect, no life at all. She refused to see that the kindest thing might actually be to put them out of their misery. Of course it is a very tough decision to make and one that needs extremely careful thought and consideration, but the fact remains that animal welfare sometimes means having to make those difficult decisions.

In some respects, those conferences felt like a vicious circle. The more experienced and established rescues like Battersea tried to help those less fortunate by sharing advice and expertise. Often, by the time the next conference came around, those rescues had improved tremendously but the frustration was that ten bad ones had sprung up in their place.

Battersea decided to put its money where its mouth was and became involved in setting up and running a shelter in Romania. The aim was to try to educate the local people that dogs not only had their uses but also made wonderful companions. Many of the street dogs led pitiful existences, debilitated by disease, attacked by larger dogs and bullied by humans. Finding food and water was a daily struggle.

The hardest part of this venture was trying to change people's perception of dogs; a tall order to begin with but over the course of many months, with the aid of publicity and education, the message started to get through and interest began to grow. The locals were intrigued and tentatively came to see what 'the crazy English' were up to.

In the beginning there was just a large fenced site, ideal for dogs to safely bound around in but barren land does not a dogs' home make. First to go up were two Portacabins, one for neutering and one for interviewing prospective new owners. Next to go up was a kennel block.

The dog's time was split between running around the large field and lazing around in their kennels so that potential new owners could get a closer look. Interest from residents continued to grow and rehoming increased from one dog a week to one a day.

After months of preparation, the time had come for the shelter's grand opening. The Romanian and British press had been invited, local publicity had been organised and everything at the centre was shining like a new pin.

By now there was great interest from the locals who patiently queued at the gate to get a piece of the action. I'm not sure if it was the dogs or the free booze that brought them; either way we were just happy they had come.

TV cameras turned up and interviewed anyone and everyone who was game. Kids from a local school came with paintings of dogs and the freshly bathed and groomed star attractions were paraded up and down for everyone to see.

What amazed me most about these Romanian street hounds was that every single one had a stunning temperament. In the Western world, dogs are often seen and treated as substitute children, leading to so many behavioural problems. Here, the dogs had never had owners to spoil and ruin them. They were never given toys to become possessive over, beds to guard or attention to become jealous of.

Due to inherent cultural differences, these types of problems were not expected to arise as most of the people wanted a dog to protect them and their families. In return, the dog would be taken off the street, fed, watered, sheltered and looked after. It was an excellent place to start.

Slowly but surely, the culture was shifting in the dog's favour and SOS Dogs Oradea now runs a successful neutering and rehoming centre.

In the name of advancement and the pursuit of animal welfare best practices, some of my colleagues had been fortunate enough to travel abroad.

Ali Taylor thought she'd hit the jackpot when a grainy fax came through asking her to give a talk on how to deal, hands-on, with extreme forms of canine aggression.

The location on the fax was written as N York and even though Ali nearly fainted at the prospect of speaking in public, a free trip to New York wasn't going to present itself every day. She immediately returned the fax accepting the offer. Excited as a puppy, Ali bounded off to the bookshop to buy a copy of the New York Lonely Planet.

A few days later when she spoke to the man who'd sent the fax, her excitement turned to horror. N York turned out to be North Yorkshire, not the Big Apple. She had been invited to help John Rogerson give a talk to a thousand people. It got worse. The B&B was full as were all the rooms in his house and she'd be sleeping in a draughty old caravan in John's garden.

I told her it would be character building – that what didn't kill her would surely make her stronger. She thanked me for those few sage words and returned the Lonely Planet book in favour of thermal underwear. Poor Ali, just as she returned from her week of hell in the freezing cold north, I announced I was off to New York.

I'd been to America before; my godparents live in Los Angeles and when I was 11 we hired a massive camper van and travelled down the West Coast and into Mexico. It was during those eight weeks that I fell in love with the States: the junk food, the push-button phones, the theme parks and the diners. It was like stepping into every American TV show I'd ever watched. Even returning as an adult, my affection for the country remained the same. But this was my first trip to the Big Apple – the coolest city in the whole world.

Tammy, my contact at North Shore Animal League, had found me a place to stay on Long Island, a lush, green, well-to-do suburb of New York City, about a 40-minute train ride from Manhattan. I took a yellow cab from the airport, gawping at everything we drove past.

After a while we crossed a large expanse of water and suddenly the freeways, motels and junk food outlets were gone. We were in a very leafy, upmarket area; Long Island, I presumed. These huge palatial houses were neatly tucked behind well-kept front lawns that overlooked quiet streets. These weren't normal streets though; they were more like 'Stepford Wives' cul-de-sacs.

'Nice place you got here,' said the taxi driver as

288

we pulled up to the house scribbled on my piece of paper.

I paid him and he drove off, leaving me standing alone, staring up at a mansion, and wondering if I'd got the address right. I dragged my case up to the front door, feeling like Will Smith in *The Fresh Prince of Bel Air*, and rang the bell.

A glamorous lady in her sixties opened the door. Her blonde hair was tied back and she wore an interesting floral tracksuit. Her hands were manicured and her make-up flawless.

'Mrs Blechman?' I asked.

She looked me up and down, raised her eyebrows when she saw my case and said, 'It's pronounced Bleckman. They said you'd be older. You'd better come in.'

She walked me through the cavernous house and into a room off the kitchen. It was small and dark, and the only furniture was a single bed and a filing cabinet.

'This is your room,' she said. Lucky me.

Mrs Blechman closed the door behind her and I looked around at my sparse room, feeling as though I'd just entered Sing Sing on a ten-stretch.

I opened my suitcase and took everything out until it was as empty as I felt. I pulled myself together. Okay, I may be in a prison cell but it was a prison cell in New York, goddammit. This was the Big Apple; the city that never sleeps, a city so good they named it twice, and I was smack-bang in the middle of it. Well, just a little off to the side.

I tentatively ventured out of my cell; I was hungry and needed to find sustenance.

Mrs Blechman was sitting on a sun lounger in the garden, wearing a big floppy hat, reading a glossy and sipping iced tea. The garden was stunning. The lawn was like a bowling green and there were big, brightly coloured flowers everywhere. Birds sang from high up in fir trees and, everywhere I looked, butterflies floated in the air. Genuinely in awe, I complimented Mrs Blechman on her garden. As luck would have it, this was the way to her heart and we spent the next half an hour discussing flora and fauna. That was all very well but it was dinner time (probably breakfast on my body clock) and I was famished.

Mrs Blechman must have read my mind and with the ice well and truly broken, she suggested we go to the local Chinese restaurant.

We spent the evening chatting about work, dogs, politics and family. She was a divorcee with two grown-up children, one in real estate in LA, the other a doctor in New York. Her husband of 30 years had walked out a couple of years previously and I was glad she got to keep the house she'd brought her kids up in. Mrs Blechman had her own successful realestate business; she was a strong, forthright woman and I liked her very much.

We got on so well that it was only a matter of days before she promoted me to the first floor of the house. I had the choice of three rooms and immediately moved my belongings out of the ten- by six-foot cell and into the second largest, brightest, most homely room in the house, which came complete with a double bed and TV.

On my first full day in New York, I took the train from Long Island to Penn station in the heart of Manhattan. The journey was mostly over-ground through picturesque suburbs surrounded by water. Before we hit Manhattan, the train descended underground. I alighted at Penn station and walked up the stairs to the exit.

I will never forget my first memory of Manhattan. I scaled the steps exiting the train station and immediately felt as though I was home. Perhaps it was that big city feel, so reminiscent of London, that engendered feelings of ease and familiarity. I'd only had that feeling once before, when I walked through the door of Battersea Dogs Home for the first time all those years ago.

As I reached the top step and the sun came into view, I looked up and gawped at what felt like the tallest skyscraper I'd ever seen. Then there was another, and another. When I finally brought my eyes down to street level, there was a sea of yellow taxicabs as far as the eye could see. Suited and booted New Yorkers rushed around, yelling into their phones whilst simultaneously hollering for cabs. Horns were honking, brakes were screeching and steam was coming out of manholes in the road, but it was the delicious smell of pizza that finally brought me round.

It didn't look much but that slice of New York pizza, handed to me by a Tony Soprano lookalike, was the best I'd ever tasted.

I spent the whole day just wandering around, marvelling at a city I'd seen a million times before in magazines, on TV and of course on the big screen. Even though I was to be in New York for a total of six weeks, I took in the Empire State Building, the Rockefeller Center, the Statue of Liberty, Macy's and Bloomingdale's all on my very first day.

For the entire time I was in New York, I spent every second of my free time in Manhattan. I was in love with the city and never wanted to leave. It pulled me back like a drug and I missed it when I was back on Long Island, sleeping and working. Work. Had it not been so interesting I would have viewed it as an annoyance, an inconvenience keeping me away from my new-found lover.

I always thought Battersea Dogs Home was top of the pops in the dazzling dog shelter charts until I saw North Shore Animal League. This was the canine Four Seasons; North Shore Animal League was at the top of the premier division.

It made its money through aggressive fundraising, which from what I could see must have been pretty brutal. What astounded me was the size and activity levels of the fundraising department. It was like a machine and felt as though it would be more suited to the world of big business than animal welfare.

This place was incredible and although it offered many of the same services that Battersea supplied, the scale on which it operated was much larger.

The veterinary department alone rivalled the best private human hospitals around, with 16 vets on site. No veterinary procedure was too big or too small – I wondered if they offered canine plastic surgery.

On the surface North Shore seemed to have the perfect set-up but scratch the surface of each department and all was not as it seemed.

Although the rehoming department was clean, well constructed and efficient, it was all about the numbers. The staff area had two deli-counter number displays; one stating the previous day's adoption figures, the other displaying the current day's. The staff seemed to do whatever it took for the latter to outnumber the former, which was fine in principle, but I witnessed a good few adoptions that made me wince. Many of the dogs were returned shortly after leaving due to the unsuitability of the match.

I was glad, however, to see that some shady characters applying to take a dog home were turned down but my happiness soon dissolved as I watched them walk straight across the road to the pet shop and buy a puppy from there instead. The shopkeeper must have known that his customer had just been rejected by North Shore. Sadly there was nothing anyone could do about this; some things are the same the world over.

Like Battersea, North Shore had a rehabilitation section although the training methods employed were somewhat dubious, encouraging the use of outdated and harsh training aids such as choke chains.

Educating children played a big part at North Shore and a whole department was assigned to all things kiddie, from dog-training classes to introducing responsible dog ownership into the school curriculum.

North Shore practised selective intake of dogs and in this respect felt like an elite club. Once a dog was in, it would want for nothing, but getting in was the trick. Like the humans in New York, it seemed that only the beautiful people made the grade. If you were an ugly old mutt in the Big Apple, you'd had it. Previously I had only wondered, now I hoped that North Shore offered canine plastic surgery for the more aesthetically challenged hound.

One morning I accompanied Stacey, a peroxide blonde with a thick Brooklyn accent, on her daily trip from North Shore Animal League to the various state-run dog pounds in the city. They were as grim as you would imagine: unhappy places, packed to the rafters with miserable-looking dogs that had 48 hours to be claimed or die. Stacey and I visited five of these pounds to rescue as many dogs as we could.

Being partial to elderly mongrels, I was straight in there, picking all the canine Jim Brannings but

Stacey told me in no uncertain terms that we were there to collect as many young breeds as we could find – space was limited and they were the ones that people wanted.

Give me Battersea's ethos any day. Battersea Dogs Home was far from perfect but it never turned a dog away and did its very best for every single one of them.

I found our visit to the various city pounds extremely hard, particularly knowing that the dogs we didn't take would almost certainly be put down. This aspect aside, being involved in the working throng of the city gave me a fascinating snapshot of what it was like to be a native New Yorker.

Stopping for bagels and coffee, whizzing through traffic on the Brooklyn Bridge and even being asked by an English tourist for directions made me feel as much a part of New York as the Statue of Liberty.

It happened to be my birthday whilst I was there and that evening, one of my childhood dreams was fulfilled. I was taken to a New York Mets baseball game at Shea stadium and kitted out in all the paraphernalia. It was just as I had imagined. The atmosphere was electric, everyone (including me) had their baseball glove on in case the ball came zinging their way and the beer and popcorn were free-flowing. One of the girls that worked at North Shore had an evening job at the stadium and came down our aisle chanting,

'Beer here, beer here.' I obliged; it would have been rude not to.

Everyone at North Shore Animal League looked after me so well whilst I was in their city. They were warm, friendly, hospitable people who made my time in New York truly special. Mrs Blechman and I had also become good friends. During our six-week house share we'd been shopping together, out to restaurants, to the movies and she had even taken me to her beach house in the Hamptons for a weekend by the sea. When the time came for me to depart, Mrs Blechman and I said our emotional goodbyes and I left for the domestic airport with many happy memories and the determination to return to my new-found favourite city as soon as I could.

My next stop was Fort Lauderdale, Florida and The Humane Society of Broward County. Whilst I waited for my flight, I decided to call home and make sure that Gus was okay – or rather that he was behaving himself.

'Hi Steph, it's me,' I said crossing my fingers in the hope that Gus hadn't consumed anything he shouldn't have.

'Oh hi, how's it going?' she asked.

'Fine, thanks,' I said. From her voice, I couldn't gauge if I'd left her with the hound from hell or an angelic furry friend. If it was the former I didn't want her to know I was having the time of my life whilst my dog was ruining hers.

I bit the bullet.

'Er, how's Gus been?'

'Oh, he's been an absolute dream,' she enthused.

'No flooring ripped up?' I pressed.

'No, nothing. He hasn't even hurled himself through a window! I thought he'd be much more fun than this. Maybe he just does that at Ali's house. I'm dropping him off there tomorrow,' she said, laughing.

I laughed back, nervously.

'What about the trip? Everyone's been wondering how you're getting on,' she asked.

'I've fallen in love with New York and might never come home.'

'Oh yes, you bloody will; there's a black dog with a grey face sitting at my feet with your name on it!' she reminded me.

After a bumpy flight, we disembarked in Florida. It was July so the temperature was as hot as Hades with 100 per cent humidity. As soon as I stepped off the plane I became an instant frizz ball, dripping with sweat.

Happy that all was well back home and once again feeling like a native Yank, I jumped in a cab and headed for the Best Western hotel, my home for the next week. It was near the beach and I wasn't working until the next day so I made straight for the sea. I desperately needed cooling down but to my amazement the sea did nothing to ease my discomfort; it was like taking a warm bath. This was the warmest sea I had ever been in and it took some getting used to. I persevered. Life was hard.

The next morning I was collected bright and early by I'am, a short, round, jolly lady whose smile reached from ear to ear. We drove straight to the animal shelter which looked smart, professional and modern.

Inside, everyone was going about their business but stopped to give me a warm welcome when I arrived. Americans really are the most hospitable and friendly people.

I'am handed me over to Carol-Ann who took me on a tour. I liked The Humane Society of Broward County very much. It felt real and as I walked through the kennels, I was struck by the similarity between these dogs and those at Battersea. Rescue dogs, it seemed to me, were the same the world over: cute, cheeky cross-breeds, desperate to escape their internment and return home, wherever that was.

That was except for one inmate. He was short, fat and bristly. I did a double take but my eyes were not deceiving me. Lying in a dog bed, playing with a red and yellow squeaky hotdog, was a Vietnamese pot-bellied piglet.

A week earlier, when the staff came into work, they found him tied to the front door of the Humane Society. He was sitting next to a box, looking a little lost. On further investigation, the box was found to contain a light blue blanket, a soft brush, the squeaky hotdog and a note.

The note was written by a child. It read, 'Nemo loves peanut butter but doesn't like jelly. Please look after him.'

Nemo's past was a mystery but his future at least looked bright. I'd never seen a Vietnamese pot-bellied pig close up before and asked if I could go into the kennel with him. As I walked through the kennel door, Nemo came trotting towards me, just like a dog. I knelt down to his level and gave him a gentle stroke. He felt like a friendly Brillo pad. To my amazement he brought the toy over to me. Maybe being surrounded by hundreds of hounds, Nemo thought he too was a dog.

Boy, my life was weird; I was in a dog rescue in Florida, playing fetch with a Vietnamese pot-bellied piglet.

I asked what would happen to Nemo. As luck would have it, the aunt of one of the staff kept Vietnamese pot-bellied pigs as pets. Her favourite pig recently died and she jumped at the chance to become Nemo's new owner.

This predominantly canine rescue centre had a good adoption set-up with interviews, home visits and common sense. However, their rehoming figures were low. I put that down to two things: a lack of adopters and turning down too many of the few they had.

Rehoming is a fine balance and at the other end of the spectrum to North Shore's 'sell, sell, sell' policy, some animal welfare organisations are too strict. Misguided good intentions and an overprotectiveness generated by genuine love for the animals can lead to no one ever being good enough to adopt.

During my week, I participated in every aspect of life at The Humane Society including cleaning out the kennels. Having spent recent times behind a desk at Battersea, I had forgotten what a good cardio-vascular workout this provided; however, this wasn't my main concern. Many of the dogs were pit bull terriers and I was a little reticent about going in with some of them. I couldn't let my American colleagues know how lily-livered I was so I bit the bullet – hoping that was the only thing to get bitten, and got scrubbing.

The most interesting experience I had whilst I was there was accompanying Mary-Lou on a school visit to educate Florida's mini dog owners. Mary-Lou was a large woman with lots of make-up and big red hair. She was also the head of education and like most Americans was friendly and outgoing.

The school was a fair distance away but we made a stop en route. We'd only been on the road for ten minutes before pulling up outside Krispy Kreme donuts which was drawing Mary-Lou in like a moth to the flame. She asked me if I wanted anything but considering we'd both eaten breakfast only 20 minutes before, I declined. Mary-Lou came back with three of the sickliest donuts I'd ever seen and a coffee the size of the Chrysler building.

The school was in a rundown part of town and the kids were predominantly African-American. We were giving a talk to a class of 30 six-year-olds. The children sat quietly and listened attentively. Mary-Lou asked how many of them had dogs to which about half the class put their hands up. When she asked what type of dogs, nearly all had guarding or fighting breeds. I suppose this was indicative of the security necessary in a rough part of town.

One little boy told us how a neighbour had poisoned his dog over a dispute involving money. Another told us the police had taken his dog away for attacking people in the street and another how his uncle's dog had been shot by a burglar. If these were their experiences of dog ownership and responsibility, Mary-Lou had her work cut out and I wondered if our message would ever get through.

The rehoming department was also of great interest to me. One rule steadfastly upheld by Battersea is not to rehome dogs to live outside. Aside from dogs that go on to join the forces, Battersea dogs are rehomed as pets and as such live as part of the family unit. Climate conditions in the UK are another factor that favours indoor living but in Florida the opposite applies. Most dogs are rehomed to live in the backyard, which is considered fine as long as the animal has shelter from the sun and water to drink. The main stipulation is that the animal is not chained. It was interesting to discover that such a stringent rule in one country is business as usual in another.

My week in Florida went as fast as the local food outlets and before I knew it, I was packing my bags and heading off to my next destination: Dallas, Texas.

We flew over the vast salt flats near Salt Lake City and arrived in Dallas on a scorching Saturday morning. I was to spend the next week at the Dallas SPCA, although my overnight accommodation was a little more upmarket than a kennel and I checked into the local Holiday Inn.

I wasn't due at work until the Monday so I spent the Sunday being a tourist. I found the infamous Texas School Book Depository from where President Kennedy was assassinated, now a museum dedicated to the tragic events that unfolded on 22 November 1963.

The various artefacts, including television newsreels, newspaper articles, clothing and of course the famous Zapruder cinefilm, made for an enthralling exhibition.

I had begun my tour at 11 a.m. I looked at my watch and was shocked to see it read 4 p.m. I'd never spent this many hours at a museum before; my mother would be proud.

I left the exhibition and took a walk to the grassy knoll on Dealey Plaza where one of the many conspiracy theories placed an accessory. It was very easy to get swept up in the history and drama of it all. The road looked exactly as it did back then and I sat on that bank imagining what it was like to be there when it happened.

After the longest time, I gathered myself together, returned to my hotel and prepared for work the next day.

The shelter was only a ten-minute walk from the hotel but the temperatures were merciless. Once again, I was a red, sweaty ball of frizz, not exactly the first impression I wanted to proffer. That said, my first impression of the shelter was not what I had in mind either. Amongst the signage on the door was a picture of a gun with a line through it. Oh well, I suppose, if anything, at least firearms were discouraged here.

I walked in and gave my name. Almost immediately a large man, approximately nine months pregnant and with a handle-bar moustache, greeted me with a slap on the back. Mert was larger than life and laugh-a-minute. He took great pride in his shelter and was delighted to show me around.

The SPCA of Texas faced more challenges than the other two rescues I'd visited. Firstly there was the demographic of the location. People were much poorer and the area was far more densely populated. Animals seemed more dispensable here and the figures of unwanted dogs received by the SPCA were startling.

Like North Shore and The Humane Society, the SPCA had many great animal welfare programmes in place; however, in some ways it was trying to run before it could walk. For example, although the education department had an impressive offensive, back then the kennels seemed cramped, dirty, over-crowded and falling apart compared to what I had been used to.

In the main, the dogs were just the same as those at Battersea. Puppies were ten-a-penny as were the faithful black-and-tan mongrels, with pit bull terriers and Chow Chows vying for third place. There was one notable exception to the canine similarities – a trio of baby racoons. They had been found by the side of a busy road, their mother nowhere in sight and the SPCA were caring for them until the appropriate authorities could take them in.

This was turning out to be a surprising trip, with pot-bellied pigs in Florida and racoons in Texas, and the very next day Mert announced he had another surprise for me. First we had to take care of business and check out a man who had adopted a pit bull terrier the previous month. A neighbour had contacted the shelter to report that he was keeping the dog on a chain with no water and no shelter from the blistering sun.

I felt a mixture of excitement and nerves. I kept replaying in my mind something I'd once seen on the television. An animal warden in America had come to seize a pit bull from a house but the owner set the dog on her as soon as she arrived. It grabbed the warden's arm and wouldn't let go, ragging her as though she were a doll. In the end, it took a bullet to get the dog off.

I tried to put this out of my mind and concentrate on the Texan landscape but this tactic didn't help as most of the hour-long drive was over dry, brown, flat terrain with not much to look at. I did get a thrill, however, when I saw my first oil pump. The enormous praying mantis machinery bobbed up and down just like in the opening scenes from *Dallas*, my favourite TV show from the eighties.

We arrived at the house and parked around the back. The owner wasn't home which was good because it meant we could see for sure if the neighbour was right. That, and the owner couldn't set the dog on us.

We peered over the fence to find the dog asleep under a tree, resting his head on a pink toy bunny rabbit. There was no chain in sight and the dog had a shaded doghouse and plenty of water to drink. At that moment a van pulled up outside the front.

A large man wearing a Stetson and cowboy boots and carrying a brown paper bag got out of the truck, slamming the door behind him. I held my breath; my radar for impending doom stirred. The dog lifted his head and his tail began thumping the ground.

'Diesel?' he boomed in a long southern drawl. 'Diesel, Daddy's home! Where's Daddy's best boy?'

Mert and I looked at each other. This man

certainly didn't sound like the hard, uncaring beast described by his neighbour. We watched through two small holes in the fence as the man entered the backyard and was almost knocked off his feet by an over-zealous dog that obviously adored him. Through dog-slobber kisses and excited leaps, the man produced from his bag a bright pink squeaky toy, and so began a game of fetch.

Mert and I left, satisfied this was a malicious call made by someone who obviously had a beef with Diesel's owner.

It was now lunchtime and a full 45 minutes since Mert had last eaten. We stopped at his favourite haunt: a rib shack. I said I'd have whatever Mert was having and five minutes later an entire cow was placed before me.

Between mouthfuls, Mert and I chatted about dogs, our respective families and places of work. He told me all about his wife who drove a red convertible and was 'the most gorgeous woman in town'. He produced a photo from his wallet. She was the spitting image of Dolly Parton.

After I had consumed a meagre one-sixteenth of my cow, and Mert had polished his off piranha-style, he told me it was time for my surprise. I hoped it was a crane to lift me out of my seat and deposit me into the car. Instead, half an hour later we pulled up outside the most famous ranch in the world.

Southfork ranch was exactly as I remembered it

from hours glued to the TV. The sun shone in the deep blue sky and a dozen majestic tan-and-white bulls grazed on the ranch's vivid green grass. The house made up the glorious centrepiece and the only thing I was a little disappointed with was the swimming pool. I had clear memories of Bobby Ewing ploughing up and down this pool but it was about a third of the size it looked on the television. The tour guide told us that whenever there was a swimming scene, the actors had weights dragging behind them so they didn't reach the other end of the pool before the take had finished.

Inside the house, the gun that shot JR stood in pride of place, secured in a gold and glass cabinet. I made poor Mert photograph me as I posed with just about everything and had to remind myself once again that I was not on holiday.

The remainder of my week was spent as a member of the SPCA staff, cleaning out the kennels, taking in unwanted dogs, assessing and rehoming. It was just like home from home, only it wasn't home and after two months away I felt ready to return to south-west London and an elderly mongrel with bad breath and a wonky heart.

My time in the USA had come to an end. I'd travelled to three different states and seen three very different rescues. We'd learned much from each other and our respective organisations would reap the benefits. I'd also met some wonderful people, visited some amazing places and tasted real life in America.

I returned home, dumped my bags, jumped in the car and headed for north-west London. I was supposed to be picking Gus up from Ali the next day but I couldn't wait. This dog had well and truly wormed his way into my heart and mind. With all his doggy mates for company, he probably hadn't given me a second thought for the past two months but I had missed him desperately.

I called Ali.

'Hi, it's me. I'm on my way to yours.'

'Hey, welcome back! I thought you weren't coming until tomorrow. We're not at home, we're in the park,' she said.

'I'll meet you there.'

Being the good dog owner she is, Ali doesn't just take her dogs to the local green for exercise; she takes them to the massive Fryent Country Park for their daily constitutional. In my enthusiasm to see my boy, I hadn't thought about logistics or geography.

For the next hour I trudged around the muddy country park, jet-lagged to the eyeballs. Every time I saw a black dog my heart leapt but when I realised it wasn't him I wondered if I was hallucinating, like some weary traveller lost in the Sahara.

I was practically on my knees when, in the

distance, I saw a party of two humans and a gaggle of dogs. Yes, it was Mr Taylor, Ali, their dogs and my boy.

I called him. Everyone in their party looked around except for my cloth-eared dog. Ali waved and Tessa began trotting over. I called him again. This time, in recognition of my voice, he looked up. When Gus started bolting towards a tree stump that some wag had put a traffic cone on top of, I realised he badly needed glasses.

I called him again and he changed trajectory. I had to wave my arms up and down like a lunatic in order for him to lock on to me but it worked. When he finally saw me he morphed into a grey-hound. Ears down and at full stride, he raced towards me like a speeding bullet, tongue hanging out, smiling.

Approximately six feet from me, Gus became airborne as he hurled himself into my arms. I'd never seen him this excited before. I didn't know he had it in him.

At that moment I decided they could keep New York. If it came to a choice between the Big Apple and the apple of my eye, I knew which one I'd pick.

# CHAPTER 13

# THE FAME GAME

Why go all the way to Hollywood for a day's celebrity spotting when you can just come down to Battersea Dogs Home – especially now that the latest must-have accessory is a handbag dog? At the world's most famous dog's home you'll see the world's most famous stars strut through the door, all glitz and glamour, only to find their egos quickly and quietly extinguished by Battersea's hard-working staff who have more important things to worry about than whether the paparazzi is snapping their best side.

Some celebrities think adopting a homeless little wretch from a dog's home will improve their public image. This may be the case and if they have a genuine love of dogs and can meet the rehoming criteria by offering a stable, loving, permanent home to one, then it's a win-win situation. If they can't, they will be told in no uncertain terms.

When I first started working at Battersea Dogs Home, a female rock star had been turned down for a dog on the grounds that her lifestyle was too unstable for a rescue dog. The rehomer in question didn't realise who she was, which I suppose allowed her to come to an unbiased decision based on the facts presented to her.

Indeed, when a soft-spoken American walked into Jade's interview room to offer his home to a Battersea dog, no one could blame her for not knowing who he was. He was an ordinary-looking man, middle-aged, with dark receding hair and brown eyes. The only thing that might have given him away was the expensive suit he was wearing, not that Jade noticed things like that. She'd be more likely to notice dog hair on people's clothes and mentally award them brownie points.

Jade was consumed by her love for dogs and there was little room for anything else, least of all celebrity. She introduced herself to the gentleman and began the interview.

'What is your occupation?' she asked.

'Oh, I'm an actor,' he said in his quiet American accent.

'Are you aware of the financial costs involved in keeping a dog? Feeding, vaccinations, pet insurance, boarding kennels, flea treatment and worming? Battersea will of course neuter and microchip the dog which will save you approximately £125 but do you feel you are able to meet all other financial costs for the duration of the dog's life?' she asked.

He said he felt that he would be able to and they proceeded.

Judging by the man's enthusiasm for his previous dogs and the way he spoke about hounds in general, Jade identified him as a genuine dog lover with a good dog-owning history. He had chosen a little black mongrel that she felt would suit his lifestyle and experience levels well. After reading him the dog's assessment, Jade walked the man to one of the meeting rooms in the Kent building and asked him to wait whilst she went to get the dog he had chosen.

I had just taken Gus to the veterinary section for his booster vaccination and yearly MOT. As the needle went in, Gus let out a squeal – most un-general-like behaviour – and proceeded to sulk. Shaun gave him a Schmacko and a clean bill of health – heart murmur notwithstanding.

On returning Gus to the PR office, I walked past the ground-floor meeting room, glancing through the door's glass porthole as I went. I did a double take. Is that Kevin Spacey? There was no one around to confirm or deny this. I had another look and just at that moment he looked back at me. I didn't want to seem like a stalker so ducked below porthole level.

'What on earth are you doing?' Jade asked, looking down at me and struggling to contain a wriggly youngster in her arms. At the sight of another dog, Gus forgot all about his vaccination and instantly perked up.

'Is that your customer in there?' I asked.

'Yes, and what a terribly nice man he is,' she replied

312

as only Jade could and began telling me the story of his last dog. I cut her off mid sentence.

'Yes, yes, but is he Kevin Spacey?' I asked.

'Kevin who?' Jade said.

'Kevin Spacey.'

Jade looked blank.

'You know, *The Usual Suspects, American Beauty, Seven.*'

Not getting anywhere I pulled his form out of her back pocket.

'Oh my God, it *is* him, it's Kevin bloody Spacey.'

Looking singularly unimpressed, Jade snatched the form back and returned to her customer, mumbling 'never heard of him'.

Jade walked into the meeting room and when she gently placed the little black dog on the floor, she knew she had been spot on in her character analysis of the man. He immediately knelt down and slowly put his hand out for the dog to sniff. Having had rescue dogs before, he knew only too well the damage inflicted upon some of them by previous owners and that only a softly softly approach would do when meeting new people.

This little scrap obviously hadn't had it too hard. She bypassed his hand and bounded straight into him. Within two leaps she was on top of him, her tail wagging furiously, her tongue in his ears. He was enchanted and reciprocated by throwing himself on the floor, the two of them cavorting around together like old pals.

I watched in wonderment as the quiet American

superstar rolled around a filthy floor at Battersea Dogs Home with a small black mongrel from the streets of London.

Jade took the two of them to see a veterinary nurse for the dog's final check-up before allowing them to go home. The dog was given a clean bill of health and Jade escorted her customer up to the shop, not something rehomers usually did. Having discovered she had a celebrity on her hands, Jade made him buy as much as she could sell him from the Battersea shop, including one of everything for the dog and a Battersea Dogs Home sweatshirt for him.

A few years prior to this, another busy Saturday was unfolding at Battersea Dogs Home and the rehoming waiting area was beginning to fill up. Retired couples sat patiently alongside families with young kids, trying to avoid sticky little fingers and snotty noses. Dogs sat uncomplainingly with their owners who had come to find a canine companion for them to play with (whether they wanted one or not). They must have wondered where the hell their owners had brought them to – some sort of cross between the vets and a lunatic asylum. If they were ex-Battersea dogs, they probably thought they were being returned. Having successfully adopted one dog from Battersea, customers often came back looking for a second. Gluttons for punishment, some might say; heroes, I'd call them.

It's true what they say about the Great British public; they love to queue. And thank God, because as far as weekends at Battersea went, they'd be queuing for a long time. Having dutifully filled out their forms, they'd sit there and wait for up to three hours for the chance to enrich their lives by becoming a member of the seven-million-strong dog owner's club of Great Britain.

A DVD explaining the rehoming process played on a loop in the rehoming reception. It was presented by me, which really flummoxed people when I flung open the doors and shouted for the next number to come through. On this particular afternoon, however, it was I who did the double take. I called the next number and Paula Yates stood up with three of her daughters.

It is a strange feeling when you unexpectedly meet someone famous. For a split second you think they are friends or acquaintances you haven't seen for a while. I have an appalling memory for faces and when I see someone I recognise but don't remember, I tend to overcompensate for my bad memory by greeting them like long-lost friends. Paula was no exception. 'Hi, how are you, God it's been ages,' I said.

After embarrassing myself for a whole hammy five minutes with this routine, I realised that Paula wasn't a forgotten acquaintance but someone from the telly. She must have been thinking '. . . and people think *I'm* mad!'

I invited her into my interview room, introduced

myself and began the interview. She was after a cat and her set-up was certainly favourable for one of Battersea's feline guests. She had a house with a garden that backed on to other gardens, good previous cat-owning history and a nanny who was at home all day.

Like all children, Paula's were animated at the prospect of owning a pet. I think the two older girls were Fifi Trixibelle and Peaches Honeyblossom but there was no mistaking the little one. She was the spitting image of her father, and I knew straight away that this sweet-natured, shy little girl was Tiger Lily, daughter of the late Michael Hutchence.

Paula was eccentric but no more or less so than other members of the public who had successfully gone on to rehome Battersea dogs and cats. I arranged a home visit, which came back with a thumbs up, so the family became the proud owners of a pair of sibling Battersea cats.

The follow-up home visit also came back with a thumbs up – satisfied customers, both two-legged and four.

When Paula died my thoughts of course went out to her daughters. First and foremost I prayed for them and when it was decided the girls would live with Bob, I also prayed Bob's retriever wouldn't eat the cats.

My promotion to Rehoming Manager meant spending weekdays sitting behind my desk, but at weekends I could be found on the frontline with the rehomers, interviewing the hordes of people waiting to rehome a dog or cat.

One particular Sunday, I was grabbing some lunch in my office, checking emails and phone messages, when I received a call from Carol in reception. She informed me that an Eighties pop star was in the rehoming reception performing t'ai chi to the entire waiting room of around 70 people. Under normal circumstances, a statement like that would have made the recipient ask the caller to repeat themselves. I'm not sure that normal circumstances ever applied at Battersea Dogs Home, so with a resigned sigh I threw the rest of my sandwich to Lolly and told Carol I'd be right down.

I arrived to find exactly what she had described: the former pop star performing t'ai chi to a packed waiting room, smoking a fag with another behind his ear. It was well after his heyday and he was looking a little the worse for wear. Time had not been kind to him but he still had incredible eyes and cheekbones.

The people sitting in the waiting area had mixed reactions to what they were seeing: some showed great interest at having an ex-pop star in their midst but others just laughed at him. I felt it best to get him out of there and took him into a vacant interview room. I explained that smoking was not permitted to which he made no attempt to extinguish the cigarette. He stared at me for about ten seconds. I stared back. I'm not sure whether he was weighing up his options, hoping to get one last drag in or just being dramatic, but a few seconds later he stubbed it out and we began the interview.

I glanced over his form and under 'name' he'd written his stage name rather than his real name. Maybe he'd changed it by deed poll but as the interview progressed it struck me that he was trying to hang on to his past celebrity.

He had been to see the dogs before having his interview and had fallen in love with a Staffordshire bull terrier cross. She was a five-year-old, brought into Battersea by her previous owner for separation-related problems. She became so distressed, whenever she was left alone, that she'd start gnawing her own paws. Self-mutilation is a severe form of separation anxiety and the rehabilitation department had been working with her for many weeks. The problem had improved dramatically, but Betty needed an owner experienced enough to continue Rehab's work.

Our ex-pop star had had dogs previously but none with such severe behaviour problems and Betty was not the right dog for him. The interview lasted longer than usual because I wanted time to establish what was going on inside his head. This was a tough case. He was obviously an eccentric but many eccentric people make fantastic dog owners and relate to animals far better than to humans.

Having interviewed thousands of people over many years, I could usually decide whether my interviewee was sane enough to own a dog or barking mad enough to be turned away. I once interviewed Mr Sunshine Bongo, who fell into the latter category. He came into Battersea dressed only in a sheet, carrying a mango that he tried to make a telephone call on. I also interviewed a lady dressed as a cat, and the king of England who came in complete with crown and sceptre made out of cardboard, toilet roll and cotton wool. They weren't bad either – perhaps he should have applied for a job on *Blue Peter*.

With this fellow, however, I just couldn't decide. This case needed further investigation. I explained that someone from Battersea would come to see him at his home and tried to bring the interview to a close, but he liked a chat. An hour later we said our goodbyes.

The home visitor called me just after he left the former pop star's house. He said it was like stepping back in time. There were posters and memorabilia everywhere. The house had a back garden, was clean and tidy and there was more than enough space for a dog. As much as he would like to be, our ex-pop star was no longer in the limelight so had time on his hands. He was still involved in the music business but also spent a lot of time at home.

Like me, the home visitor had spent longer than usual with him to try and ascertain a full picture.

319

He decided that he was indeed eccentric, but met all of Battersea's criteria for rehoming a dog. Battersea still reserved the right to turn people down if it was felt that the risk factor was too high; Battersea dogs and cats had been through enough trauma already and stability was what they needed more than anything.

Based on the facts presented to us, both the home visitor and I decided that the risk of things going wrong was low. How wrong could we be?

The very next morning the papers were full of stories of our ex-pop star being drawn into an argument in a pub which had become heated enough for the landlord to throw him out. Ten minutes later he returned and lobbed a car engine part through the window. He was arrested and two days later committed to a psychiatric unit.

Up until then, I'd prided myself on my ability to judge people's characters but, as one supportive colleague reminded me, you can't get it right every single time.

Well, if you're going to get it wrong, might as well do it in style. The most important thing wasn't that my pride was bruised; it was that this aging rocker never took home a Battersea dog.

Kenneth Branagh did manage to rehome a Battersea dog but got slightly more than he bargained for in the process. He came to Battersea with his friend and fellow actor, Derek Jacobi, who was looking for a dog at some point in the near future. They were both charming and after interviewing Derek, I turned my attention to Kenneth.

He lived in a large house with his retired mother and also had the option of taking the dog to work with him should its temperament lend itself to film sets. The house came with live-in staff and plenty of secure grounds for the dog to run around in. What more could a dog want than a big, safe garden, someone at home to be with and plenty of love and affection?

Kenneth had done everything back to front and when he walked into the Home, went straight up to look at the dogs. All signage requested that people had their interview before seeing the dogs to prevent them falling for one that might not be suitable. Kenneth had fallen head over heels for a small middle-aged Jack Russell cross. He gave me her number and I pulled her details up on the computer, hoping she wasn't the worst-behaved dog in the Home. As luck would have it she wasn't; he had picked a winner. Her name was Suzy and although she was little, she was feisty. She came into Battersea as a stray, picked up from Blackheath on the edge of south-east London. We guessed the reason she was 'let go' was because of her crabby, cantankerous nature towards other dogs.

Ali and Ann had assessed her and carried out extensive tests with other dogs. They decided she wasn't the type to go looking for a fight but neither would she tolerate other dogs in her face. Perfect.

Mr Branagh had a house with acres of secure grounds and no other dogs in sight.

The meeting between canine and human went swimmingly and he adored her. He gave her a Schmacko and in return she brought him a squeaky pork chop. I was witnessing a scene from *Romeo and Juliet*, just with more fur and squeak.

It was a weekday and very quiet at the Home. Suzy had met no other dogs whilst Kenneth was getting to know her but as he waited with her at reception to pay, Steve and his bulldog, Bertie, walked past.

At that moment it was as if little Suzy had changed into her Exocet missile costume (complete with hat and goggles), put on her rocket launcher boots and lit the fuse. Her ears went right back, pinned flat to that little head, her bark – which no one had heard all morning – sounded like a crazy mezzo-soprano screech, and she jumped around in all directions on the end of the lead like a kangaroo on crack. Kenneth went pale, I thought Derek Jacobi was going to faint, Steve and Bertie jumped out of their skin and I put my head in my hands.

I gave the poor man the option of changing his mind or at least deferring until we had carried out further tests on Suzy's incontrovertible personality disorder. But in true 'the show must go on' style and once he was over the initial shock, Kenneth said he too had days like that and he thought Suzy and he would get along famously.

A few months later Kenneth appeared on the front cover of Battersea's quarterly magazine, *Paws*. He was in full costume on the set of his latest film, *Shackleton*, proudly holding Suzy, who was behaving impeccably. By a strange coincidence, the huskies that accompanied the real Shackleton on one of his expeditions were kennelled at Battersea before setting out. Here's hoping Suzy never met any of the huskies on set; Shackleton had enough problems to deal with.

Working at Battersea Dogs Home certainly had its perks, as we found out one sunny afternoon when Robbie Williams came in. He was looking for a friend that could provide unconditional love with no hidden agenda. Although many of the kennel staff (predominantly female and in their late teens/early twenties) offered themselves up for the role, Robbie was looking for a four-legged friend.

As Robbie walked through reception to the interview room, the entire female staff of Battersea Dogs Home lined the way. Our security man, whose day usually consisted of throwing out drunks and stopping kids from teasing the dogs, suddenly found himself having to control most of his own colleagues.

Robbie didn't act like the megastar he is. Perhaps he knew that, for once, money and fame weren't enough to get him what he wanted. He was applying to an organisation that rated the happiness of one of London's strays above his.

He filled out the interview form, which read like most other famous people's; the dog would go everywhere with him and on the odd occasion it couldn't, 'staff' would be there to look after it. The dog would have acres of secure ground to run around in and would want for nothing.

Ordinarily I wouldn't be so crass, but being a big Robbie fan I couldn't resist asking him for his autograph. He duly obliged (and I don't just mean by signing that he was over 18 on the interview form).

After the interview, Robbie, accompanied by his mum, looked around the kennels which for once didn't smell of disinfectant and odour eliminator but more of perfume and hairspray. Sadly the efforts of excited kennel maids to hook a pop star were wasted that day. Robbie fell neither for the charms of a kennel maid nor the brown eyes of one lucky hound and left empty-handed.

One rock star, whose success eclipsed most others, had always wanted to come to Battersea Dogs Home but was afraid it would be too distressing. Ringo Starr and his wife, Barbara Bach, are one of millions of couples in the UK who are dotty about dogs. One of the Battersea trustees knew Ringo and, dismissing his fears as nonsense, arranged for him and his wife to have a guided tour of the Home. Their guide, unbeknown to me, was to be me.

It was another one of those extraordinary

moments during an otherwise ordinary day, when I picked up my office phone and heard, 'Can you give Ringo Starr a tour of the Home, please?' uttered back at me.

'Sure,' I replied. 'Can he hang on for five minutes? Someone's just put a Schnauzer in my office and it's thrown up everywhere.'

Five minutes after my right hand was clearing up Schnauzer vomit, it was shaking the hand of music royalty.

Ringo and Barbara were very friendly and down to earth. I could tell immediately they were genuine animal lovers as he enthusiastically told me all about their dogs, cats and horses.

As we walked through the kennels, Ringo removed his obligatory rock-star sunglasses so as not to frighten the dogs and bent to gently stroke the dogs through the kennel bars. He asked about their stories and couldn't resist going in for a cuddle with some of them.

Both Ringo and his wife were extremely impressed by the scale and professionalism of the Home. Ringo said he'd almost declined the invitation, imagining Battersea Dogs Home to resemble a scene from a depressing Dickens novel. Instead he was delighted and relieved to find such a happy place, full of well-looked-after and adored dogs en route to a better life.

As I watched Ringo wrestle with a young and unruly Rhodesian ridgeback, I looked into his eyes and wondered about all the things he'd seen and done, all the people he'd met, all the memories he had.

Ringo Starr was the only person whose presence I was a little star-struck in. With the exception of Elvis Presley, it didn't get much bigger than the Beatles. They were the trail-blazers who redefined the music world and whose popularity is almost unequalled.

Ringo hadn't lost his touch and was proving just as popular with this outsize teenage hound. The dog didn't know or care that this man was an ex-Beatle, he was just having fun wrestling him to the ground and redefining his Gucci sunglasses.

The general feeling amongst Battersea staff was that if they had to deal with a celebrity and all the nonsense that went with them, at least let it be a big one or a nice one. Of all the celebrities I met during my dog days at Battersea, Jemima Khan was without exception the nicest.

Her people called Battersea's people (me) to say that she was interested in adopting a Battersea dog. I told them I would have to speak directly to Jemima in order to find out, amongst other things, what type of dog she was looking for. Five minutes later she called me and even from the other end of a phone, I instantly liked her. She was humble, unassuming, down to earth and really friendly. She had grown up with many dogs, some of whom were rescue dogs, so was also refreshingly knowledgeable.

Jemima was open to any age group and type of dog but had two young sons who, like most three- and five-year-olds, were into everything, so asked that the new dog be good with children. She had a large house and secure garden and there was someone at home all day.

I recommended a puppy but explained to Jemima that the puppies currently in the nursery were reserved for people who had already been through the interview process. She would have to be patient and wait for me to call her when one came in. Jemima replied that she fully understood and the most important thing was to wait for the right dog: music to my cars.

About a month later a drunken man came swaying into the Home holding a can of extra-strong cider in one hand and a yelping 12-week-old puppy in the other. He practically threw the little black-and-tan puppy at a kennel maid, cursing that while he was at the pub the dog had messed in his house. We couldn't get his signature on the transfer-of-ownership papers quickly enough.

The dog was pretty traumatised. We settled him down in the nursery and gave him some food, which he wolfed down. His name was Max but that name was probably only ever used in the context of yelling and abuse. The puppy would no doubt have a bad association with it so with the start of his new life, we decided to rename him Scruff.

Another puppy had come in that morning so we put her and Scruff in a playpen together with some squeaky toys. Within five minutes they were jumping all over each other and it was as if Scruff's previous owner had never existed. However, things are never quite that simple.

A few days later, Jo, the nursery kennel maid was playing with the pups and all was well until Shaun the vet walked in. At over six feet tall, to a puppy Shaun must have seemed like a giant. Scruff took one look at him, wet himself and ran into the corner, shaking. Most of Battersea's staff were female so Shaun was the first man that Scruff had seen since his unpleasant owner had brought him in. Picking up some treats and avoiding eye contact with Scruff, Shaun sat down on the floor next to him. Scruff's eyes grew bigger and bigger and he pushed himself back into the corner as far as the corner would go. Shaun didn't pressure him; he just sat there quietly talking to Scruff, all the while avoiding eye contact.

After a while, Shaun threw a treat to Scruff which he pounced on and gobbled up. Scruff's love of food would make the trusting process a whole lot easier. Still not looking him in the eye, Shaun held a treat in his hand for Scruff to take. Little by little, the puppy edged over to Shaun's hand but he backed off every time it came to taking the treat. Shaun spoke to Scruff in a very soft voice and after 15 minutes Scruff took the treat from Shaun's hand. He then began to rub Scruff's chest all the while looking away from him.

After a little trust had been established through physical contact, Shaun used some more food to slowly gain eye contact with Scruff. Within 30 minutes of first walking into the nursery, Shaun had won Scruff over with food, patience and a silly voice.

Over the course of the next week, the male members of staff (outnumbered ten to one by females) were asked to come in and socialise Scruff. With kindness, patience and of course food, Scruff was no longer terrified of men. Rather than seeing them as big scary monsters to be terrified of, he now saw them as big friendly treat dispensers.

All Scruff was missing was a good home to go to; one phone call to Jemima Khan soon rectified that. I asked Jemima to bring her children in to meet Scruff. Not only did she comply with this request, she also brought her mother, Lady Annabel Goldsmith, in.

I took Jemima, the kids and Granny to a meeting room and before I brought Scruff in, I told them everything they needed to know about him; his difficult short life so far and his previous anxiety around men. Lady Annabel Goldsmith was a well-known dog lover who had many dogs of her own; if I thought Jemima was experienced around dogs, her mother put us both in the shade with her wealth of knowledge.

The children were as well behaved and as attentive as youngsters of that age can be and I just knew Scruff was going to be okay with this family. Even though I was talking to people who probably knew more than I did, they were never impatient, pushy or superior. Jemima listened intently to everything I had to say and asked lots of questions. She told me how excited they had all been and how grateful she was to me for finding Scruff for her family.

Many families like Jemima's came to Battersea to open their hearts and their homes to a dog that was down on its luck. They wanted to take it home, look after it and give it a better life. I was always humbled when anyone, be they prince or pauper, said how grateful they were and how lucky they felt to be entrusted with a Battersea dog. Surely, we were the ones who should be grateful.

It was time to bring Scruff in but before I left the room, Granny gave the kids a stern talking to about not rushing up to the puppy when it came in. They were to sit on the floor and let him come to them.

I opened the nursery door to find Scruff jumping all over Erik, one of the rehomers who'd popped in to help with Scruff's socialising. It looked to me like Scruff was well and truly cured. I scooped him up and took him to the meeting room. I walked in and put him on the floor. He made a beeline for the kids who were much more his size but Lady Goldsmith intercepted him, picking him up in a no-nonsense kind of way.

'Well, let's have a look at you then,' she said. He licked her cheek. 'Yes, you'll do nicely,' she decided, putting him back on the floor. Jemima had a soft, gentle air about her and crouched down to stroke Scruff, speaking softly to him. He climbed into her arms and just lay there with his head on her shoulder, looking at her with his big brown puppy eyes. They say dogs have a sixth sense about people and Scruff looked as though he knew she was kindness personified. At that moment I'd have gladly given her Gus, let alone this lucky pup.

About a week later I had a card from Jemima. It was a custom-made postcard of her two boys in stripy T-shirts, weeing against a brick wall! In the card she said that Scruff was doing fine and everyone loved him. She once again expressed her thanks and gratitude to me and to Battersea; 'a wonderful institution', as she put it.

Battersea Dogs Home never really needed to court the press. Seeing TV cameras, journalists with microphones and photographers at the Home was a common occurrence. What was less common, however, was when celebrities turned up with their own TV cameras.

Geri Halliwell wanted to give a home to a Battersea dog and at the same time was filming her own fly-on-the-wall documentary. She came in with George Michael who was extremely sensible and knowledgeable about dogs, imploring

Geri to choose carefully. She was scatty, emotional and wanted to 'take 'em all 'ome'.

Being an experienced dog owner, George had come along to advise Geri, but as she proceeded to pick every dog in sight, all he could do was raise his eyes heavenward and shrug his shoulders. He need not have worried. Once we had interviewed her, we knew it was going to be a case of us choosing the right dog for her rather than her choosing the cutest dog.

Geri gave it a pretty good try though. She chose about ten dogs, all of whom were small, long-haired and beautiful, but about half of them had come into Battersea for being over-dominant with their owners, also known as small-dog syndrome.

Small dogs often like to think of themselves as leaders of the pack, especially if they've been spoilt, which can lead to serious confrontation. Knowing that Geri would spoil any dog, the dominant ones were immediately ruled out. If one of these little darlings had gone to live with Geri, I would have laid odds on a bite before the first week was up.

Grooming is an essential part of any long-haired dog's routine. To give an inexperienced owner a long-haired dog that hated being groomed would be insane. Due to her lack of experience and the specialised homes that these dogs needed, Geri was turned down for each one. On the up side, after a long and thorough interview, we recognised that she would give the right dog a great home.

From the start, Geri had said she'd like a small dog that she could take everywhere with her. Most rescue dogs would probably have a nervous breakdown if thrust into the limelight of Geri Halliwell's world. Her new dog would have to cope with coming into contact with a multitude of people, environments and situations on a regular basis. Any dog of Geri Halliwell's would need to have an extremely sound temperament and be able to adapt to every eventuality. Puppies do just that and as luck would have it, a shih-tzu puppy had been brought in the previous day. The fact that it was a small breed was a bonus.

When she met the dog she burst into tears. Even George Michael, a confirmed Labrador man, went a little weak at the knees. The puppy's long fur was as soft as a feather duster. It was sticking out in every direction as if he'd put his paw into an electric socket. At first it was difficult to tell which end was which but on closer inspection his little curly tail could be differentiated from his snub nose.

To begin with he was sleepy, floppy and cuddly and yawned a long puppy-breath yawn, but when George Michael squeaked a squeaky toy, the puppy shot into life, zigzagging around the room trying to seize control of the screaming plastic.

Geri picked him up; he could fit into the palm of her hand. This was a done deal but before being allowed to take him home, she was given the same intensive lesson in grooming, feeding, exercising, training and general dog care that all Battersea's customers go through.

The rest is history and now whenever you see a picture of Geri Halliwell in the tabloids, she is usually accompanied by Harry, her Battersea shih-tzu.

A few days later Geri phoned up to give us a progress report. She was so delighted with Harry she said, 'He's marvellous and I feel so lucky, how can I ever thank you?'

'Well,' I said, 'two tickets to the Brit Awards tonight wouldn't go amiss, thanks, Geri.'

I was of course joking but there's no harm in asking. What did I have to lose? She could only, as I was fully expecting her to, say no.

To my amazement that afternoon, two tickets to the Brit Awards were couriered over to Battersea so Steph and I donned our glad rags and headed for Earl's Court.

The note attached to the tickets said that a coach would pick us up in a car park, ten minutes away from the venue. A bit strange we thought but went along with it anyway.

The coach was waiting just as the note had said it would be. We boarded and were met by a wave of squealing, giggling, over-excited teenage girls from a local school for the performing arts. We looked at each other, had a closer look at the tickets and realised they were for the mosh pit. The mosh pit? We thought we'd be on a table with Geri, quaffing champagne and consuming fine food. But no, we were in the mosh pit, an unruly den at the front of the stage, where minors excitedly throw themselves around, screaming at anything that moves.

By now, the excitement on the coach had reached fever pitch, with renditions of chart songs past and present being belted out. A grinning child sitting in front of us turned around and, realising we were far too old to be from any performing arts school, asked us how we got our tickets.

'We're friends of Geri Halliwell,' I replied with all the nonchalance I could muster, resulting in a wide-eyed gasp from the girl and a kick under the seat from Steph. From that moment on, we were the A-list on that coach.

As soon as we walked into the venue, our mosh pit snobbery disappeared. The set was stunning and the atmosphere electric. We could barely contain our excitement. We could see the music glitterati having dinner at their tables, the champagne flowing. I even spotted the Gallagher brothers, Coldplay, Destiny's Child and Fatboy Slim but they could keep their tables and their food and drink. Suddenly, from our mosh pit, we realised just how close we were to the stage.

Pulling age rank, Steph and I muscled our way to the front, leaving sparkles and lip-gloss flying in our wake. And then, without warning, the stage exploded into light. Indoor fireworks spewed everywhere and the opening bars of 'Rock DJ' hit us like a juggernaut. The bass thumped through every sinew of our bodies and the entire pit (including Steph and me) screamed in anticipation of Robbie's arrival. He didn't disappoint. Fifteen seconds later he was standing in front of us and, love him or loathe him, the man has stage presence. He set the place on fire and had everyone, including many of the stuffed shirts, rocking in the aisles.

The show went from strength to strength, and Steph and I watched another stunning performance, this time from Destiny's Child who mesmerised us with their exquisitely choreographed dance moves. Boy, could those girls dance; it was intoxicating.

Traditionally, after all the awards have been given out, the show culminates with the bestowal of the 'Lifetime Achievement' award. This year it was U2's turn. They graciously accepted the award and began their own mini-concert, showcasing a sample of their life's work. They too were sensational and seeing these stars close up made me realise exactly why they were so successful.

Then something unexpected happened. Bono dived head first into the pit. I doubt if he would have done the same, faced with a crowd of hungry U2 fans, but somehow a crowd of teenage girls must have seemed altogether less risky.

Forget the teenage girls, he practically landed on me. Everyone in the pit lunged towards him. I grabbed Steph and we ran as far away from this short, sweaty, unattractive Irishman as we could. If he had landed on me, I wonder whether any incapacity incurred would have qualified as an industrial injury. I shall never know.

That night was certainly one to remember. When I woke up that morning, I could never have dreamed I'd end the day almost buried beneath Bono. But then again, as I'd learned so many times before, with a job as unique and incomparable as mine, anything could happen.

# CHAPTER 14

# BATTERSEA'S ROYAL PEDIGREE

There are many things that make Battersea Dogs Home one of a kind. For starters, at almost 150 years old, it is the oldest dogs' home on the planet. As such, it is steeped in history and tradition and has an impressive pedigree boasting more royal connections than the Palace Internet.

In 1886 Princess Alice adopted her Jack Russell, Skippy, from the Home and Princess Michael of Kent, the wife of Battersea's current president, owns three Battersea cats.

Queen Victoria was Battersea's first patron and when she died, King Edward VII assumed the mantle, followed by King George V.

When Battersea's current patron paid the Home a visit in my early dog days, everything was polished and scrubbed to within an inch of its life. From Dobermanns to doorknobs, West Highland terriers to windows, everything was buffed and gleaming. I wonder if the Queen really knows the world is actually quite a grubby place, or whether she thinks it is naturally sparkling, where everyone smiles all the time like village idiots.

In 1991, 30 minutes before the arrival of our Sovereign, Battersea's diligent staff were polishing the last of the cats, and not one dog had a hair out of place. Beefy Palace security milled around, talking into their lapels.

A line of six staff, including Keith, Jacky and Ali, each with their own dogs, waited nervously to greet Her Majesty. The dogs were the best behaved of the bunch; their temperaments were known, tried and tested and therefore could not possibly bite the royal hand who was by now only 15 minutes away. Just at that moment, Keith's Labrador (who had been a little agitated) squatted and let rip splattering diarrhoea everywhere.

It was like watching a car crash. Nobody moved; everyone just stared, appalled, unable to react. Thankfully, Dot took charge and from behind the scenes came ten kennel maids with buckets of water, brooms and potpourri odour eliminator.

A decision had to be made. Either risk turning the royal shoes (usually white) an unacceptable shade of brown if the Labrador had more in reserve, enlist June and Tootsie – whose temperament was high risk at the best of times, or use a dog from the kennels to meet, greet and hopefully not chomp on the Queen. Using any other staff dogs was out of the question; most of them were more badly behaved than those in the kennels.

The Labrador was removed in disgrace and from a cast of hundreds, I suggested Benjamin take his place. Benjamin had become my project and I was determined to find him a home. He was a long-stay resident in my sales block, a cream lurcher that had been at Battersea for 12 months waiting for a new owner to pick him. He was a stray so we didn't know his history or why he had been turfed out and hoped to God it wasn't for biting royalty. Benjamin had never shown any signs of aggression during his time at Battersea, quite the opposite in fact, but the dogs get to know the staff and one can never guarantee how a dog will react in a new situation when faced with a stranger. Deep down, we knew he would be fine and attributed our hyper-sensitivity to the fact this wasn't just any old stranger – this was the Queen.

I knew Benjamin wouldn't let me down but as confident as I was, I couldn't get the saying 'never work with children or animals' out of my head. What if Benjamin was having an off day? What if he had an adverse reaction to being patted by white-gloved hands? I imagined the worst-case scenario splashed all over tomorrow's newspapers: 'Pooch Punctures Patron's Paw', 'Battersea Dog in Double Dog House', or 'Benjamin Bites Betty'. None of them particularly appealed to me.

We didn't have much choice and even less time so with optimism in our hearts, got on with the job in hand. Poor Benjamin didn't know what hit him; he was dumped in the bath, then under the industrial-sized dog dryer and finished off with a nice blue bow in the Battersea Dogs Home colours. The look on his face was a cross between shock and mortification.

Encouraged by the fact the Queen had a one in six chance of patting the 'iffy one from kennels' – favourable odds for the house, I'd say, we took our places. The plan was that Ali would stand a step in front of the rest in an attempt to subconsciously lure the Queen into patting Tessa, her sublime Border collie.

Things began well enough. The royal car pulled up, the Queen stepped out in her white shoes and everybody donned their best village idiot grins. As soon as she saw the dogs, the Queen broke into a smile that came straight from her heart. How do dogs do that?

Her gaze fell from one to the other until she had eyed all six. Tessa's chest was puffed out and Ali was doing her best to will the Queen over, but to our collective horror, she made a beeline for Benjamin. Everyone tensed, held their breath and rose at least two inches off the ground. You could have heard a pin drop as she reached her hand out to Benjamin.

Keith, who was holding him, immediately lost all colour. I thought he was going to faint. The Queen asked him how Benjamin came to be at Battersea. Keith, now in a state of high anxiety, didn't even look at the Queen. Instead, he just kept his eye on Benjamin and the royal hand and mumbled, 'Stray, I think.' The Queen, probably thinking she was actually talking to a real live village idiot, moved on. Everyone dropped two inches back down to earth.

We needn't have worried. Not only did Benjamin behave impeccably as we knew he would, we'd forgotten that the Queen was a genuine dog lover. She approached Benjamin as any dog person would; with the palm of her hand held out for him to sniff and waited until he had given the tacit 'you may now pat me' before scratching his ear affectionately. I watched in wonderment as this stray dog from the streets of London kept the Queen of England waiting until he was ready to be stroked.

The next day the newspapers were full of pictures of the Royal visit and the Queen stroking Benjamin (no adverse headlines in sight). Thanks to the power of the press and perhaps a little Royal help, Benjamin found the home he'd been waiting so long for. A lovely family who'd recently lost their elderly lurcher saw the pictures and drove the four hours from Devon that morning, in the hope they might have just the right home for Benjamin. They did. I missed him terribly when he left but Benjamin was off to a better life, spending his days lying in front of an open farm-house fire, punctuated by long walks on Dartmoor and swims in the sea.

He is regarded as somewhat of a celebrity in his village: the mutt that met the Monarch.

★   ★   ★

As famous as Battersea Dogs Home is, not many people know it actually began life in 1860 in a stable yard in Holloway, north London.

Battersea's founder, Mary Tealby, was an ordinary Victorian lady who happened to adore dogs. She couldn't bear to see them suffer abuse and neglect, so set about helping as many as she could. In those days, animal welfare barely existed and public opinion did not understand or support the idea of rescuing starving dogs when there were human beings suffering on the streets of London.

Mary Tealby was separated from her husband, a timber merchant from Hull, so had little financial support. Thankfully her brother, a clergyman named Edward Bates, persuaded his wealthy and influential friends to support her.

Mary's campaign also received a vital boost from Queen Victoria, which did a great deal to promote her extraordinary work at a time of negative publicity. It was largely due to her patronage and the support of people like Charles Dickens, who wrote positive articles in the press, that the public began to see Mary Tealby's work in a different light.

Although she didn't live to see it, by 1871 Mary's vision had become a firm reality and up to 200 dogs a week were being cared for. The stable yard became far too small to accommodate London's waifs and strays and the dog shelter moved from Holloway to a large house with grounds in Battersea, southwest London, where it remains today. Battersea Dogs Home has grown beyond all recognition and now encompasses an area of 4.9 acres which can house up to 700 dogs and 300 cats.

As a result of Mary Tealby's compassion, dedication and vision, millions of dogs have been rescued and will continue to be, for as long as necessary.

Mary Tealby did more to help life's canine cast-offs than she could ever have imagined. Colonel Green and his assistant, Shirley, recognised this and felt she had to be honoured in some way. Through robust research and dogged determination, they found the final resting place of this remarkable pioneer who began it all 150 years ago. Battersea's founder is buried in a small cemetery in the Bedfordshire town of Biggleswade. No one knows exactly why this place is of such significance to her, and we probably never will.

Colonel Green and Shirley arranged to meet the vicar of St Andrews Church the very next day. He took them to a remote corner of the run-down churchyard and beneath a large tree, he pointed out an unremarkable slab of mossy granite which turned out to be a horizontal tombstone. It had an inscription on either side, stating that two people were buried there. One side spelled out the name of Mary Tealby's brother, the Reverend Edward Bates. The other read: 'Mary Tealby, widow, born 30 December 1801. Died 3 October 1865.'

Colonel Green and Shirley rolled up their sleeves and, with bleach, hot water and steel wool, began restoring the headstone to a state befitting one so important as this great lady. It was the very least they could do after all she had done.

With a little help from Benjamin, the first multi-storey kennel block to be built at Battersea was opened by Her Majesty the Queen in 1991. It is three storeys high, air-conditioned, has two lifts and can house over 100 dogs. In an inadequate but heartfelt gesture, the block was named 'Tealby Kennels', after the lady whose legacy will never be forgotten.

Battersea Dogs Home began life amidst humble beginnings and its extraordinary rags-to-riches story is reflected by some of its very own residents.

After being dumped at an East End police station, Fergus, the little scruffy white terrier with brown ears and a broken leg, could never have imagined whose lap he would end up leaping into.

I had been tasked with selecting a 'likely candidate' for the Canadian Ambassador and his wife who were looking for a canine companion. The new dog would meet very important people, live in a large house with valuable antique furniture and staff, and therefore had to be small, trained and amiable. Fergus sprang to mind. He was all of the above and I just had to hope he wouldn't bring shame upon the Battersea name with any disreputable behaviour.

When Roy MacLaren first met Fergus, the BBC were filming at Battersea. Amidst cameras jostling for position, the tall Canadian High Commissioner knelt down to Fergus's level with a Schmacko and asked, 'Would you like a cookie?'

With his accent he sounded like Ernie from *Sesame Street*. I had to stop myself from laughing out loud. Fergus, of course, was more enamoured with the big, fluffy microphone being pointed in his direction. By now his leg had healed nicely and he killed the microphone with little effort. When dogs are convalescing, it is hard to gain a true picture of their character. They are below par and feeling sorry for themselves and as a result are usually subdued. During his leg-healing process, Fergus had been a model dog. He was obviously feeling more himself now; I just hoped the murder of the microphone was not a sign of things to come.

Mr MacLaren and his wife took Fergus home to live with them at the Canadian High Commission in Grosvenor Square. The crew followed them and caught on camera the moment when the little stray from Plaistow swaggered into the Canadian Embassy, ignored everyone that came so effusively to greet him, and peed on an antique chair. Things could only get better. Or worse.

The BBC stayed for three days and filmed Mr MacLaren and Fergus as they took their daily constitutionals in Hyde Park, met diplomats and High Commissioners, dined in style and signed

346

important papers together at their enormous mahogany desk.

Delighted with the footage they had, the crew packed up and returned to their Battersea base. How could they have known what they'd be missing?

When Mr MacLaren met the highest dignitary of them all, Fergus jumped uninvited into her lap, to which a horrified Mr MacLaren apologised profusely, citing, 'He's from Battersea.' The Queen replied, 'I should have known, I'm the patron!'

Not content to stop there, Fergus was also hand-fed chocolates by the Queen Mother, presented with a Hermès collar made especially for him and watched by 6.5 million viewers when the BBC series went to air.

Feeling it only right that the present-day patron should have a Battersea dog, an attempt to foist an unwanted corgi on the royal household was shamelessly set in motion. The puppy had been bought from a pet shop as a Christmas present, but now that the holidays were over, the children were back at school and the parents back at work.

Left to its own devices for eight hours a day, the dog had spent the last week weeing and pooing everywhere, ripping up carpets, toys and furniture and upsetting the neighbours by howling.

Situations like this always made me mad. The family would have known that the dog would be left alone after the holidays were over but still went ahead with the purchase, not giving one of the most important decisions of their life the consideration it deserved. I just had to bite my tongue though; Battersea was not there to judge, rather to take in and care for animals let down by someone else. Some cases were more genuine and on occasion I was brought to tears by people who were in such dire straits that they really had no other choice but to give up their beloved pet.

We took the corgi puppy in and settled her down. Even as a pup, she was a feisty one and, once assessed, the behaviourists felt she'd be better off going to live with someone who had previous experience of the breed. If she didn't, she could easily turn from an obnoxious youngster into a really problematic adult and would probably be back at Battersea within a year or two.

So, who did we know that had had corgis for the best part of 70 years? She could only say no, right?

Helen from the PR department was in the middle of assisting with a fundraising photo-shoot, starring none other than the devastatingly handsome Gus, who would do anything for a sausage. Her phone rang and, distracted by the call, she put the sausage down.

'Hello? Yes, this is Helen. You want me to do what? You want me to call the Queen and offer her a corgi puppy?'

Gus stared at the discarded sausage on the table and then stared back at Helen, willing her with his mind to refocus on the sausage. He was fighting a losing battle because two calls later she had reached the Queen's private secretary and was launching into an impressive sales pitch to rehome Battersea's finest (and only) corgi puppy.

Even though Helen couldn't see it, she knew an eyebrow was being raised at the other end of the phone. Still, the secretary dutifully marched off to put this highly irregular offer directly to the Queen. He returned saying, 'Her Majesty thanks all concerned for the generous offer and for thinking of her; however, she currently has ten corgis and feels that is probably more than enough to be going on with. Good day.'

Oh well, it was worth a try.

This news didn't worry us too much and within a week the little dog with the big character had found another home.

When the couple came to meet their new corgi, it was love at first sight. They confessed that they'd been bickering over what to call her but when we told them who they might have lost out to, the problem was instantly solved. They named her Lizzie.

A few years later I found myself at Lizzie's London residence; the real Lizzie, not the corgi. An envelope, complete with royal seal, dropped through my letterbox and into my dusty communal hallway. I couldn't help feeling that envelopes like this one shouldn't fall into hallways like mine. I had absolutely no idea why Buckingham Palace should be writing to me; surely I was too young to become a Dame.

I ripped open the envelope to find an invitation written in gold leaf, asking me to attend a party. As I read on, the penny dropped. Lady Weatherall's husband was retiring and his party was to be held at Buck House.

I checked my diary. Damn: Book Club. I'm sure they wouldn't mind if I missed a week and, besides, it would give me an excuse not to have to read *The Shining*. Having an overactive mind and a delicate constitution, horror has never been a good genre for me. I scribbled my acceptance.

I had no idea how long a rave at Buckingham Palace might go on for, so decided it best to find a dog-sitter for Gus. The timing of my invitation, however, was a little off. Both Ali and Steph were away and all my other possibilities were either out themselves or fostering crazy dogs that, coupled with their own, meant they already had a houseful.

I only had one option left: my mother.

'Do you want the good news or the bad news?' I asked her over the phone.

'The good news,' she replied.

'I'm going to Buckingham Palace.'

'Buckingham Palace? Oh my goodness! That's wonderful.'

There was a pause and I just knew from that moment on, the subject of my chosen career would never come up again.

'What's the bad news?' she asked hesitantly.

'You're looking after Gus.'

'What? Are you mad?'

I was beginning to wonder that myself.

'Oh please. It'll only be for a few hours. I'll walk him, feed him and wee and poo him. You won't have to do anything. He'll probably sleep for the whole time anyway.'

What was I thinking? She'll never agree to this. My mother in charge of a dog?

Then it came to me.

'If I brought Gus over to you on my way to the palace, you could see what I was wearing and tell me if it's okay.'

I knew I had her.

'Good idea, because you know you can't wear jeans, don't you?'

Yes, thank you, Mother, I had worked that one out for myself.

The big day arrived. The weather had turned hot and humid and as I was getting frocked up, clouds were gathering. Please, no, I thought, don't thunder. Of all the days, don't thunder when my mother is looking after Gus. I looked at him. He didn't seem agitated so, trying to stay positive, we left for my mother's.

When I dropped Gus off at her fourth-floor riverside flat, she looked me up and down.

'Turn around. Yes, you'll do. Now, what about this hound?' she said, looking Gus up and down. He wagged his tail at her.

I put his bed down and he obediently settled himself into it.

'Thanks for this,' I said. 'He won't need anything. I'll only be a few hours.'

'Now you'll take a taxi won't you? I don't think they'll let you in if you drive up to the gates of Buckingham Palace in your car.'

'What do you mean?' I asked, half knowing she was right.

My car had a fair few rust patches and the gears stuck every now and again, resulting in a sound resembling a rooster being strangled, but other than that, my new second-hand £125 sky-blue Lada was as sound as a pound. And besides, I couldn't afford to take taxis.

I took one more look through the window at the ominously building clouds. My doom radar was twitching but there was nothing I could do. Walking through my mum's front door to leave, I glanced back to hear her say, 'You're a good boy, aren't you? Yes you are. We'll be just fine together.' I was even more shocked to see her kneel down and stroke him. This was indeed progress. Maybe I wasn't adopted after all.

As I drove up to Her Majesty's house, the tourists parted to let me through, peering in to see if I was anyone important. When he saw my car, the security man's jaw dropped but he stood firm, arms crossed in front him. He wasn't about to raise the barrier for this jalopy. I rolled down the squeaky window and showed him my special pass to which he raised his eyebrows in disbelief. He checked it three times before stepping aside to let me through. I put the car into gear and drove on, leaving a group of Japanese tourists in a cloud of exhaust behind me. As I changed from first to second, the gears stuck and the rooster screeched. Not wanting to attract the attention of M15, I quickly changed up to third but didn't have the required speed, so stalled the car. I felt the eyes of the tourists, the security man and the two Irish guards in their red tunics and bearskins bearing down on me. I even thought I saw a curtain twitch on that famous balcony. Oh, the embarrassment, why didn't I listen to my mother?

I parked in between a Jaguar and an Aston Martin and disembarked. As I was brushing the dog hairs off my clothes, a beautifully tailored footman wearing a red and gold coat and a white wig came to greet me and ushered me into the Palace.

I followed him down a long corridor with high glass ceilings. The carpet matched his coat, as did the wallpaper. I gawped at the paintings hanging from the walls. They were enormous, with ornate gold frames, and contained people from a bygone age, all looking terribly serious. Almost every one of the paintings included a dog.

I had been on the tourist tour of Buckingham Palace before, so had seen how sumptuous some of the rooms were, but I wasn't a tourist now;

there were no queues or roped-off areas keeping me out.

I turned the corner and found myself in the room where the party was being held. Much to my disappointment, it looked a little tired. The walls were an uninspiring beige and the carpet a plain dark blue. Perhaps the best rooms were saved for the tourists. No matter, another colourfully dressed footman was bringing me champagne.

Always having preferred food to alcohol, I furtively craned my neck, checking to see where the nibbles had got to. I was expecting spectacular canapés or at the very least a pyramid of Ferrero Rocher but was disillusioned to find crisps and peanuts. I knew the Queen had a reputation for being thrifty but this was ridiculous.

Without anything culinary to concentrate on, I decided to find someone to chat to. That someone turned out to be Lady Jane Fellows, Princess Diana's sister. She was extremely warm and friendly and when she found out where I worked, she excitedly told me about her own dogs and asked all about the less-fortunate hounds at Battersea. It transpired that many of her friends had rescued Battersea dogs, reminding me once again how effortlessly dogs transcend class.

At that moment, it also became apparent that the opposing worlds of my double life were merging into a single exquisite existence.

Suddenly I saw a brilliant white flash followed by a massive thunder clap. The heavens had opened.

The thunder was so loud it earned a few 'oohs' and 'aahs' from the floor. I had visions of Gus on my mother's head and my mother calling 999.

I was just about to sidle off and rescue both my mother and Gus when Lady Weatherall spotted me and bounded over. With a squeal of delight she flung her arms around me and gave me a hug. Wondering what all the commotion was about, her husband turned around. When he saw me he strode over, all smiles, and produced an envelope of photos he'd brought in especially for me to see. I pulled out a dozen photos of Fred, successor to their beloved Nelson, looking the picture of health and happiness, lying on a Louis XVI chaise longue, sunbathing. Talk about landing on your feet, or in his case a priceless antique. The Weatheralls waxed lyrical about Fred and how, even though no dog could replace Nelson, Fred was doing a damn good job of trying.

I had been there for three hours in total and an hour after the first thunder clap. It was time to leave. I said goodbye to my hosts and climbed into my battered old banger. I pulled my phone out of the glove compartment to find 23 missed calls, all from my mother. I chose not to listen to the messages; I'd be there soon enough.

The thrill I had driving out of Buckingham Palace was just as spine tingling as the feeling driving in – although this time it was nothing to do with my clapped-out car stalling. As I drove through the gates with the Palace behind me, I paused and turned around, making sure I'd imprinted the scene on my memory. It was, after all, a view that only the Royals and few besides ever got to see.

I arrived at my mother's to find a pair of dishevelled neurotics. They both looked as traumatised as each other, the only discernible difference being that my mother wasn't drooling. Both looked like they had aged ten years, the carpet by the door was pulled up and Gus had wee'd, thankfully in the kitchen.

She handed me Gus's bed and his lead (with him attached to the other end), walked me to the door and said, 'Phone me tomorrow and tell me all about it; I can't take anything in right now.'

I'd been at Battersea for long enough to know that extraordinary situations were par for the course but when I found myself paying my respects in front of the Queen Mother's coffin courtesy of Whippet Rescue, even I did a double take.

Battersea Dogs Home was fortunate enough to have the assistance of many breed rescues to help with the monumental task of rehoming thousands of dogs every year. The breed rescues that Battersea dealt with had been carefully vetted before any Battersea dog was entrusted into their care. Once officially on Battersea's books, the rescues set about vetting potential homes for those specific breeds that found themselves dumped at the Dogs Home.

Not only did every breed of dog have its very own rescue organisation, the more popular breeds had dozens representing them. Anyone could set themselves up as a breed rescue, but only the good ones were accredited and made it into such publications as the *Kennel Club Breed Rescue Directory*, which was updated annually.

Workloads varied enormously from breed rescue to breed rescue. For example, Staffordshire bull terrier rescues always had more dogs to find homes for than there were homes available. In 2005, for the first time in Battersea's history, Staffordshire bull terriers outnumbered mongrels at the Home. In 2007, a third of all the dogs Battersea received were Staffies or discernible crosses.

On the other hand, rescues for smaller breeds such as chihuahuas, miniature pinschers and whippets often sat twiddling their thumbs, waiting for dogs to fill the dozens of homes waiting.

Most breed rescues found exceptional homes for their Battersea charges, which was of course a good thing, but it did lead to some shameless boundary stretching, if it meant getting a dog rehomed quickly. Where the dog's heritage was concerned, Battersea's staff sometimes stretched the realms of possibility and alerted breed rescues to a particular dog, knowing it wasn't perhaps the real deal. One example of this blatant distortion of the truth was when I invited Whippet Rescue to Battersea, to look at a 'whippet' named Walter.

Jean and Jessica, two very English ladies, ran a

very tight whippet ship. Jean, a sort of present-day Miss Marple, lived in Dover and sourced some wonderful country homes but could not always get up to London. This is where Jessica came in. Jessica was the personal assistant to the former MP Claire Short and worked at the Houses of Parliament just along the embankment from Battersea Dogs Home.

Jessica would cycle between the two establishments with her own young whippet, Lenny, comfortably secured in her rucksack. I'm not sure that this was the best advert for responsible dog ownership (or even if it was legal) but Lenny seemed to love it.

Obviously when Jessica came to collect dogs from Battersea she drove. Even though the rucksack was large, two dogs would have been stretching the boundaries of acceptability.

On this particular day, Jessica cycled because she was only coming to view the Battersea whippet and begin the process of finding him a new home. Walter was a stray so had to wait seven days in case his owner came forward. This was unlikely to happen as he was grossly underweight.

I took Jessica up to the kennels and stopped outside Walter's temporary home. He was sitting down, looking up at us with soulful eyes. Jessica looked at Walter and then looked at me.

'I can't see the whippet. Is he hiding in the back?' she asked.

'No, that's it,' I said confidently.

'That's not a whippet, it's a skinny mongrel, and well you know it.'

'But Jessica, he's got a pointy nose and he's awfully sensitive, so I'll bet his grandfather was a whippet.'

I unlocked the kennel door and shoved her in with Walter, knowing this would do the trick. I'd been in with him the previous day and I knew he'd win her over. He gently sidled up to her and pushed his nose under her arm. She threw her eyes up to heaven and folded.

My blatant cheekiness may have earned me a black mark with Whippet Rescue, but it prevented poor skinny Walter from having to sit in the rehoming kennels at Battersea, waiting God knows how long for someone to choose him.

Jessica and Jean came up trumps and Walter went off to live in Folkestone with a retired lady of slightly better breeding than himself. I saw a photograph of him six months later. He had filled out and looked every inch the . . . mongrel.

I was obviously forgiven because the next week, Jessica invited me for lunch on the terrace at the House of Commons. From the other side of the Thames, I'd often seen MPs quaffing champagne on that famous terrace and wondered who they were and what their lives were like. Now I could see for myself, as I quaffed along with the best of them. Mostly they were fat, old, bald men with red faces and shirts that were too tight.

Jessica kindly invited me back to those hallowed

halls on two other occasions. The first was to take a fascinating tour up St Stephen's Tower to Big Ben and stand behind the iconic white clock. They timed the tour so we were up in the bell tower as the midday chimes rang out across London. Thrilling, if a little deafening. The tour also included the great Westminster Hall, once used as a court of law. This centuries-old building had many chambers, nooks and crannies, one of which was the tiny room where the suffragette Emmeline Pankhurst hid from her would-be jailers. I crouched in the room, bent double as it was so small, trying to imagine what she must have felt. I also stood on the spot where King Charles I was sentenced to death. I finished the day by staring down the barrel of the present-day royal toilet, used only by Her Majesty on state occasions.

The next time I returned to Westminster Hall was a little more sombre. It was to see the lying-in-state of the Queen Mother. The queue of people paying their respects was miles long, but Jessica's tickets allowed us direct entry into the Hall. Just as we got there, the four guards standing at each corner of the coffin changed. In their place, the Queen Mother's four grandsons, Princes Charles and Andrew, dressed in full military uniform, Prince Edward, and their cousin Lord Linley, took their positions, heads bowed in respectful silence.

Although full of people paying their respects to the Queen Mother, the Hall was completely silent, an atmosphere of peace and reverence prevailing.

Westminster Hall's splendid stature and high ceilings allowed shafts of sunlight to come through its elegant windows and permeate the grief.

What an incredible privilege this was. As I walked past one of Britain's best-loved Royals, in one of the country's most beautiful and historical buildings, I wondered if, as well as having her grandsons and thousands of adoring public there, the Queen Mother, a confirmed dog-lover, was glad to have me there too.

# CHAPTER 15

# THE LAST RESORT

The Queen Mother reminded me very much of my own grandmother. Both were loved by everyone, both liked a tipple and both wore high heels right to the end. Gran Gran, as she was known by all, was like a second mother to me and when she died I was utterly lost. She was my kindred spirit; the only other person in the family that loved dogs the way I did and she meant the world to me.

Gran Gran was 88, still living in her own home and spending her pension on wine and make-up. To visit her was always a joy, never a chore and her love and warmth enveloped me like a hot bath. Everywhere she went, laughter accompanied her like a loyal dog.

I was in my office when my mother called to tell me that Gran Gran had been rushed into hospital. She was gravely ill and needed an emergency operation that night. This shocking news came totally out of the blue and it hit me hard. My mother tried to convey the severity of the situation but couldn't quite get the words out, frightened that if she said it, it would be true.

Nevertheless, I understood. I immediately left work and caught the next train from Clapham Junction to the south coast.

Knowing how much Gran Gran loved Gus, my first thought was to take him with me but this was impractical and the unwavering and dependable Ali Taylor kindly stepped in to take care of him.

On the train journey, hundreds of priceless memories of my grandmother swirled around my mind but as each memory formed, it was ruthlessly obliterated by one grim possibility. The more I tried to keep the thought of losing her at bay, the stronger and more real it became.

I raced through the hospital, frantically trying to find her. When I did, she was conscious but looking frailer than I'd ever seen her. I kissed her on the forehead and she smiled at me, apologising for all the trouble she'd caused. My voice broke as I told her it was no trouble but I knew I couldn't fall apart; when I looked at my mother and saw how devastated she was, I realised someone had to be strong. We stayed with Gran Gran until the doctors told us it was time to leave her. She looked frightened and as I kissed her on the forehead, a terrible feeling washed over me; I just knew something bad was going to happen. That was the last time I saw her conscious.

For the next week, my family and I took turns to sit by her bedside but she never regained consciousness. The doctors told us there was nothing more they could do. My mother had to make the unthinkable decision to switch the respirator off.

Gran Gran was 21 years old when she had my mother. Always young at heart, she and my mother were more like friends, enjoying the same sense of fashion, family and fun. My mother didn't know a life without Gran Gran, couldn't imagine it; didn't believe the time would ever come.

They asked if we would like to stay with Gran Gran until the end. My mother couldn't do it, any more than I could if it was her lying there. My brother, who also adored Gran Gran, couldn't do it either. I knew this was something I had to do and although it would be the hardest thing, I somehow knew I could.

Perhaps it was due to the heartbreak I'd experienced at Battersea that I felt strong enough to be with my beloved grandmother at the very end.

I'm glad I was there when Gran Gran died. It gave me the chance to tell her how much I loved her and to say a very personal goodbye. She was one of a kind, and had enriched my childhood and my life and would leave an indelible imprint on my soul.

It may sound strange but I truly believe that over the years, Battersea had helped me come to terms with and understand death. It taught me how to deal with grief and how to be strong. Somehow coming face to face with death and having had my heart broken on more than one occasion, I had gained an inner strength.

At Battersea, putting animals to sleep was the absolute last resort after every other option had been exhausted. It was a sad but necessary part of Battersea's work and indeed animal welfare, and I was glad that Battersea had the option to euthanise. Sometimes it was the kindest act a human could bestow upon an animal.

The most common question I was asked when people discovered I worked at Battersea Dogs Home was, 'How many dogs are put down?' My response was always one of genuine bewilderment. Why would they want to know how many dogs were put to sleep, when they could ask me how many lost dogs were reunited with their owners or how many unwanted dogs were rehomed and went on to live better lives?

I never dodged the question though. In fact it gave me the chance to dispel a deeply unfair myth that saddened all of us who worked so hard at Battersea. People seemed to think that Battersea arbitrarily put dogs to sleep on a whim. If this were the case, I doubt whether the dedicated staff would work there; I know I wouldn't have.

Battersea Dogs Home did not randomly put dogs down after seven days. If a dog was rehomeable, it would stay for as long as it took until Battersea had found exactly the right home to suit the dog's individual needs.

Battersea was one of the very few rescues left that did not practise selective intake. At Battersea, no dog was ever turned away and as such a staggering 10,000 were taken in every year. Even when the Home was packed to the rafters, space would always be found for every single dog that came to its door.

Not all animal welfare organisations employ the same policy. Many are selective in their intake and promote themselves as 'no kill shelters' in a clever ploy to gain the upper hand in a market fiercely contesting for the public's generosity. Although the statement may be true, what they omit to mention is that in their selectivity, they simply won't take any dog arriving on their doorstep that they deem unrehomeable due to temperament, age, previous history or a tricky medical condition. Instead they take the cute, cuddly, healthy, non-problematic, rehomeable dogs.

But where does that leave those that have been turned away? I hate to think how many of these poor creatures end up dumped on the streets. I knew of several people who travelled the length of the country especially to bring their dog into Battersea, because no rescue in their area would take it.

Sadly, of the thousands of dogs Battersea received every year, a proportion were simply not rehomeable. The decision to put a dog to sleep, however, was far from simple.

There were two reasons why Battersea euthanised.

One was behavioural, the other medical. Battersea's vets treated a myriad of medical conditions on a daily basis and sophisticated facilities and equipment, afforded by the generosity of the public, ensured that the majority of cases were remedied. However, if the dog could not be cured, if its long-term quality of life was compromised or if it was suffering, the veterinary surgeons would make that difficult final decision.

Many of the dogs put to sleep on medical grounds were extremely old and not well enough to be rehomed. Often upwards of 15 years old, blind and deaf, many could barely stand up. I used to be terribly affected by these cases; it seemed so harsh that a dog who had lived a full life, probably much loved by someone, should end its days dumped at a dog's home.

Battersea also euthanised dogs that were deemed dangerous as it had a responsibility not to rehome aggressive animals to the public.

The fearless Rehabilitation team had proved on countless occasions that some forms of aggression could be trained out of a dog; however, unpredictable aggression is where the real danger lies and dogs displaying this type of behaviour were put to sleep. In many cases, for a member of staff to even try to rehabilitate these dogs would have meant putting themselves and others at risk.

Battersea received many large, powerful breeds and bull terrier types that had been bought for their natural guarding and fighting instincts by ruthless owners who relentlessly encouraged these traits. Many of these proud, strong animals were turned into aggressive attacking machines by ignorance and machismo; products of a human's desire for status and security in a violent world. When the owner could no longer manage the dog's size and aggression, it was invariably dumped.

In some ways seeing those large, magnificent animals now sedated and muzzled, prematurely at the end of their days, seemed the most pitiful of all. They weren't born that way; neither did they come into the world wanting to inflict pain upon people and other dogs. They were made that way by people that never saw the big picture, never understood the consequences; by those who were nowhere to be seen when the syringe went into the dog's vein and the liquid was released.

But the staff at Battersea Dogs Home were there. They were there to hold the dog and wonder how different its life could have been in the hands of a responsible owner. They were there to stroke its head and whisper words of comfort in its ear as the syringe emptied and the dog exhaled its final breath.

That was the worst part for me, knowing that just a few seconds ago this dog was a living, breathing creature. Knowing in those few seconds that a life had been taken and could never be given back. But I also knew there was no alternative. Everything humanly possible would have been done to try and avoid this ending, this empty shell of a dog, this body devoid of life lying before me.

Putting any animal to sleep – even if you don't know it, is one of the hardest things to witness, let alone have to do. For the staff, the unfairness of it all was almost more difficult to cope with than actually putting the dog down. It felt like we were doing other people's dirty work, people who should have taken responsibility for the mess they'd made of their dog's life and done the decent thing by taking it to their own vet to be put to sleep.

At Battersea, the decision to put a dog down on behavioural grounds was made after thorough assessments by at least two experienced behaviourists, with consultation from others who had seen the dog's behaviour on a daily basis. A senior behaviourist (Battersea's had had approximately 40 year's experience between them) would then sanction the decision.

The veterinary staff bore the brunt of the physical deed, assisted by a rehomer. Kennel staff were exempt from this duty; they worked too closely with the dogs to ask them to bear such a heavy burden.

Battersea euthanised by injection, essentially an overdose of anaesthetic. It was quick, painless, dignified and calm, and allowed the dog to just fall asleep. Even so, it used to break my heart to watch a life ebb away. I loved dogs after all and had come to work at Battersea to help them.

But help, I realised, sometimes came in un-expected ways.

It was an unusually slow afternoon in the intake department. I had only taken in two strays, three unwanted cats and a litter of chunky black Labrador puppies and the day was nearly over.

At five minutes to five, a middle-aged man walked towards me, struggling to carry his Old English sheepdog. The dog was wrapped in a blanket which I thought was rather odd as it wasn't a cold day and the dog didn't seem particularly old.

The man was upset and explained to me that his landlord was forcing him to give the dog up. I comforted him as best I could, knowing this was always a difficult situation and he signed the papers. He left in a hurry, due to what I assumed was the distress of having to part with his dog.

Steve helped me carry the dog over to the clinic to be vaccinated and checked over. When we got to the clinic, we placed Jake carefully down on the table. He was struggling to breathe and was in obvious discomfort, but allowed the veterinary staff to check him over.

One of the nurses pulled the blanket back and the sight that greeted us made us gasp in horror. Jake had hundreds of maggots crawling around a massive open wound at his rear end. One nurse was physically sick and another ran out of the room in tears. With 20 years at Battersea between us, this was one of the most distressing sights Steve or I had ever seen. The wound was raw and infected and covered about 20 per cent of Jake's body. At that moment he vomited, spewing up maggots.

The RSPCA was called straight away but it transpired that the man had given a false name and address. Even though the long arm of the law could not redress this unjust balance, I hoped Jake's owner would pay for this appalling neglect in some other way.

Jake's prognosis was about as bad as it could be and the vets made the decision to put him out of his misery then and there.

On the whole, euthanasia was a blessing but sometimes it felt uncomfortably like playing God, especially when one's hands were tied by, of all things, legislation.

The Dangerous Dogs Act came into force in the early nineties, after a spate of dog attacks on the public (mostly children). There were four dogs on the 'dangerous list', one of which was the pit bull terrier. The other three were the Japanese tosa, the Dogo Argentino and the Fila brasileiro. The latter three were fairly rare in the UK at that time, so it was the pit bull that was most affected by what I always deemed to be a hastily constructed parliamentary bill.

The bill stated that with immediate effect, all pit bull terriers must be neutered, microchipped and, for identification purposes, tattooed. They must also be muzzled and kept on a lead whilst in public, and registered on a central police database. Failure to comply would result in the animal being seized by the police, with a high possibility it would be destroyed.

I knew immediately that this was practically a death warrant for pit bulls.

Although some pit bull owners were responsible enough to adhere to the conditions, the vast majority were not. Whether this was due to lack of money, understanding or inclination was up for debate, but I was correct in my prediction that pit bull terriers would soon come flooding into Battersea.

Another condition stamped on pit bull owners was that it was illegal to pass their dog on to another party. This same condition applied to Battersea Dogs Home and effectively meant that if Battersea rehomed a pit bull, it would be breaking the law. I had to somehow come to terms with the fact that no matter how sound their temperaments were, there was no option but to put all pit bulls to sleep.

Some were brought into Battersea by their owners, who could not, or would not, adhere to all the stipulations laid down. After being given the choice to either leave the dog at Battersea to be destroyed or take it back home, some owners opted for the latter whilst others signed the forms with little or no compunction.

Other pit bulls were dumped and ended up at Battersea as strays. Their owners had already broken the law by allowing them to stray so were unlikely to come forward to claim them. If they were brave enough to come into Battersea and identify their dog, the police would cart the animal off to secret holding kennels, whilst a lengthy court case against the owner ensued. As usual, the taxpayer picked up the bill, which often ran into thousands.

But it was the indiscriminate slaying of hundreds of pit bulls ranging from puppies to the elderly that was the hardest to come to terms with. I felt that once again, we were doing someone else's dirty work, this time the government's.

As ever, if it had to be done, I was glad of the painless method Battersea adopted which, coupled with the Home's caring staff, made sure the end was as kind and compassionate as it could be.

In the years since the Dangerous Dogs Act came into operation, one would have thought that with the passing of time and the government's insistence that every pit bull be neutered, the breed would have slowly died out. But as with everything in life, if something is forbidden, it goes underground and pit bull terriers continued to arrive at Battersea throughout my time there.

Battersea was not in the business of storing dogs. If a dog could not be rehomed, it would not be kennelled for the rest of its natural life. To do this to a dog would have dramatically diminished its quality of life, not to mention its sanity. In human terms it would have been comparable to a life sentence in prison, only without having committed a crime.

All too often it was the owner that committed the crime, the crime of irresponsible ownership, but sadly the animal usually paid the price.

Ali Taylor and I stepped out of the Home to head for the pub one lunchtime, and unwittingly walked straight into a fracas involving Battersea's Spanish security guard. Carlos was leaping out of the way of a speeding car whilst cursing the driver in his mother tongue.

After we had calmed him down, he explained that on his security cameras he'd seen a woman pull up in her car, take out a cat box and dump it outside the gate. He'd raced up to catch her but she had jumped into her car and almost ran him over in her rush to get away.

There wasn't much we could do about that now; we just had to concentrate on looking after the cats.

The next four minutes were unimaginable.

Carlos picked up the cat box containing both cats and to our horror, the bottom of the box just fell away. The terrified cats were out on the pavement and we knew it was only a matter of time before they ran into the road. Battersea Park Road is an extremely busy main road and drivers often use the wide stretch outside the Home as a race-track. With no thought for his own safety, Carlos jumped into the road to try and stop the speeding traffic.

He was too late and I watched both cats run into the oncoming traffic. The scene unfolded in slow motion.

A car instantly hit one of the cats but the driver just drove on. The other cat had followed its mate and was hit by another car, the driver of which at least had the decency to stop and get out.

Neither cat was killed outright. They were both flailing around in the road. Everyone was in shock, frozen in time, until Ali screamed, 'Pick them up!'

This jolted everyone out of their daze and Carlos, who was closest, picked them up. As he rushed them past me and back into the Home, I could see that one of them had been hit in the head. Its eye had exploded. It was fitting and trying to bite Carlos at the same time. I grabbed the other one from him which by now had gone limp.

We rushed them into the veterinary department. The one I was holding had died in the 30 seconds it had taken to get him to the vet. His body was intact so he must have died from internal injuries. The one that had been hit in the head was instantly put down. At that moment, I thanked God we had the privilege to end this kind of suffering. Euthanasia is always upsetting but there were plenty of times, especially when witnessing animals in extreme distress, that it could not come quickly enough.

Later that day, the driver who failed to stop called Battersea to find out if the cat he had hit had survived. We told him the bad news.

A couple of hours after that the owner of the cats phoned. Oblivious to the drama that had unfolded, she immediately began explaining away her irresponsible behaviour with a list of pathetic excuses, excuses we had all heard a million times before. She could never have imagined the trauma she had caused by not having the guts to hand the cats safely over to Battersea instead of just dumping them outside the gate. When she was told what had happened after she sped away, there was a gasp followed by the clatter of a dropped phone and then silence.

Nothing could have prepared me for the sudden death of my beloved grandmother, and four months after she died I was equally unready to lose Gus. His initial six-month prognosis had stretched into three and a half wonderful years, so no one was more shocked than me when out of the blue, the day that all dog owners dread finally came.

It was a beautiful, sunny Monday morning. Gus and I walked into work across the Common just as we had done every day since he decided I was his. Nothing was amiss. Gus made straight for the bushes where he performed his morning ablutions;

he met and greeted his usual doggie friends with tail-wagging glee, and dilly-dallied, sniffing everything along the way. He went back on the lead for the walk up Queenstown Road and we reached the Home bang on 7.50 a.m. You could set your watch by us.

I handed him over to Helen in the PR office and left two Schmackos by his bed. Gus settled down for a hard day's sleep and I walked over to my office for a hard day's work.

At about 10 a.m. I collected him from Helen for his mid-morning wee and as usual found her and the rest of the PR team attending to his every whim, such was their fondness for Gus. Everyone loved this friendly, gentle, well-mannered old fellow.

Everything was as it should have been until about 11.30 a.m., when I received a phone call from Helen, telling me something was wrong with Gus. I wasn't overly concerned; they'd call me if he so much as sneezed.

I ambled over to their office to find Gus unable to stand and unable to focus. My heart lurched and my mind began to race. I scooped him up and carried him over to the veterinary section. At that time of day, all the vets were usually in theatre but luckily one of them was available.

Breeony was fairly new to the Battersea family but had settled in and was one of the gang. From the start we knew she was a good vet. Not only did she take time talking to and comforting

Battersea's residents rather than just prodding and diagnosing them, she also took time with the staff. She understood how much the dogs and cats meant to them and would explain in detail what was wrong, and how they could help make them better.

Breeony examined Gus who by now was having trouble breathing. She knew about his heart murmur and said he needed oxygen to help him breathe.

The news about Gus had spread like wildfire throughout the Home and within minutes Ali Taylor was at my side. When Breeony held my hand, I knew bad news was coming. She told me as gently as she could, that Gus had had a stroke and that the situation was extremely serious.

Her words echoed around my head, over and over again, as she took Gus away to give him oxygen. Fighting back the tears I turned to Ali and asked, 'Is she saying what I think she's saying?'

At that moment in time, there was no one I would rather have had with me. Not only was Ali a good friend, but over the years she had been through this exact same situation a hundred times before with all the oldies she had fostered. She, more than most, knew all about heartache.

Ali also knew exactly what Breeony was saying. She nodded and took me back to her office where I sat stunned. I knew he was old, I knew he had a bad heart but there'd been no sign that anything was wrong and I just wasn't ready for this. Losing a much-loved pet is, of course, not the same as losing one's own flesh and blood but I felt the same kind of panic I felt when I first heard Gran Gran was sick.

At that moment Breeony came in. She discussed the prognosis with me and it wasn't good. She said he was comfortable at the moment and we should wait and see how he was by the end of the day.

I knew I had to remain objective and not let Gus's quality of life become compromised. I'd seen too many instances where people let their dogs go on longer than they should, not that it's ever easy to know when the right time is to let your beloved friend and companion go. It is a horrendous situation and I knew I'd have to be really strong if it came to having to make that impossible decision myself.

What a strange day that was. I didn't know what to do with myself, especially at lunchtime; for the past three and a half years, that was when Gus and I took our stroll in the park together.

By 5 p.m. he'd perked up a little and Breeony said I should take him home and see how he was overnight. He could walk but was very unsteady and reminded me of a newborn foal.

Gus and I had walked into work that morning but there was no way he could walk home. Kirsty kindly offered to drive us and when we arrived home I made him as comfortable as I could. I made him the tastiest dinner possible, knowing there might not be many more. You might think lamb, beef or chicken would have been on the menu but you'd be wrong. My boy was as quirky as he was unique. Melon and banana were his favourites. He regularly turned his nose up at fillet steak in favour of a piece of honeydew melon.

'Is your dog a vegetarian?' people would often ask. Whether he was or wasn't didn't matter because for dinner that night, Gus had his favourite: fruit salad. I took some comfort and hope from the fact that, as always, he wolfed his food down.

The night was so-so. I think he actually had a better night than I did. I was awake for most of it trying to imagine what life would be like without him. It had just been him and me for three and a half years and I couldn't bear the thought of losing my buddy.

The alarm went off at 6.30 a.m. but I was already awake, looking down at Gus as he slept peacefully at the bottom of my bed. As I set about my routine of getting ready for work, he stirred. For a moment it seemed just like every other morning.

When I was ready, I gently woke him. I wanted to see how his coordination was and whether he could stand up on his own. He managed to stagger to his feet but after taking two or three steps, fell over. Knowing what that meant, I burst into tears but being a firm believer that dogs know when people are upset, quickly tried to pull myself together. I figured Gus had enough to cope with without worrying about me too.

As part of our routine, I always gave Gus a Schmacko before we left the house each morning. I held out the treat for him but he didn't want it. This was a very bad sign. I held it there for a few minutes willing him to change his mind and to my delight he did. My joy was short-lived. He tried to take it but snapped at the air about 20 inches from where the treat was. The stroke had shot his coordination to pieces. It was clear that I only had one option, one decision to make.

We drove to the park so Gus could do his ablutions. He needed help every step of the way and when he'd finished I picked him up so that I could carry him to the car. At my touch he wagged his tail. My heart almost broke right there.

At work, we didn't park in the Home's car park. Instead, I drove Gus all the way to my office, on the way passing Ali and Steph. They knew what this meant and having looked after Gus on many occasions, they too adored him and were devastated at the news.

I spent the next hour sitting on my office floor beside Gus, waiting for Breeony to arrive. His head was in my lap, his breathing unsteady. The news was out and a procession of friends and colleagues filed in to say their final goodbyes to the General. Many were in tears; he was far more loved than I knew. The PR team was inconsolable. Gus had been a big part of their lives for three and a half years and they would undoubtedly feel his absence more keenly than most.

It was 9 a.m. and with my door open, I could see Breeony walk through Battersea's gates and head straight for my office to see how Gus was. She saw immediately. We both agreed that he had been too severely damaged by the stroke to let him suffer any more and that he should be put to sleep straight away.

Breeony went to the veterinary department to get the necessary injection and I sat looking down at my dog – his head in my lap, the same lap he'd landed in all those years ago. His floppy black ears twitched a little as he dozed. I stroked his head and tried to count the grey hairs around his face but there were too many. Twenty-four hours ago he'd been fine; this was all happening so quickly.

Breeony returned and although I knew it would be the hardest thing to stay with him whilst she put him to sleep, for his sake I knew I had to. It was only right that I should be the one holding him and that my voice was the last he would hear.

Breeony asked me if I was ready. I would never be ready but, unable to speak, I nodded. I held Gus and watched as the liquid left the syringe and entered his vein. With his head in my lap, I stroked him and whispered that I loved him. At that moment he looked up at me and seemed to relax, as though all the pain of the last 24 hours had just faded away. He exhaled deeply. I knew that was Gus's last breath.

I was too upset to work that day and went straight around to my mum's. I knew she secretly loved Gus and she too was devastated. For someone who wasn't a dog person, he had completely won her over and she bawled her eyes out. We both did.

I had him privately cremated and received his ashes back in a small wooden casket with his name engraved on the top. I also had a plaque engraved, which was put up in the rehoming building at Battersea. It read: 'To the world he was my dog, to me he was the world.'

Life after Gus took a bit of getting used to. I missed him most at the oddest times. Driving around in the car, I'd absent-mindedly look in the rear-view mirror expecting to see his handsome grey face and those lovable floppy old ears and when I didn't, the tears would freefall down my face.

Those early worries I'd had about the responsibility of taking on another life were completely outweighed by the love, happiness and truly wonderful times we shared. I wouldn't have been without Gus for the world. He was a pleasure, an absolute joy, but it's true what they say about all good things.

In the following days, weeks and months, when I felt saddest and missed him the most, I'd take great comfort from knowing that I'd given Gus a happy last few years; that he'd lived life fully to the end and that when it came, the end was quick. It would be the way I'd choose to go; running around the park right up until the finish.

# CHAPTER 16

# BILLY AND THE BALLET

As my mother zipped me into one of her frocks, I wondered how these extra-ordinary things kept happening to this very ordinary dog lover from south London. I had no choice but to borrow one of her dresses. My one and only good outfit (the one I was given by those kind people from the *Style Challenge* TV show, the one I'd worn to Buckingham Palace) was in the dry cleaners and the rest of my wardrobe consisted of jeans, T-shirts and sweat-shirts. She also insisted I put on a bit of slap.

'We're going to the ballet, you know, not the local grey-hound track.'

Yes, thank you, Mother, I was aware of that. We were off to see the Royal Ballet performing *Romeo and Juliet* at the Royal Opera House, Covent Garden.

As a child, I'd done a bit of ballet but it wasn't really my scene. You know how it is: your mum makes you sign up for Brownies, violin lessons and ballet. To me, Brownies was like having my teeth pulled, violin lessons sounded like I was having my teeth pulled and, as for ballet, I think I would rather have had my teeth pulled.

We stepped out of the taxi and walked towards the Royal Opera House. I only stumbled twice on the way in, not a bad effort all things considered. High heels, worn by a novice on cobbles, was an accident waiting to happen.

Just as he had promised, our behind-the-scenes tour guide was there to meet us. He was performing that night and was already in make-up but not yet in costume. I'd never been to the Royal Opera House before. My mother had tried to bring me but, having little interest in the arts, I politely declined. As uncultured as I was, however, even I recognised that this was a bit of a coup; my very first time and here we were being given a private tour of one of the most spectacular theatres in the world.

I expected behind the scenes to be slightly more work-in-progress but everything was in perfect order; there wasn't even a ballet shoe out of place. I looked up, mesmerised by the enormity of the place: the lights and the pulleys, the walkway in the roof, and all around me were props, costumes and bustling people.

The theatre itself was sumptuous and grand. Red velvet drapes, emblazoned with the royal crest, hung majestically from the high ceiling above the stage. The seats were scarlet – tasteful, elegant and deep, and the orchestra pit was somewhat more civilised than the last pit I'd been in.

It was too early for patrons to be admitted so

we stood there, taking in the eerie silence of this enormous, opulent, empty theatre.

Our host had to leave us to get ready, so my mother and I decided to have a drink. We found the bar, which was almost as grand as the theatre itself, and I ordered two glasses of wine. From my borrowed handbag I pulled out a crumpled ten-pound note. When the barman told me how much the drinks were I nearly had a heart attack. I may have been at the Royal Opera House but I was still on an animal-charity wage. As quick as a flash, my mum whipped out her purse and saved both the barman and me any further blushes.

We sat down with our most expensive drinks in the world and I thought back to that cold December morning when I received the phone call that would, a month later, see my mother and me enjoying some culture – for once, courtesy of me.

In an effort to help take my mind off Gus, people had been practically throwing dogs at me to foster. It was too soon to take any home but I compromised by helping to take care of a litter of tiny puppies in my office. Lolly was decidedly miffed at having to share her space with four squealing hamsters. I was bottle-feeding them when I received a call from Perry, asking for a favour. In his capacity as local dog walker, Perry had done Battersea enough favours in the past so I was more than willing to oblige. His best friend, Phillip, was looking for a special dog for his parents and knowing Battersea's forte was special dogs, he called me.

The dog-walking business had treated Perry well. He had an army of loyal customers who entrusted their hounds and their homes to him. He also had a large custom-built van in which he collected said hounds every morning and whisked them off to doggie heaven, also known as the park. In addition to this he had a house in the country with sprawling grounds.

Most people in this day and age work Monday to Friday, nine to five, so dog walking has become big business. Plenty of chancers have jumped on the bandwagon too, thinking it's easy money. Well, how hard can it be? Take a few dogs out for a stroll, catch a few rays, get a bit of exercise and fresh air; nice work if you can get it.

Those in the know understand it's not quite that easy. For starters, to make it financially viable you need to build up a substantial client base, not easy in itself. Dog walkers can be a cut-throat bunch and, just like some of their four-legged clients, fiercely guard their territory.

The business side apart, you need to be extremely dog savvy in order to be able to keep your charges under control at all times. I've watched many an inexperienced dog walker and winced as they let their dogs off the lead one by one, only to find that some or all of the scattered pack won't come back. The ensuing scene keeps me entertained for hours, as the hapless walker runs the length and breadth of the park, at first calmly calling their names, but whose voice steadily rises to a scream when none of them return. Sometimes, however, things get serious.

One particular dog walker had in his care a young, naive cocker spaniel. The adolescent decided to pick a fight with an enormous Rhodesian ridgeback; not a wise move. Realising it would do little for business to return a half-dead dog to its owner, the dog walker waded in, trying to pull the spaniel to safety.

Classic schoolboy error. As I found out all those years ago, never put your hands into the middle of a dogfight. I watched as our poor, unfortunate dog walker yanked his hand away and thrust it under his armpit, bent double in pain. The inevitable had happened. Deciding a young spaniel wasn't worth the effort, the ridgeback released him but the youngster was so spooked, he ran straight out of the park and into the road. He was immediately hit by an oncoming car.

At this point I ran into the fray. I told the dog walker to round up the other dogs and that I'd take the cocker spaniel to Battersea Dogs Home (just around the corner) and meet him there.

The driver of the car was in shock. I didn't have time to comfort him although I desperately wanted to. The same thing had happened to me and I knew how devastating it was. I ran over and killed a terrier that bolted across the road after a cat.

Its 14-year-old owner was walking it in the street without a lead. What a waste of a life. The distress caused to the owners and to me, all so easily preventable by something as simple as a lead.

I cannot bear seeing dogs off lead in the street. Even the best-trained dog in the world can be unpredictable. All it takes is a car backfiring to spook the dog or a cat to pique its interest and the dog is gone for ever.

The cocker spaniel was still breathing but wasn't moving. There was no blood but my concern was internal bleeding. I picked him up and ran him into the Home. Just as I reached the veterinary clinic, the dog drew a huge breath and as he exhaled, blood started pouring out of his mouth. He died, then and there in my arms.

Dog walkers have a massive responsibility to their charges and of course the owners. It isn't as simple as some might think, or as pleasurable. A good dog walker must be consistent. Those dogs are relying on their walks and they don't care if it's sunny or pouring down with rain, or whether you're in rude health or as sick as a dog. Good dog walkers never phone in sick.

Dog walkers must be in control at all times. That means knowing which dogs can and cannot be let off the lead and which ones will pick a fight with dogs in the park, and indeed each other. They must have cast-iron stomachs for all that poop scooping and definitely cannot worry about the cleanliness of their vehicle's upholstery.

Perry had all these attributes.

His friend Phillip was born and bred in Yorkshire and his retired parents still lived there. Over the years they'd had three dogs, a Labrador and two Labrador crosses, and were looking for a similar make and model once again.

Aside from Phillip, their dogs were the love of their life. Their last Labrador cross had died two years ago and they only just felt ready to welcome a new dog into their home.

Labradors are an extremely popular breed in Britain. Sadly the trend in popularity of any breed is usually reflected in the numbers that are subsequently abandoned and find their way into rescue homes across the country. Labs are actually one of the few exceptions to this rule, probably because they are biddable, trainable, good-looking and don't slobber.

Labrador crosses, however, were a common sight at Battersea and always held a special place in my heart. They usually had all the good qualities of their pedigree cousins but with their own quirky personalities thrown in for good measure, quirks lovingly handed down from their non-Labrador parent.

The Robinsons wanted a female and it had to be middle-aged – the same age as them, but in doggie years. How refreshing: someone that had actually thought about the reality of dog ownership, rather than seeing it through rose-coloured spectacles and automatically wanting a puppy.

As a rehomer, I'd spent so much of my time trying as diplomatically as I could to steer elderly people away from the wild, untrained youngsters that needed so much more time, energy and attention than they could usually provide.

It is true that pensioners have plenty of time on their hands, but to give them a crazy youngster would be the equivalent of leaving hyperactive, tantrum-throwing toddlers with them on a permanent basis. Isn't it widely recognised that the best thing about having grandchildren is that they can be given back? Not so easy with one's own dog.

I asked Perry for Mr and Mrs Robinson's phone number so I could speak directly to them. I needed to find out in detail about their dog-owning history, their current situation and what type of canine personality they were looking for. I also wanted to get a sense of them.

It didn't take me long to decide that Mr and Mrs Robinson were the perfect dog owners. They were delightful, telling me everything from how they hadn't had a holiday for over 30 years because they couldn't bear to put their dogs into boarding kennels, to how their dogs began every day with a cup of tea and a rich tea biscuit in bed with them.

Credentials established, the search was on. They asked how long it would take. I explained that this was an impossible question to answer. The ideal dog for them may already be sitting in the kennels waiting patiently, but then again it might not come in for weeks or even months. I explained to the Robinsons that their preference for a middle-aged female might increase their wait. They told me timescale wasn't important; that they'd rather wait and be sure to get the right dog.

I asked all of my colleagues to look out for a special middle-aged female Labrador (or cross) – there was a box of chocolates in it for the one who found her first. Unaccustomed as I was to giving away boxes of chocolates, I knew I'd better get looking too.

Two weeks later, Pauline came into my office.

'I've come to claim my prize,' she said. 'I've just picked up a Lab from Dulwich. She's a bit stressed but I reckon she's just what you're looking for.'

Just then the phone rang. It was Shaun.

'I've just vaccinated a middle-aged female Lab. Shall I come and get the chocolates now or later?'

Before I had time to answer him, Jade came in.

'There's a lovely Labrador in Tealby. I've put her on hold for you,' she said as she held out her hands for the booty.

Bloody hell.

It turned out they were all talking about the same dog.

Cookie, as Jade had named her, was indeed just what I was looking for. She was terribly underweight, her coat was dirty and her claws were overgrown but she had a beautiful face and a temperament to match.

I read her card, which said she had been found

running across a busy main road. A car had clipped her but thankfully no damage was done. A man walking his own Labrador had managed to catch Cookie, clip his dog's lead on her collar and take her to a local police station, from where Pauline had collected her.

Jade had taken her from the van to the veterinary clinic where Shaun had given her the once-over and vaccinated her. He had written on her card that she was in surprisingly good nick, all things considered. Physically, that may have been so, but she looked pretty shell-shocked to me and the kennel environment wasn't doing much to help. Cookie sat in her kennel shaking like a leaf stuck to a pneumatic drill.

She began to lose weight she could ill afford to lose and even cut her mouth trying to bite her way out of the kennel. I knew that fostering was the only option for Cookie and went to find Rebecca.

'Room for a small one?' I asked.

'Ooh, yes,' she said. 'Another Scottie? Or is it a Jack Russell? I don't mind, Buster hasn't put me off you know,' she said, opening her filing cabinet drawer and pulling out a freshly laundered blanket, four squeaky toys and a packet of Schmackos.

'It's more of a Labrador. When I said small, I meant skinny.'

Once in Rebecca's care and away from the kennels, Cookie was a model dog: calm, well behaved and housetrained. In short, perfect for the Robinsons.

Cookie's seven days came and went without any sign of an owner coming forward. She was assessed by Ali and Jacky who wrote her up as 'Middle-aged and delightful – seeks similar for love, country walks and tea and biscuits'. Uncanny! I called the Robinsons, who immediately set off on the long journey from Yorkshire to London.

Phillip, who lived in north London, met up with his parents at Battersea, as did Perry. Mrs Robinson gave me a vice-like bear hug and Mr Robinson shook my hand, so earnestly he nearly broke it. They were wonderful people, really warm and friendly. Mrs Robinson gave me a big box of chocolates for finding Cookie for them. I thanked her, swallowing hard, knowing the chocolates would have to be split four ways.

I went through the formal interview with them and Mr Robinson produced a letter of recommendation from their vet. It was a glowing report.

Particulars in order, I told them all about Cookie, her history and the information that Rebecca had provided. Mrs Robinson dabbed her eyes.

I dropped them all off in a meeting room whilst I went to get Cookie. When I collected her from Rebecca's office, I was struck by how much her condition had improved in a week. She was now a healthy weight and, thanks to a bath and groom, her beautiful golden coat shone like the sun.

Poor Rebecca was crying again; another one she had to say goodbye to. She fumbled around in her filing cabinet once more, this time producing a Polaroid camera. Nichola took a photo of Rebecca and Cookie together and handed it to Rebecca. Cookie and I left the office with Rebecca wiping her tears away, furiously shaking the picture, willing the image to process quickly.

I brought Cookie into the meeting room and let her off the lead. She completely ignored the Robinsons and jumped all over me.

'I'm not having you,' I told her. 'Get over there and sell yourself.'

Perry and I left Phillip and his parents alone to become acquainted with Cookie, over a packet of Schmackos.

Once out of the room he said to me, 'You know who Phillip is, don't you?'

I didn't have a clue.

'He's the real Billy Elliot. He's the ballet dancer whose life the film was based on.'

I loved the film *Billy Elliot* but my childhood memories of ballet had left me decidedly cool on the whole tights and tutu thing.

After 15 minutes, Perry and I went back in to see how things were going. Cookie was lying on her back having her tummy tickled by Mr Robinson. I thought of Gus and had to quickly pull myself together.

Mr and Mrs Robinson were ecstatic. They thanked me profusely and left with the latest addition to their family. After his parents had gone, Phillip pulled me aside.

'I can't begin to thank you enough,' he said. 'I haven't seen that spark in my parents' eyes since our last dog was alive. I'd like to offer you two complimentary tickets to watch the Royal Ballet performing *Romeo and Juliet* at The Royal Opera House.'

I thanked him but said it really wasn't necessary. However, I couldn't resist showing him my childhood ballet moves – positions one to five, finishing off with a particularly clumsy pirouette. He told me not to give up my day job; we all had a good laugh and said our goodbyes.

I stopped off at my mother's for dinner after work that night. She asked me how my day had been and I told her about Cookie. I said how lovely the family were that took her and:

'Oh yeah, their son Phillip is the real Billy Elliot.'

I explained about his kind offer which, having no interest in ballet, I had politely declined.

She nearly choked on her lamb chop. After attempting the Heimlich Manoeuvre and getting a clout in return, she said to me, 'Are you mad, two tickets to the Royal Ballet? Do you know how expensive, not to mention scarce those tickets are? Don't you know how wonderful the ballet is and to see the Royal Ballet perform at the Royal Opera House, it doesn't get much better than that. Have I instilled no culture in you at all? You're to get on the phone to Phillip first thing tomorrow, tell him your mother is very cross with you and ask him if the offer is still on.'

Why is it that even as adults, when our mothers put on that tone of voice, we still jump? I did as I was told and rang Phillip the next day. Embarrassed, I explained to him what had transpired and asked if the offer was still there. He laughed and said of course it was.

The bell at the Royal Opera House rang, signalling it was time for curtain-up. I hadn't finished my wine but at those prices I wasn't going to leave it. I downed it which was not the most brilliant idea considering I had to stay upright in unfamiliar heels. We took our seats and waited in anticipation as a hush descended upon the theatre.

The curtain went up and the orchestra exploded into life. What happened over the next two hours took my breath away. I was transfixed, totally consumed by the beauty and emotion, the costumes and the setting, the sheer grandeur of this stunning spectacle. When Phillip burst on to the stage I could barely contain my excitement and felt a rush of pride at knowing him. I couldn't look away, not for one second. The dancers were so elegant, their bodies toned to perfection, as they flitted around the stage like mercury. I felt goose bumps, and the hairs on the back of my neck stood up throughout the performance.

I was a little quiet on the way home, in awe of what I had just seen.

'See,' my mother said with a knowing smile.

Perhaps there was something to this culture thing, after all.

# CHAPTER 17

# BATTERSEA'S ANNUAL REUNION

When the pain of losing Gus had subsided a little, I decided it was time for a good old-fashioned wake to celebrate the life of my beloved old soldier. It was supposed to be a low-key affair. I put up a couple of notices which included the intended time, date and place, the dog-friendly pub opposite the Home.

I wasn't sure if many people would come – after all, it was a bit of a kooky idea. But in true inimitable Battersea style, whether it was because people could relate so heavily to having loved and lost dogs of their own, or whether it was simply because they adored Gus, the staff turned out in their masses. There were about 50 Battersea faithful there ranging from Colonel Green, to veterinary staff, kennel hands, rehomers, behaviourists, office staff and even Margaret the Tea Lady. Most were accompanied either by their own dogs or dogs from the kennels that they were fostering. Both laughter and tears flowed freely as everyone swapped memories of an elderly black-and-grey mongrel with a dickey ticker.

Gus's ashes were in a little wooden casket and

it seemed entirely appropriate to take him along to his own wake, so the casket took centre stage on the pub's main table. Someone even bought him a pint of Guinness which stood, like the occasion, slightly to the left of centre.

Photos of Gus lay strewn across the tables and someone even recited a poem they'd written especially for him. Helen and the PR team had put together a folder of all the publicity shots and fundraising campaigns that Gus had taken part in, doing his bit for the cause.

It was about 5.30 p.m. and workers from surrounding offices were spilling into the pub to have a quick one for the road. A lady on the next table leaned over and asked what the occasion was. Someone told her. She didn't quite know how to react, unsure if she was having her leg pulled.

Unusual as it was, it was a wonderful evening and a fitting tribute to the General. Primarily this was a celebration of Gus, but it was also an opportunity for all of us to recognise why we were there that night and why we chose to spend every day doing what we did.

The Battersea Dogs Home Annual Reunion was just celebrating its fourteenth anniversary. I was there for its inception but, alas, can take no credit for this brilliant idea.

Every year around the middle of September, under the watchful gaze of the iconic Power

Station, a corner of Battersea Park would be transformed into an extension of Battersea Dogs Home, with one or two subtle differences. Nowhere within the Home's four walls, for example, would one find a bouncy castle, dogs jumping through flaming hoops, innumerable ice-cream vans or such a large volume of proud dog owners.

When the Reunion began, it took up a modest space and attracted a couple of hundred nosey parkers, out for their Sunday stroll. But as the years went on, thousands of people and their dogs came from all corners of the country, specially to take part in what could only be described as one of the most heart-warming events of the year.

I was always dumbfounded by how well behaved the dogs were. Knowing what many of them were like when they left the Home, the transformation was impressive. There were very few scraps, hardly any escapees, never any bites, and Shaun, who manned the dog first-aid tent, usually sat twiddling his thumbs.

One of the busiest stands at the Reunion was the 'Battersea Buys' where one could procure all things Battersea, ranging from bowls, books and badges to porcelain pooches, pencils and poo bags. I walked over to find out what was on offer this year and was delighted to see Lady Weatherall chatting animatedly with Bill Turner at the counter. Once again I was reminded what a social leveller dogs are. She was buying Fred a new

Battersea collar and lead and he was buying Tom a new Battersea bowl.

'Hello! How are you?' I enquired, genuinely pleased to see them both. They greeted me as though I was their long-lost pal.

'Very well thanks,' Bill answered. 'I was just telling this lady about my mate, Tom.' He pointed to Tom. ''E looks good, the old git, doesn't 'e?' he said, bursting with pride.

I looked down at Tom who was looking back at me, wagging his tail. He appeared to be smiling. His smile was contagious and I knelt down to stroke him. He snorted his approval. Not wanting to miss out on a free pat, Fred poked his head under my arm and was rewarded with an ear massage.

'They both look great,' I replied. 'Are you entering them in any of the events?'

'Oh yes,' Lady Weatherall said enthusiastically. 'Fred and I have entered the main competition – something about Dandiest Dog.'

'And we're going for back-to-back "Dog that Looks Most Like its Owner",' Bill announced and I remembered back to the previous year when he and Tom had beaten 40 other hopefuls to claim the title.

He took Tom's new bowl from Rebecca who was manning the Battersea Buys stall with Steph. Even though it was still early, they were rushed off their feet.

'God, this is like the January sales in Oxford

Street,' she wailed as someone handed her a china spaniel to wrap. Lady Weatherall, Bill and I left her to it with the sound of the tills ringing in our ears.

We wandered over towards the grooming stall, another popular feature at the Reunion. Here, Rover could receive a shampoo and set, have his anal glands squeezed and even purchase a pedicure. I looked in to see Jacky and Jade wrestling an unruly Bearded collie into the bath. His owner wanted him to have the full works – he had other ideas.

'You okay?' I enquired.

'If God had intended dogs to have baths, he would have given them hands with which to turn the taps on,' Jade replied, flustered. We beat a hasty retreat and I left Lady Weatherall and Bill at the tea and cake stall swapping stories and comparing notes on the delights of dog ownership.

By far the most popular attraction at the Reunion was the fancy dress – for dogs, you understand. Some dog lovers might find this offensive but take my word for it – the dogs loved it. Some of the costumes were ingenious and ranged from Posh and Becks, the Tellytubbies and Superman, to the Queen and Prince Philip, Snow White and the Seven Dwarfs and the entire cast of *The Wizard of Oz*.

Judging this competition and singling out a winner was almost impossible and the dilemma usually fell to a celebrity guest. The year Lily

Savage judged, fisticuffs almost broke out between a Staffie dressed as Mike Tyson and a poodle in a cat suit. Peace was only restored when Mike Tyson's owner produced a sausage to distract him with, and the poodle, suddenly seeing Lily's wig, fell deeply in lust and had to be dragged off.

The Reunion was a fantastic opportunity for the staff to become reacquainted with some of the dogs they had rehomed over the years. Some you remembered straight away according to either how special they were to you or the length of time since the dog was rehomed. One thing I always found remarkable was how the owners never ever forgot you. It might have been years since you rehomed them their dog, but they'd come straight to find you and proudly show off their adored canine companion.

Many organisations and groups came to showcase their talented hounds at the Reunion. The Essex Dogs Display Team were perennial favourites and every year would show off their amazing training skills and their even more amazing dogs, who would jump through flaming hoops, herd geese and were experts on the agility course. In order to manage the crowd's expectations, we made sure The Battersea Flyers went on before The Essex agility dogs.

The police also liked to show off their high-performing hounds, but sometimes displayed more brawn than brain. One year they were demonstrating how their specially trained dogs could take down armed criminals, a perfectly respectable profession for a German shepherd. What they didn't take into account was that to shoot a gun, albeit a fake one, into a crowd of semi-neurotic rescue dogs probably wasn't the best idea. As the gun fired, everything with four legs – and some with two – jumped ten feet in the air. When they came back down to earth, the four-leggeds scattered in every direction. Pandemonium! People were running everywhere to try and catch their terrified hounds. The terrified hounds were running everywhere to try and get away from the gunshots. Some dogs were caught straight away but others were seen running out of the park, cars and bikes swerving to avoid them, horns beeping, bells ringing and expletives exploding into the balmy air.

Back at the Home that afternoon, the Lost Dogs Department had its work cut out. Happily, every dog was reunited with its owner within 12 hours of the first shot ringing out. Many, somewhat ironically, were reunited with their owners at police stations, none of them any the worse for wear. As for the police, we let them off with a caution and told them not to be so silly next year.

One of the main attractions at the Annual Reunion was the judging of 'Dandiest Dog' and 'Bonniest Bitch'. This was taken very seriously – of course by Battersea, but even more so by the proud parents, each more determined than the others to walk off with the coveted trophy.

Registration started early, as did the queue of owners who lined up patiently with their dogs, waiting to register for whichever category they fell into. The heats were divided into male and female, then sub-divided into age categories: under three years, three to five, five to seven and my own personal favourite, the over-sevens.

I loved seeing all those happy grey faces, some of whom were bought from Battersea as puppies and had reached their dotage as much-loved family pets. Some of them were more recent purchases but they all had a special place in my heart and I couldn't help but think of Gus as I gave each and every one a scratch behind the car.

My role at the Reunion was to run the main ring where all the judging took place. The judges were selected from a random bunch of dog-loving Battersea contacts, ranging from police dog-handlers (unarmed) and breed rescue representatives, to Battersea trustees, celebrities and council dignitaries.

Carolyn had flown in from St Tropez especially to be a judge and when I saw her, we had our own mini-reunion and spent more time than we had catching up on each other's news. I grabbed her hand to inspect her Battersea battle-scarred finger.

'Can you still pick your nose?' I asked.

'Oh yes,' she replied.

'No harm done then,' and we both fell about laughing.

We were yanked from our silliness by a tannoy announcement rallying those that had registered in the Dandiest Dog and Bonniest Bitch heats to seek whichever ring their group was being judged in. This was our cue to do the same and we got serious; the judging was about to commence.

Some groups were larger than others, for example males under three years usually accounted for the largest group with anything up to 160 dogs in the ring at one time. In order to deal with this many dogs, four judges were brought in, one for each side of the ring. If there was going to be any trouble, this was where it was most likely to be. With so many males in such close proximity, the odd scuffle had been known to break out. Between the judges, the owners and me, however, we managed to keep everyone under control.

I shadowed the judges mainly to keep them on track because with such a large volume of dogs to judge, there was always the danger we would still be there after dark. It wasn't just a question of them giving the dog the once-over; it was about the dog's story too. Their sometimes pitiful histories were relayed by the Master of Ceremonies through his microphone to the crowd who listened, captivated by the often sad but always fascinating stories. I knew some of them to be true but others were shamelessly embellished in an attempt to secure the coveted trophy. I had to stifle the odd giggle as I listened to each owner ham up their dog's story to make it sound more heart-wrenching than the previous dog's.

The first person in line usually began with how their dog was found abandoned on a rubbish tip aged four days old. By the time the judge reached the end of the line, he was being told how the dog in front of him was fished out of the Thames after being given up for dead, kept alive only by mouth-to-mouth resuscitation administered by a passing vet.

The four judges would pick one dog each, an impossibly tall order when there were so many fantastic dogs to choose from. They'd then huddle together in the middle of the ring and fight over which place – first to fourth – their chosen dog should take within the heat. Even though the placing didn't really matter (being chosen automatically secured the dog a place in the grand final), the judges would seldom compromise and each remained steadfast as to why their dog should be given the top spot. Actually, it was a bit like hearing the owners' stories all over again but exaggerated once more so that by the time the judges had given their version, a new canine Hollywood weepy had practically been born.

Whether a dog was placed or not, everyone was a winner at the Reunion and no dog went away empty-pawed. Those that didn't make it to the grand final each received a 'Special Dog' rosette because let's face it, in their own right, they're all Rin Tin Tins.

Biggles, a young spaniel cross, made it through from the under-threes category. Even though he only had three legs, his tail had not stopped wagging since he and his owner registered at 9 a.m. I remembered when he was brought into Battersea as a pup.

His back right leg had been severely deformed and had become a useless, ulcerated hindrance that dragged behind him. His owner obviously didn't have the compassion or the inclination to take him to the vet for a simple operation that would have dramatically improved his quality of life. Anyone who could not or would not acknowledge the pain and suffering this poor dog must have been in shouldn't have had the privilege of calling himself a dog owner.

Biggles was brought into Battersea not because of his leg, but because the other dog in the house kept attacking him. Thank God it did. Once at Battersea, Biggles useless appendage was amputated and he was rehomed to a family with no other dogs and two well-trained children to play with.

To see him at the Reunion, bounding around unencumbered, tongue hanging out and a new-found love of life oozing from every follicle, was poetry in motion.

A scruffy black-and-tan mongrel named Myrtle made it through from the three- to five-year-olds. Myrtle exuded love and happiness and she had what most dogs have: the ability to instantly make you smile. If you have an idea in your mind of bliss taking on a physical form, Myrtle was it.

She had been dog number 7,682 the previous year and had arrived at the Home on a cold November morning. No one came to claim Myrtle, quite why I don't know.

She progressed from the stray kennels to the rehoming kennels via a sparkling assessment. She was rehomed but a week later brought back to Battersea because of a death in the family. A month later she was rehomed again but this time brought back because the child was allergic to her. Luck was not on the side of this particular hound.

Being a quiet sort of dog and bearing in mind she looked like many other black and tans patiently waiting in the rehoming section to be picked, Myrtle stayed in the rehoming kennels for six months, waiting to be chosen again.

Quiet, unremarkable dogs should never be overlooked but people were mostly attracted to handsome hounds and noisy dogs. What they didn't realise is that those that liked the sound of their own voices often went on to display attention-seeking behaviours. The sympathy vote also played a big part and people often chose dogs with some sort of physical deformity – Biggles being a case in point. But it took a keen eye to pick out a really good dog.

When Sophie, an ex-RSPCA vet, knelt down and called Myrtle over, she obediently came. Sophie then asked Myrtle to sit, upon which the scruffy mongrel gave the very best one she could; chest out, bum firmly planted on floor, tail wagging. Sophie asked Myrtle for her paw – she gave one and then the other, just to be sure. Myrtle then pushed herself sideways against the bars for a better stroke. Sophie's trained eye had picked out a winner and after six months of patient waiting, Myrtle found her home.

In the crowd, I spotted my old schoolteacher, Ann Hooper, and her husband. On the other end of the lead they were clutching was an over-excited Floyd. He was getting on a bit now but with his short legs and big ears he hadn't lost any of his cuteness or his *joie de vivre* and it took all of my willpower not to call out to them. So fierce was the competition, if Floyd was picked by a judge I didn't want anyone to think it was due to foul play.

On the other side of the ring Cookie spotted me and slipped Mr Robinson's hold on her. I was unaware of the Exocet missile heading my way until she knocked me off my feet and was on top of me in a hail of licks and squeals. The whole ring exploded into laughter whilst a highly embarrassed Mr Robinson came to retrieve his nutty hound. Although a little bruised, I was moved by this show of canine affection.

Amber Melody, an ex-racing greyhound, made it through the five- to seven-year-old category. Amber was a fairly unsuccessful racer at the best of times but a freak incident cut her faltering career short, and led to a life of misery at the hands of a man who beat and starved her. She was one of hundreds of ex-racers that found themselves discarded at Battersea (if they were lucky), once their careers, shining or otherwise, were over.

Her demise came about due to her love of chocolate. One of the staff at the racing kennels had unwittingly dropped a square of Cadbury's Whole Nut just outside Amber's kennel. She got down, belly to the floor, and reached under the kennel door with her paw. She had to extend her front leg to its full length and stretch for all she was worth to reach the chocolate. Just at that moment the kennel owner's pet Jack Russell escaped from the house and hurtled through the kennels. He spotted Amber's outstretched leg and grabbed on to it, tugging hard as though pulling a rat from a hole.

Amber's screams were drowned out by all the other dogs barking and it was a full five minutes before the owner realised his dog was missing and went to look for him. As soon as he saw what was happening, he rushed to Amber's assistance. By now the Jack Russell had let go of her leg but, instead, latched on to Amber's paw. The man managed to extract it from the terrier's jaws but her leg and paw were too badly damaged for Amber ever to race again.

Once she had healed, Amber's owner sold her to what he thought was a good home but after six months, thanks to a concerned neighbour's intervention, the RSPCA were called and Amber was rescued from the violent drunk entrusted to take care of her. They brought her to Battersea to be rehomed and the rest was history. At the Reunion, she still walked with a limp, but otherwise Amber was as healthy and happy as any dog could ever wish to be.

Colonel Green and Nichola were judging the five- to seven-year-old males. Knowing how many they had to see, I tried to chivvy them on. The lady Colonel Green was talking to was saying something about a very special collar. My ears pricked up and I immediately looked down to see Marcus proudly showing off the collar the Queen had given him. It looked like it had been polished and shone in the sunlight. Apparently it only came out for special occasions such as the Reunion, but however handsome the collar looked, it was outshone by its wearer. In this case the clothes didn't maketh the man; it was most definitely the other way around.

Amongst the dozens of veterans, I thought I saw an old friend but he was obscured by the other dogs around him. I altered my position, eager to see if it really was him. The shine from his black coat almost dazzled me and when I saw that it was him, my heart skipped a beat. It was one of my most-loved dogs, one of the very first I fell in love with. It had been over a decade since I had seen Roscoe and I watched transfixed as he sat to attention for the judge. He was proud and handsome and he took my breath away. By now, Roscoe was old. His black coat was still luxuriant but his face was grey and he reminded me of Gus. He still had stature as well as a playful side and as the judge approached, Roscoe could hold his composure no longer. He rolled over, willing the judge to rub his tummy. He got his wish and the crowd loved it.

I looked to the other end of the leash and saw James's face, partially hidden by the now-battered Trilby hat which shaded his eyes from the September sun. He rolled his eyes at his dog's shameless flirting but I knew he was brimming over with pride. I followed his line of sight and picked out Sarah from behind a camera. She blew him a kiss but continued to snap away, determined to capture the moment.

After a minute or so, Roscoe sat up and as the judge stood talking to James, Roscoe gently took her hand in his mouth and held it, just held it. Just as I fell for Roscoe all those years ago, so did the crowd. When his story was read out by the MC, I sense that Roscoe was the people's favourite.

The judge pulled Roscoe into the centre of the ring. He was through to the grand final.

These were just some of the 32 dogs – 16 of each sex, whittled down from the initial 500, that made it through to the grand final of Dandiest Dog and Bonniest Bitch.

★ ★ ★

Away from the drama of the ring, a multitude of other events were taking place, one of which was 'Temptation Alley' manned by Kirsty and Ali. Kirsty took the owner's money whilst Ali held their hound. The owner then walked to the end of the long, straight course and frantically called the dog. The rules stated that the dog had to go directly to its owner without deviating. What could be simpler? But between the dog and its owner lay a myriad of temptation, ranging from sausages and steak to Schmackos and saveloys. If the dog went straight to its owner it won a prize; if it was tempted, the owner had to cough up a pound. Aside from the Battersea Buys stand, Temptation Alley generated the most revenue at the Reunion. And they say there's no such thing as a safe bet.

At the approximate midpoint of the Reunion, those that had stayed behind to look after the 500 or so dogs at the Home came over to the park to join in the fun. They each brought a dog from the kennels that needed a special home: Ann and her team would usually bring a few ex-Rehab dogs and the others brought dogs that might be struggling to find a home. These dogs may have had behavioural issues that needed the expertise of experienced owners to help them stay on the straight and narrow, or they may have simply needed to live in the country with wide open spaces. It might have been that, like Myrtle, they had just been inexplicably passed by and sat depressed in their kennels as the calendar months peeled away.

Each dog was led into the main ring, where the Master of Ceremonies read its history to an absorbed audience. This was a fantastic opportunity to secure new lives for these dogs and this very popular and extremely successful part of the proceedings resulted in many of the dogs finding their perfect partners.

At about 4 p.m., once all the heats of Dandiest Dog and Bonniest Bitch had been completed and the finalists selected, the two grand finals took place. Reminiscent of Crufts, each owner back-combed and fluffed their dog's fur as though their lives depended on it. They got them to face front, wag their tail, stop sniffing other dog's genitals, pay attention and hoped for the best. Though they would never experience the grandeur and high stakes of Crufts (thankfully, some might say), this must have felt just as good, if not better. Here was their dog in all its glory, their pride and joy, probably rescued from a pitiful existence, now on parade for all to see in the final of the ultimate rescue dog show.

In the girl's ring I saw Myrtle, Amber, Dusty and Cookie as well as a dozen other beautiful hopefuls. The photographers were out in force, as were the local TV news cameras, and by this stage the atmosphere was electric. A new team of judges set about their impossible task. The MC repeated the dog's histories, adding to the drama as the suspense built.

After speaking to each and every owner about their protégé, from a possible 32, the judges pulled out a shortlist of four dogs and four bitches.

The judges had to compromise now, in order to whittle down and then place the eight shortlisted into four; the Bonniest Bitch and runner-up, and the Dandiest Dog and runner-up. I saw some of them shaking their heads and pointing fingers at each other, obviously not wanting to budge from their original choice. However, in the name of good manners and not wanting to appear argumentative on TV, the judges signalled that they had made their final decision.

A drum roll resounded around the park, as the Master of Ceremonies strode into the centre of the ring.

'Lay-dees and gentle-men,' he said, drawing out every syllable in his best ringmaster's voice. 'After much deliberation, the judges have come to a decision. I am delighted to announce that the runner-up of the Bonniest Bitch goes to everybody's favourite mongrel. Let's hear it for Myrtle!'

Great cheers and excited leaps came from Myrtle's camp. She looked in the prime of her life with a shining coat, bright eyes and a cold, wet nose. Myrtle wasn't really sure what was going on but she liked the judge and as he attached her rosette to her collar, she jumped up and planted a big wet smacker right on his lips. A collective 'ahh' came from a delighted crowd.

The male runner-up was about to be picked and I watched as Marcus, Biggles and Roscoe, and all the other finalists, received a final brush from their owners.

'Lay-dees and gentle-men, the prize for runner-up of the Dandiest Dog goes to Biggles!' Like Myrtle, Biggles wasn't sure what all the fuss was about but when a big bag of food was placed at his feet, he didn't really care and had no hesitation about tucking into his prize.

'And now, the moment you've all been waiting for . . .' the MC announced. I looked around the park. There must have been a thousand people around this ring, most of whom had dogs with them, all waiting in anticipation.

'The Battersea Dogs Home Annual Reunion prize for the Bonniest Bitch goes to . . .' The crowd held its collective breath, waiting for the announcement and I was amazed by the total silence that had descended. Even the dogs were quiet. Perhaps they sensed something too.

'. . . Amber Melody!'

A huge roar, which I'm sure could be heard all the way to the top of the Power Station chimneys, went up from the crowd. Amber's story seemed to touch everyone in the park; the people's choice had won. The judge handed Amber's owner her winning rosette, an armful of edible goodies and a big silver cup. He knelt down to Amber who gave him her paw – her good paw. Her owner wiped away tears as she thanked the judge and shook his hand. He put his arm around her and she crumbled into his shoulder, overcome with emotion. Amber never won any racing trophies but her new owner didn't care. She knew that this piece of silverware was far more worthy of her exceptional dog.

'And now, ladies and gentlemen, boys and girls, and of course all you lovely dogs, it is time to award the final prize of the day.'

I looked at Roscoe gleaming in the late summer sun and crossed everything, willing him to win, but the competition was stiff this year. 'Go on, say it, say Roscoe,' I mumbled to myself under my breath.

'The Battersea Dogs Home Annual Reunion prize for the Dandiest Dog goes to . . .'

'Say it, please . . .'

'Roscoe!'

I gasped and then to my surprise I was both laughing and crying. I couldn't believe it. Things like this only happened in Hollywood, not south-west London. The crowd was cheering and the judge strode dramatically towards the dog that once stole my heart, and who had now stolen the show. James threw the Trilby up in the air and he and Sarah screamed with delight. Sensing the family joy, Roscoe joined in and leapt into James's arms, almost causing him to collapse. Sarah held the cup aloft and the crowd roared as though their team had just won the FA Cup. Just as Amber was the crowd's Bonniest Bitch, so too, Roscoe was their Dandiest Dog.

I walked over to James, Sarah and Roscoe. I didn't expect any of them to remember me. Roscoe saw me first. He suddenly pulled away from James and ran towards me.

I was surprised that Roscoe remembered me so vividly but when he leapt up to greet me there was no mistake. He took a good few minutes to calm down, by which time James and Sarah had caught up with him.

Roscoe and I stared at each other, doe-eyed, whilst James and Sarah breathlessly filled me in on life with Roscoe. We all delighted in his victory and they told me that they felt like the luckiest people in the world. The feeling must have been contagious because as I looked around the park I got the sense that anyone who had ever owned a Battersea dog felt the same way.

I saw Dusty nuzzling into Val, wagging her tail harder than ever, and as they began a game of fetch, they did not seem the slightest bit troubled not to be taking home the cup. Just to be taking Dusty home seemed more than enough for Val.

At the other end of the ring Biggles escaped and bounded around gleefully with an embarrassed owner hot on his heels. Even with only three legs, Biggles dodged his owner, ducking and diving like a professional rugby player. She only caught him because he stopped at the famous 'end of show cake' and started helping himself.

And what would any event be without cake? The cake was specially made so that both dogs and humans could indulge. No one missed out on this sponge that was large enough to feed the five thousand, let alone the one thousand that attended the show. Margaret was in charge of dishing out the cake. She tried to run a tight ship but by the end of the day everyone was famished and the orderly queue descended into a free-for-all. The gigantic cake was consumed within minutes.

As I was tucking into my piece, a disgruntled Bill found me. He had no trophy to show for his and Tom's striking likeness.

''Ere, me and Tom was robbed,' he said. 'Just because that fat woman has big white hair, doesn't mean she actually looks like her Old English sheepdog.' Realising how ridiculous that sounded, both he and I started giggling.

'Don't sweat the small stuff, Bill. Have a piece of cake,' I said.

Margaret handed him a large piece of cake.

'Don't mind if I do. Thank you, young lady,' he said to Margaret with a wink and a cheeky grin. I thought about matchmaking him and Margaret but I was too exhausted and the idea dissolved almost as quickly as it came to me.

The MC brought the day to a close, thanking staff, volunteers, public and hounds alike for making this Reunion another unrivalled success.

For the staff, the hard graft was just beginning and the mass clear-up got under way. We loaded up Pauline and Martin's vans with everything that belonged to Battersea and carted it back to the safety and security of the Home, leaving the park as we found it. Then it was off to the pub for a pint. As the dogs snored under the table, we shared our own personal stories of the triumphs and cock-ups, and mad dogs and equally mad Englishmen, that had made up this year's Reunion.

On the next table I recognised some people who had also spent the day in the park. They asked if they could come and join us and we were delighted to include them. Not many things provoked this kind of spontaneous friendliness between strangers in a big city like London. But dogs did and so did Battersea Dogs Home. They wanted to know all about us, our dogs, the Home and how the Annual Reunion produced such a fantastic atmosphere year after year.

The answer was easy. With a recipe of happy dogs, the people that adored them, a bouncy castle and a giant cake, how could the Reunion be anything but a huge success?

Everything I had experienced in the last 12 hours had an extra poignancy. This was my very last Reunion as part of the Battersea Dogs Home family and I savoured every last bark, every last tail wag and every last loving look from owner to dog and back again. In two short weeks I was to leave London for a new life in Australia.

I couldn't begin to imagine how much I would miss my Battersea life, but if there was ever a perfect way to end a perfect 15 years, this was it.

# EPILOGUE

## LET SLEEPING DOGS LIE

When I left school, I didn't go on to further education. Instead I went to Battersea Dogs Home and learned about real life. To me, this was education in its truest sense and since leaving Battersea I have, on a daily basis, drawn from the lessons I learned and experiences I gained at this remarkable institution.

Being exposed to people from every conceivable walk of life every single day, I also gained a broader understanding of humanity than money or books could ever have given me. How strange that I should learn so much about human nature from a dog's home, one of the biggest lessons being that the vast majority of people have good hearts.

But it was London's waifs and strays that taught me what is really important in life: that kindness goes a long way, love is at its purest when it is unconditional and that the simple things make us the happiest.

I began working at Battersea Dogs Home when I was 18 years old and left at 34. During that time, I bought my first home, my first car, I had my first dog, I lost someone close to me and I experienced many other life-defining moments.

Battersea Dogs Home also gave me unlimited access to the best things on four legs. I had always loved them but now I understand them – validation in full for my once eyebrow-raising career.

I would never have left Battersea to take another job in London. Why would I when I had the perfect job? Sure, there were parts that were far from perfect; but every day I was surrounded by the creatures I loved, whilst doing some good with my life.

I always knew that when the time came, it would be something big that took me away from Battersea.

My parents are adventurous types and both my brother and I were always encouraged to explore the world, experience as many things as we could and, most of all, find happiness. I definitely had the third one nailed; maybe it was time to have a crack at the other two.

After 15 years at Battersea Dogs Home, the opportunity arose for me to sample the Australian way of life. I thought long and hard and eventually decided to bite the bullet. I somehow felt the time was right; nevertheless, I knew leaving Battersea would be a wrench.

My last day was a surreal affair, spent reminiscing with old friends, cuddling up with the dogs, and looking at the place through the various different lenses of my many Battersea lives. I walked through Unders, where it all began, and smiled as the dotty bus-hopping Tulip popped into my mind. She was one of the first dogs I met on my very first day all those years ago.

And now, here I was at the end of my very last day. Ali Taylor and some of my other closest pals threw a party where they presented me with a 'This is your Battersea Life' slide show, commemorating 15 wonderful years. It was quite a night and one I will never forget. These people weren't just my friends, they were my family, many of whom I'd quite literally grown up with.

Looking back, I ask myself if I stayed too long; after all, we only get one life. My answer is: I don't think so. The years I spent at Battersea were immensely important to me, therefore the length of time I invested felt right.

Almost more than my last day, I was dreading the morning after, waking up no longer a part of Battersea Dogs Home. Thankfully, I didn't have one second to think about what I was leaving behind. I was heading off to a new life in one week and had so many things to sort out: renting my flat, selling the car, tying up loose ends and, most importantly, saying my goodbyes.

The day of my departure came all too soon. I stood on the platform at Clapham Junction station with London's commuters and waited for the 7.30 a.m. train to take me to Gatwick airport.

It was 7.20 a.m. and I realised I could have been on my way to work. But I wasn't, and for the first time since leaving Battersea I knew this was real. Angst shot through me like an electric current and I could suddenly feel a huge pit in my soul. I missed my friends and I missed the dogs. It would be the longest time before I would see either again.

But I knew I'd made the right decision and when I thought about what I was heading for, the excitement of exotic lands and unexplored territories eased the sense of loss that threatened to engulf me.

En route to Sydney, an itinerary lay before me that would have made Judith Chalmers envious. A trek in Nepal, India's Taj Mahal, an elephant orphanage in Sri Lanka, a sun-kissed beach in Thailand and a cookery course in Vietnam all beckoned.

Whatever happened during my travels and on into the next chapter of my life, Battersea Dogs Home would always remain a part of me, as would those lifelong friendships I'd made along the way. Should the need ever arise, I knew my unforgettable memories from that incredible time would always be there to rescue me.

# ACKNOWLEDGEMENTS

There are many people I must thank for making this book exist other than solely in my own heart and mind.

Thanks to my agent, Jane Burridge, whose knowledge and guidance were invaluable and whose belief in my dog-eared manuscript secured its first injection of possibility.

Thanks to Pat Sheppard and Alison Urquart for early introductions and to Tina Betts for expertly steering the book towards publication.

Thanks to my editor and publisher Charlotte Cole for her invaluable advice, direction and enthusiasm, and for giving my book the necessary platform to reach an audience.

My heartfelt thanks also go to my partner, Alison Grigg, whose trusted opinion and valued suggestions I sought throughout this literary journey. Alison's belief in me never wavered and, during times of frustration and self-doubt, she gently reminded me that this was my Plan A for fame and fortune and that I didn't have a Plan B. You truly are my *raison d'étre*.

I had tremendous support from friends, both

Battersea and non-Battersea, and would especially like to thank Gemma Daniel for her help, generosity, support and friendship.

Thanks, of course, go to Battersea Dogs Home for the unforgettable memories that will always be mine and to its staff, past, present and future, for the heroic work they perform every single day.

Finally, I would like to thank my parents for giving me the best start in life anyone could ever hope for, the education required to write this book and enough love to always feel safe. I hope I have made you proud.

I hope you have enjoyed reading about my
life and times at Battersea Dogs Home.
If you did, I would love you to support the
organisation by donatingwhatever you can.
Their details are:


Battersea Dogs & Cats Home
4 Battersea Park Road
London SW8 4AA
020 7622 3626

www.battersea.org.uk